MW00720881

The Tongue of
FIRE

The Tongue of
FIRE

OR

The True

POWER

of Christianity

WILLIAM ARTHUR, A.M.

 seedbed

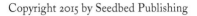
SEEDBED PUBLISHING
Franklin, Tennessee
seedbed.com
Sowing for a Great Awakening

And now, adorable Spirit, proceeding from the Father and the Son, descend upon all the Churches, renew the Pentecost in this our age, and baptize thy people generally—O baptize them yet again with tongues of fire! Crown this [twenty-first] century with a revival of "pure and undefiled religion" greater than that of the last century, greater than that of the first, greater than any "demonstration of the Spirit" ever yet vouchsafed to men!

—William Arthur, concluding prayer in the 1856
original edition of *The Tongue of Fire*

The Lord, who has graciously granted to it His blessing, will not now withdraw that blessing. Its theme is one of interest as enduring as are the relations of the spirit of man to the Spirit of God. May this new edition go forth with a fresh mandate of usefulness from Him who worketh all good. May everyone who shall pass peruse these pages rise from them refreshed for his task in the Church; and may he, endued with new power, seek and behold triumphs of our Redeemer's kingdom such as will cause him to rejoice with exceeding great joy.

—William Arthur, preface to 1880 new American
edition of *The Tongue of Fire*

CONTENTS

PUBLISHER'S FOREWORD
THE JOHN WESLEY
COLLECTION

John Wesley's profound legacy and impact on world Christianity during and since his lifetime can be viewed through a number of lenses. The revival that arose under his leadership changed the social and political structure of eighteenth-century England as the poor and lost found hope in the gospel of Jesus Christ rather than in revolution against the crown. The influence of Wesley's Spirit-inspired teaching continued unabated as the Methodist movement spread(s) scriptural holiness across the American continent and lands far beyond.

Wesley's influence as a publisher, if considered separately from all other of his extensive accomplishments, represents an astonishing record in its own right. Wesley lived in a time when Gutenberg's invention of movable type, which had immediately preceded Luther's reformation, had coalesced into specialized printing trades in London. Typefounders and printeries were becoming established and were offering exciting new pathways for the spread of the gospel through inexpensive printed text.

Perhaps more than any other figure of his day, Wesley embraced this new technology and issued sermons, tracts, commentaries, abridgments, biographies, and a host of other items that he considered relevant to the spiritual growth of maturing Christians.

Wesley was vitally driven by the reality of the inner witness of the Holy Spirit. His teaching on entire sanctification, or Christian perfection, is the capstone of his legacy. He worked tirelessly to abridge and republish seminal works by historical figures of previous generations, reaching as far back as the apostolic fathers of the first-century church. He constantly curated voices that communicated the work of the Holy Spirit in bringing believers into the fullness of salvation and lives of holy love.

These writings resourced the early Methodists in their quest to spread the gospel by providing the intellectual and spiritual moorings for the messengers of the movement. Seedbed believes these writings are as relevant to our context today as they were in the eighteenth and nineteenth centuries. Consequently, we consider it a sacred calling to join with those who are recapturing John Wesley's publishing vision for the twenty-first century.

With great joy we present The John Wesley Collection. In the years ahead, Seedbed will reissue selections from this vast collection, which include his fifty-volume Christian Library, some 150 sermons, countless items from his journals and letters, as well as innumerable tracts, hymns, poems, and other publications, most of which have been out of circulation for decades, if not centuries.

The John Wesley Collection is Seedbed's offering to the ongoing Wesleyan tradition, providing rare insight into the heartbeat of a movement whose greatest days are yet to come.

We encourage you to enter these texts with determination. Readers who persevere will soon find themselves accustomed to the winsome tenor and tempo of Wesley's voice and vernacular.

Seedbed's editors are constantly examining this extensive collection of more than 250 years of vital spiritual writing by the Wesleys and successive generations to find the most relevant and helpful messages that will speak to today's body of believers. We commend this old-new publishing work to you as one ready to be transformed by the latent power of these ancient truths. It is our prayer that these timeless words will add fuel to the fire of an awakening ready to ignite once again across the world.

Sola sancta caritas! Amen.

Andrew Miller
Seedbed Publishing

INTRODUCTION TO THE
SEEDBED EDITION

If we settle for the assumption that God cannot renew the movement of apostolic zeal we see in early Christianity, the church will die and the world is lost! This is the central challenge of the book you now have in your hands. Read it, and be prepared to have your mind purged of disbelief, your heart kindled with a new passion for the glory of God, and your ministry enflamed with a new expectancy of his transforming power.

William Arthur (1819–1901) was a native Irishman. He was born in Glendun, County Antrim, and moved with his parents to Newport, County Mayo, where he worked as a corn merchant in his early teens. Though raised in the Church of Ireland, he was converted at a Methodist meeting in Westport, and started preaching at the age of sixteen. After training for the Wesleyan Methodist ministry, he set out for India in 1839 on missionary service to work as an evangelist. He returned to England in 1841 due to ill health, and served churches in London and France between 1842–50. He was then appointed as general secretary of the Wesleyan Missionary Society from 1851–68, after which he spent three years as principal of Methodist College in Belfast. During this time, he was elected a member of Wesley's Legal Hundred in 1856 and became president of the Wesleyan Conference in 1866. Having become a well-respected leader of the church, he traveled extensively as a representative and speaker at numerous ecumenical conferences in Italy, France, and America. Following the death of his wife in 1888, he moved to Cannes for the benefit of his health and died there ten years later.

John Wesley claimed to be unafraid that Methodism "should ever cease to exist in either Europe or America." The movement was too big, too well organized, and too successful to imagine it disappearing easily. What Wesley feared was that they "should only exist as a dead sect, having the form of religion without the power." It was not until 1820 that the Methodist Conference was stirred by the first report of numerical decline, and entered a season of soul-searching about what could be done to increase spiritual religion among the societies and for the advancement of God's work in the world. Thirty-six years later, what had been a prognosis for Wesley was becoming a diagnosis for William Arthur. *The Tongue of Fire* was published in 1856 during his leadership of the Missionary Society and clearly reflects the heart of an evangelist, dissatisfied with the languishing spirituality of the church and longing for a renewal of effective ministry and mission. It could also be read against the background of the Second Great Awakening in America (1800–1830s) and the spread of revivalism in Britain and Ireland during the years after its publication.

In his preface to the original edition, Arthur describes his work as "the fruit of meditations entered upon with a desire to lessen the distance painfully felt to exist between my own life and ministry and those of the primitive Christians." Drawing from the book of Acts, he describes the early church as full of devout and joyful believers, vibrant with spiritual gifts, growing in holiness, and multiplying in numbers. He sets before us the example of apostolic ministry driven by a zeal for the glory of God and the salvation of souls. And he causes us to wrestle with these questions: Why are we not more unsettled by the zombification of the church? Why are we tempted to settle for so little spiritual fruitfulness in our discipleship and mission? Or, to put it another way, Why are we not more hungry for the fullness of spiritual life? And, Why are we not more thirsty for the salvation of others? Arthur's answer would be: we are suffering from power failure!

In the midst of power failure, the most important need for the church is not more effective churchmanship, but a baptism of fire and the fullness of the Holy Spirit! Arthur vividly narrates the events of that first Pentecost, as the tongues of fire descended on the apostles and enabled them to declare the wonders of God in the languages of other nations. Writing some fifty years before the birth of Pentecostalism, and one hundred years prior to the charismatic movement, his imagination is not held captive to the phenomenon of glossolalia, the allure of extraordinary spiritual gifts, or the performance of miraculous signs. For him, the gift of Pentecost is a supernatural power that takes whatever natural abilities we have and enables us to communicate the truth of the gospel with a power that renews souls, revitalizes the church, and revolutionizes society, from the inside out. Pentecostal Christianity means being filled, transformed, and overflowing with divine fire, for the sake of the church and the salvation of the world.

Being baptized by the tongue of fire is about being used as an instrument through whom God speaks to the

world with the power to change lives. Although speaking in
tongues may be an extraordinary sign of this gift, the ordinary and abiding reality is a prophetic power of speech that
does not come from the art of oratory but the anointing of
the Spirit, and it is for everyone! It is a tongue of fire because
the same gift of the Spirit also makes us fit for this holy
purpose by purifying our hearts and filling us with zeal for
the glory of God and the salvation of souls. It is the tongue
of fire that calls, gifts, and empowers the most unremarkable
people to lay down their lives for the mission of God. It is
for those set apart by the Spirit of prophecy to be apostles,
preachers, evangelists, pastors, and teachers. Moreover, it is
the tongue of fire that convinces the world about the reality
of God, through the holy lives and everyday conversations of
ordinary Christians whose lives, words, and deeds become a
demonstration of the Spirit's power.

It is one thing to experience the baptism of fire, and
another thing to keep the fire burning. William Arthur
reminds us that when the Pentecostal wind died down, and
the visible tongues of fire disappeared, it was the fullness of
the Spirit that remained as a permanent gift to the church.
But he witnessed the Methodist movement becoming dark-
ened in an Age of Enlightenment; as the spiritual fire of
revival, which gave it birth, was being quenched by the anti-
supernatural spirit of modernity. Without the tongue of fire,
Arthur shows how doctrine gets judged at the bar of human
reason, while theology slides into intellectualism; how holiness gets reduced to the respectability of human behavior,
while discipline plunges into moralism; and how the church
gets organized into the machinery of a human system, while
ministry descends into management. Behind all this lay a
culture of progress and the technocratic impulse to substitute
faith in God for human ingenuity, and radical dependence

on the Spirit for the ability to predict and control our own future.

The apologetics of modernity were tinged with cessationism and deism. William Arthur laments those that relegated the miraculous power of the Spirit to the early church, and rejected the particular work of the Spirit in favor of a general divine providence, domesticated to our natural abilities. He sees it in the temptation to settle for an inevitable routinization of inward spiritual power in the outward forms of an institutional church.

Today, the visible legacy of this modernist spirit is evident in lifeless and dying churches, as well as the felt need of entire denominations to deploy institutional programs of revitalization. William Arthur would no doubt caution us that unless these efforts actually emerge from, or lead us toward, a fresh baptism of fire and filling with the Spirit, we are in danger of repeating the same mistakes. The invisible legacy of this modernist spirit is not the rejection of Pentecostal Christianity in principle, but being cessationist or deist in practice. The problem of practical atheism does not require us to deny the reality of God's life-transforming presence and power. All we have to do is treat it as either irrelevant or unnecessary for our personal discipleship and church leadership. Arthur notes that nowhere is this more evident than in the way we train people for the ministry; insofar as the call, gift, and power of the Spirit is substituted for ecclesiastical office, natural talent, and higher education.

William Arthur was a missionary, and his primary concern was evangelism, at home and overseas. His study of Pentecost also presses us to ask why we have so little confidence that our ministry will actually make disciples of an unbelieving world. The tongue of fire, and the fullness of the Spirit, endued the apostles and the early church with a power for the conversion of multitudes, not just a few here and there. Perhaps there is a cessationism, deism, or plain-old practical atheism lurking behind our inability to do great things with God and to expect great things from him. A missionary spirit cannot be attained by laboring to get our message straight, or revising our methods for getting the message out. Arthur notes that there was nothing outstanding about the character, intellect, or eloquence of the apostle Peter, or the primitive Christians in general. Rather, it was the spiritual zeal from which they spoke and the holy example of their lives that brought others from darkness into light. To receive this gift, they had nothing to do but pray and wait.

The tongue of fire that filled their hearts, transformed their lives, and spilled from their mouths was both attractive and contagious. It first landed on the apostles, who moved through the crowd, speaking in tongues and spreading the fire. It then gathered and baptized the church, as a Spirit-filled community, whose close fellowship and spiritual conversation drew people into the kingdom every day.

William Arthur reminds us that the whole world cannot be brought to Christ by professional evangelists, occasional revivals, or even mass evangelism. Rather, the legacy of Pentecostal Christianity is the spontaneous expansion of the gospel, as the tongue of fire continues to separate and spread, from heart to heart, life to life, town to town, and nation to nation. This is the permanent benefit of Pentecost to the church, and true ministers of the gospel are those who continually fan this fire into flame, seek to be filled with the Spirit's power, and look for its visible fruit in the lives of ordinary people. This, and only this, is the convincing proof of real Christianity in an unbelieving world. This is the witness of William Arthur.

I pray the same tongue of fire that inspired the writing of this book will inspire in you a holy dissatisfaction with the lukewarm life, and stir up the perennial question: What shall we do? And the response from heaven will be the same as it was in the beginning: "Repent and be baptized, every one of you, in the name of Jesus Christ for the forgiveness of your sins. And you will receive the gift of the Holy Spirit." May *The Tongue of Fire* bring us to our knees in repentance for our practical atheism, and the temptation to settle for less than life-changing ministry. May it grasp our souls with hungry, thirsty, longing prayer; earnest, persevering, wrestling prayer; for ourselves, the church, and the world. And, as we pray together in one accord, may we lift our eyes heavenward for the gift of Pentecost, and the fulfillment of God's promise.

Philip Meadows
Advent 2014

A HOLY SPIRIT CREED

I believe in the Holy Ghost. I expect to see saints as lovely as any that are written of in the Scriptures—because I believe in the Holy Ghost. I expect to see preachers as powerful to set forth Christ evidently crucified before the eyes of men, as powerful to pierce the conscience, to persuade, to convince, to convert, as any that ever shook the multitudes of Jerusalem, or Corinth, or Rome—because I believe in the Holy Ghost. I expect to see Churches, the members of which shall be severally indued with spiritual gifts, and every one moving in spiritual activity, animating and edifying one another, commending themselves to the conscience of the world by their good works, commending their Saviour to it by a heart-engaging testimony—because I believe in the Holy Ghost. I expect to see villages where all the respect-able people are now opposed to religion, the proprietor ungodly, the nominal pastor worldly, all that take a lead set against living Christianity—to see such villages summoned, disturbed, divided, and then reunited, by the subduing of the whole population to Christ—because I believe in the Holy Ghost. I expect to see cities swept from end to end, their manners elevated, their commerce purified, their politics Christianized, their criminal population reformed, their poor made to feel that they dwell among brethren—righteousness in the streets, peace in the homes, an altar at every fireside— because I believe in the Holy Ghost. I expect the world to be overflowed with the knowledge of God; the day to come when no man shall need to say to his neighbor, "Know thou the Lord," but when all shall know him, "from the least unto the greatest"; east and west, north and south, uniting to praise the name of the one God and the one Mediator— because I believe in the Holy Ghost.

—William Arthur, from *The Tongue of Fire*

The Tongue of
FIRE

INTRODUCTION

The Reverend William Arthur scarcely needs an introduction to American readers. The author of that great commercial biography, *The Successful Merchant: Sketches of the Life of Mr. Samuel Budgett*, and of other works which have had an extensive circulation on this side of the Atlantic, and one of the deputation that visited the United States on behalf of the Wesleyan Church Extension enterprise in Ireland, his name is not unfamiliar in this country.

Mr. Arthur was a native of Ireland. He entered the Methodist ministry at an early age. He was active and laborious as a preacher and a writer, and occupied the post of one of the General Secretaries of the Wesleyan Missionary Society. Notwithstanding his comparative youth, he was elected to fill a vacancy in the Legal Hundred at the session of the Wesleyan Conference at Bristol in 1856—an indication of the high esteem in which his talents and usefulness were held by his brethren in the ministry.

We will not forestall the reader's judgment by a review of the work before him. If he be a man of evangelical tastes, and can, withal, relish the classical eloquence of one of the best writers of the age, he will not be put to sleep by *The Tongue of Fire*. The design of this volume is to rouse the church to action. Its utterances are like the staccato notes of the priestly trumpet, summoning the hosts of Israel to battle. It calls for a revival of Christianity according to the Pentecostal type; not the polyglottal endowment, yet "the tongue"; not the visible flame, yet the "fire." The scope of the volume might lead one to lay undue stress on aggressive, converting agencies and immediate, prodigious results, were it not for the specific importance which it attaches to that internal economy of the church by which her members "edify themselves in love." Christian fellowship is here very properly considered as essential to the very being, not merely the prosperity, of the church. Mr. Arthur's creed knows nothing about a "holy catholic Church" apart from "the communion of saints." His Pentecostal Christians are all "filled with the Spirit"—devout, zealous, joyful believers—and he would have all who profess and call themselves Christians to be just like the Pentecostal Christians.

CHAPTER 1

THE PROMISE OF A BAPTISM OF FIRE

When John the Baptist was going round Judea, shaking the hearts of the people with a call to repent, they said: "Surely this must be the Messiah for whom we have waited so long." "No," said the strong-spoken man, "I am not the Christ (John 1:20); but One mightier than I cometh, the latchet of whose shoes I am not worthy to unloose: He shall baptize you with the Holy Ghost and with fire" (Luke 3:16).

This last expression might have conveyed some idea of material burning to any people but Jews; but in their minds it would awaken other thoughts. It would recall the scenes when their father Abraham asked Him who promised that he should inherit the land wherein he was a stranger: "Lord, whereby shall I *know* that I shall inherit it?" The answer came thus: he was standing under the open sky at night, watching by cloven sacrifices, when, "behold a smoking furnace and a burning lamp that passed between those pieces" of the victims (Gen. 15:17). It would recall the fire which Moses saw in the bush, which shone, and awed, and hallowed even the wilderness, but did not consume; the fire which came in the day of Israel's deliverance, as a light on their way, and continued with them throughout the desert journey; the fire which descended on the Tabernacle in the day in which it was reared up, and abode upon it continually; which shone in the Shekinah; which touched the lips of Isaiah; which flamed in the visions of Ezekiel; and which was yet again promised to Zion, not only in her public but in her family shrines, when the "Lord will create upon every *dwelling-place* of Mount Zion, and upon all her assemblies, a cloud and smoke by day, and the shining of a flaming fire by night."

In the promise of a baptism of fire they would at once recognize the approach of new manifestations of the *power and presence of God*; for that was ever the purport of this appearance in "the days of the right hand of the Most High."

Among the multitude who flocked to John came one strange Man, whom he did not altogether know; yet he knew that He was full of grace and wisdom, and in favor with God and man. He felt that himself rather needed to be baptized of one so pure than to baptize Him; but he waived his feeling, and fulfilled his ministry. As they returned from the water side, the heavens opened: a bodily shape, as of a dove, came down and rested on the stranger. At the same time a voice from the excellent glory said: "This is my beloved Son, in whom I am well pleased: hear ye Him."

John said, "I knew Him not: but He that sent me to baptize with water, the same said unto me, Upon whom thou shalt see the Spirit descending, and remaining on Him, the same is He which baptizeth with the Holy Ghost." Therefore, when he saw Him walking, he pointed his own disciples to Him, and said, that this was He. They heard the word, and pondered. The next day, again, John, seeing Him at a distance, said, "Behold the Lamb of God!" Now, two of his followers went after the stranger, to seek at His hand the baptism which John could not give—the baptism of fire. They were joined by others. For months, for years, they companied with Him. They saw His life: a life as of the only begotten Son of God. They heard His words: such words as "never man spake." They saw His works: signs, and wonders, and great miracles, before all the people. Yet they received not the baptism of fire!

He began to speak frequently of His departure from them, but His mode of describing it was strange. He was to leave them, and yet not to forsake them; to go away, and yet to be with them; to go, and yet to come to them. They were to be deprived of Him their Head, yet orphans they should not be. Another was to come, yet not another; a Comforter from the Father, from Himself; whom, not as in His case, the world could neither know nor *see*, but whom *they* should *know*, though they could not see (John 14:17). His own presence with them was a privilege which no tongue could worthily tell. Blessed were their eyes for what they saw, and their ears for what they heard. Better still than even this was to be the presence of the Holy Ghost, who would follow Him as He had followed John.

"I tell you the truth," He said, when about to utter what was hard to believe: "I tell you the truth; it is expedient for you that I go away." How *could* it be expedient? Would they not be losers to an extent which no man could reckon? The light of His countenance, the blessing of His words, the purity of His presence, the influence of His example, all to be removed; and this expedient for them! "It is expedient for you that I go away for if I go not away, the Comforter will not come unto you." Well, but would they not be better with

Himself than with the Comforter? No; just the contrary. They would be better with the Comforter: He would lead them into all truth; whereas now they are constantly misapplying the plain words of Christ. He would bring all things to their remembrance; whereas now they often forget in a day or two the most remarkable teaching, or the most amazing miracles. He would take the things of Christ, the things of the Father, and reveal them unto them; whereas now they constantly misapprehended His relation to the Father, and that of the Father to Him, misapprehended His person, His mission, and His kingdom. Again, He would convince the *world* of sin, of righteousness, and of judgment to come; and this is not as one teacher limited by a local personality, but as a Spirit diffused abroad throughout the earth. And He would abide with them *forever*, not for "a little while." Whatever, therefore, Christ's personal presence and teaching had been to them, the presence of the Spirit would be more.

Jesus Reveals the Great Commission

Having thus strongly preoccupied their minds with the hope of a greater joy than even His own countenance, the Master laid down His life. Stunned, dispersed, and desolate, they felt themselves orphans indeed. Their Master ignominiously executed, and neither the word of John nor His own word fulfilled: no Comforter, no baptism, no fire! Soon He reappeared, and, as they were met together for the first time since His death, once more stood in the midst of them. He breathed upon them, and said, "Receive ye the Holy Ghost." With that word, doubtless, both peace and power were given; yet it was not the baptism of fire. During forty days He conversed with them on the things pertaining to the kingdom of God; assigning to them the work of proclaiming and establishing that kingdom to the ends of the earth. One injunction, however, He laid upon them, which seemed to defer the effect of others. They were to go into all the world, yet not at once, or unconditionally. "Tarry ye in the city of Jerusalem till ye be endued with power from on high." Apparently more ready to interpret "power" as referring to the hopes of their nation than to the kingdom of grace, they asked, "Lord, wilt Thou at this time restore again the kingdom to Israel?" (Acts 1:6).

He had said nothing of a kingdom for Israel, or in Israel. His speech had been on a higher theme, and of a wider field, namely, "that repentance and remission of sins should be preached in His name among all nations, beginning at Jerusalem. And ye are witnesses of these things." Such, in various forms, are the words we find Him uttering concerning His kingdom during these forty days. When, therefore, they asked if He would at this time restore again the kingdom to Israel, He shortly turned aside their curiosity. What the Father's designs were as to Israel nationally; what the times when they might again be a kingdom—were points not for them. They had better work, and nearer at hand. "It is not for you to know the times or the seasons, which the Father hath put in His own power" (Acts 1:7). "But," He continued, passing at once from curious questions about the future of Israel, and unfulfilled prophecy, to His own grand kingdom: "But ye shall receive power, after that the Holy Ghost is come upon you." What power? of princes, or magistrates? Nay, quite another power for an unearthly work: "And ye shall be witnesses unto Me both in Jerusalem, and in all Judea, and in Samaria, and unto the uttermost part of the earth."

In these words He traces the circles in which Christian sympathy and activity should ever run: first, Jerusalem, their chief city; next, Judea, their native land; then Samaria, a neighboring country, inhabited by a race nationally detested by their countrymen; and finally "the uttermost parts of the earth." They were neither to seek distant spheres first, nor to confine themselves always at home; but to carry the gospel into all the world as each country could be reached. This was what He had before placed in their view—the filling all the earth with the news of grace, news that repentance and pardon were opened to men by the power of His atonement.

A New Kind of Kingdom

We have no hint that He ever spake, during the forty days, of other kingdom, royalty, or reign. Not to rule over cities; not to speculate on the designs of the Father and the destinies of the Jew; but to go into the whole world, tell every creature the story of Christ, was to be their princely work. To found a kingdom not over men's persons, but "within" their souls; a kingdom not of provinces, but of "righteousness, and peace, and joy in the Holy Ghost"; a kingdom to be spread not by the arms of a second Joshua, but by the "witness" of the human voice; a kingdom, the power of which would not lie in force or policy, or signs observed in heaven, but in a spiritual power imparted by the Holy Ghost, and operating in super-human utterance of heavenly truth; this was their embassy. For this were they to be endued with power from on high.

But when was this power, so long spoken of, to come? Would John's word ever be fulfilled? The Master has not forgotten it. "John truly baptized with water, but ye shall be baptized with the Holy Ghost not many days hence." At length the promise is brought to a point, and its fulfillment near.

Already had He proclaimed Himself King, and marked out the ministers and army, the weapon, the extent, the badge of citizenship, the statute law, the royal glory, and the duration of His kingdom. With His disciples around Him, standing on a mountain top, heaven above and earth below, He thus proclaimed His kingdom: "All power is given to Me in heaven and in earth": here was the King. "Go": here were the ministers and army—an embassy of peace. "Teach": here the weapon—the word of God. "All nations": here the extent. "Baptizing them in the name of the Father, and of the Son, and of the Holy Ghost": here the badge of citizenship. "Teaching them to observe all things whatsoever I have commanded you": here the statute law. "And, lo, I am with you": here the royal presence and glory of the kingdom. "Always, unto the end of the world": here its duration (Matt. 28:19–20).

Now again He is rising a hill, conversing with those who had heard this proclamation, as to their part in the establishment of the kingdom. He has clearly promised that, before many days, the long looked-for baptism of fire will come. That implies, that before many days He will depart; for He ever said that He must first ascend. He has answered, or rather rebuked, their curious inquiry as to Israel; has turned their thoughts again to the descent of the Spirit; and is just telling them that, endued with this new power, they shall bear witness to His glory not only at home but abroad. "To the uttermost part of the earth," is the last word on His lips (Acts 1:8)—a startling word for His peasant auditors, accustomed to limit their range of thought within the Holy Land. But He had already said that all power was given to Him "in heaven and in earth." Did not the faith of some disciple reel under the weight of these words?

"In Jerusalem, and in all Judea, and in Samaria, and to THE UTTERMOST PART(S) OF THE EARTH!" This word is on His lips; they are steadily watching Him: He lifts His hands,

He pronounces His blessing; and in the act (Luke 24:50) lo, His body, which they know "has flesh and bones" like their own, begins to rise! No wing, no hand, no chariot of fire! Upward it moves by its own power; and in that single action commands the homage of earth: for our globe has no law so universal and irreversible as that whereby it binds down all ponderous bodies to its surface. Here this law gives way, and thereby the whole mass of the globe yields to the power of Christ. This placid movement of that body, up from the surface of earth into the heights of the sky, is an open act of sovereignty over the highest physical law; whereby Christ "manifested forth His glory," as Lord and Maker of all physical laws. His proclamation of Kingship is thus acknowledged by earth with its highest homage. Now the heaven adds its homage, stoops in luminous cloud, and robes Him for His enthronement. The everlasting doors lift up their heads. The King of Glory enters in.

The First-begotten from the dead, the Prince of the Kings of the earth, sits down with the Father on His throne; and from Him receives the word, "Thy throne, O God, is forever and ever; a scepter of righteousness is the scepter of Thy kingdom!" And again, "Let all the angels of God worship Him." Within the veil they worship the Lamb; and down they speed to His followers, and tell them that they need not gaze. As they have seen Him go, so shall they see Him come, even in the clouds, to judge that world, of which and of its Princes He is King. Thus triply is His kingship owned. Earth permits Him to rise, heaven bows, the angels add their testimony. All things own Him. Unbelief is now impossible. Doubt vanishes away. His word shall not pass unfulfilled. The baptism of fire is at hand.

CHAPTER 2

The Waiting for the Fulfillment

It is on Thursday, probably in the evening, that the disciples return to Jerusalem. Their Master is no more at their head—indeed, no more on earth; and as yet His great promise is unfulfilled. But the scene of the ascension is in their eye; the voice of the angels in their ear. Jesus is King of Kings, and Lord of Lords. The Comforter is coming "not many days hence." Not with doubting or weeping do they enter the city, but with "great joy"; the joy of a triumph already sealed, and of hope foreseeing triumphs to come. Most probably that joy carries their first steps to the temple (Luke 24:53). Oft had they entered it with Him, but never so triumphantly as now. There they are, not mourning the absence of their Master, but "praising and blessing God." Thence they go to "an upper room." We know not in what street, or on what site; but there "abode" a few men whose names were not then great, but whose names will never more pass from the memory of mankind. With them abode also a few women, who had loved their Lord; and for the last time "Mary the mother of Jesus" is named as one of the little company. Men and women, they now began to pray, and they "continued with one accord in prayer and supplication," for the baptism of fire.

Did they expect to receive it that very night? This we know not, but we do know that then opened a new era in the intercourse of man with heaven. As they began to pray, how would they find all their conceptions of the Majesty on high changed! It no longer spread before and beyond the soul's eyesight, as an unvaried infinity of glory incomprehensible. The glory was brighter, the incomprehensibility remained; but the infinity had now received a center. Every beam of the glory converged toward the person of "God manifest in the flesh," now "received up into heaven": the glory not dissolving the person in its own tide, the person not dimming the glory by any shade, though appearing through it as the sun's body through the light.

Perhaps the change was such to their view, as would have struck the eye of an observer of nature, had one lived on our planet at the time when the sun was first set in the firmament. The light which before had been a wide and level mystery, now had to his eye a law, a center, and a spring. The indistinct view of a material form amid the seemingly spiritual glory, gave the feeling that some body akin to our own globe lay at the center of illumination. This body was not the cause of the light, not even of the same nature, but around the body the "exceeding weight of glory" seemed to hang.

The Glory of His Death Is Revealed!

O to feel as felt that heart which first discerned human nature, in the person of Him who had been "so marred," set down "on the right hand of the Majesty on high!" The glory of the Father encompassing a human form, and beaming from a human brow! "If ye loved Me, ye would rejoice, because I said, I go unto the Father; for My Father is greater than I"—was the word of Jesus. Now that they had seen Him pass within the veil; seen the ushering angels attend His entrance, and heard the music of their voices; they would not feel as if He had forsaken them, but as they had often felt when the High Priest passed from their view into the holiest, bearing the blood of atonement, to stand before the Presence. "He is out of sight, but there before the Lord." The first thought would be one of joy for Him.

Peter, how did thy breast heave when first thou didst behold, by faith clear as sight, that countenance which had looked round upon thee from the bar, now looking down on thee from the high and lofty throne! Mary Magdalena, who wast bent under the sevenfold power of the devil when first that face beamed on thee, who didst fall at His feet when, just arisen from the dead, He first appeared to thee! What was the flow of thy tears, what the odor of thy joy, when the full truth burst on thy view, that He had "overcome, and was set down with the Father on His throne"! And thou, John, what felt thy bosom when He on whose bosom thine own head had leaned, appeared to thy mind no more with such as thee; but, as "in the beginning, with God"? And thou, too, Mary the blessed, through whose soul the sword had gone, how did thy "soul magnify the Lord"! How did thy

"spirit rejoice in God thy Savior," when thy meek eye saw the
infinite accomplishment of Gabriel's word, *He shall be Great!*

Man Communes Directly with God

Mingling with this first joy for the Master's exaltation,
and presently rising to the surface and overspreading all
their emotions, would be the feeling, "He has entered *for
us* within the veil! He bears our names upon His heart for
a memorial before the Lord! He maketh intercession for
us!"—Tush! Which of the Twelve is it that starts up as if
a spirit had entered him, and, pointing upward, says to the
Brethren—"Let us ask the Father in HIS NAME! He said
to us, 'Whatsoever ye shall ask the Father *in My name*, He
will give it to you. Hitherto ye have asked nothing *in My
name*: ask, and ye shall receive, that your joy may be full'"
(John 16:23–24).

The angels had often sung together when the prayer
of repenting sinners was heard on high. Now, for the first
time, they hear prayers from human lips rising to the throne
authorized and accredited by the name of the only begotten
of the Father. That name has just been set "above every
name": and as it echoes through the host above, with the
solemn joy of a hundred believing voices, "things in heaven"
bow. Be man ever so unworthy, "worthy is the Lamb." His
name covers with justice every request to which it is set by
His authority. What must have been that moment for the
saints in paradise, who had seen the Savior afar off, but
never known the joy of praying directly in His name! Father
Abraham had "rejoiced to see His day; and he saw it and
was glad." What would be his gladness now, that earth and
heaven were rejoicing in His name! David, to whom He was
at once Lord and Son—what would be "the things" which in

that wonderful moment his tongue would speak "touching the King"?

From the hour that sin entered into the world, the Just One had never given man audience on terms fit only for the innocent. An upright inferior may approach Majesty, not without reverence, but without shame or atonement. The admission of a criminal on the same footing would be wrong. Right in our governments is the imperfect reflection of a perfect right. Had the favor of the Almighty crossed the line which divides innocence from guilt, and smiled upon the latter, that smile would have been a scathing flash, wherein all morals would have blackened. Sinful man had not been hopelessly banished from the presence of God; but he had ever been taught to come displaying a sign of wrath, of death, which is the wages of sin; thus declaring to the universe that he appealed not to a justice which had never been offended, but to a justice which had been satisfied.

The altar had been the patriarch's place of prayer. The temple, where was the perpetual offering, had been the center to which every praying Israelite turned. To approach the eternal Godhead as if no evil had been done, and no stroke merited, was never yet the privilege of a creature who had done wrong. It was wonderful, yea, mysterious, that such could be allowed to approach at all; but the Lord would ever justify His permission, by demanding clear and express reference to that propitiation, which He has set forth to declare His own righteousness, in that marvelous act of lifting the guilty into the mansions of the good.

How great the transition from these symbols of the Atonement to the full view of its reality! During the forty days Jesus had opened their understanding, pointed out to them the Scriptures which bore upon His death, and showed its connection with remission of sins for mankind. They now looked no more to temple or to altar. They had before them the true sacrifice completed. He had "purged their sins," and, in the same body wherein He had done so, was standing before the Father.

He had given them authority to use His name. With that name their petitions carried the assent of all the rational and moral creation. The eternal Father in holding communion with beings who had done wrong, exposed no sinless being to doubts as to whether right and wrong were equal. He had "made peace through" Christ's "blood," had thus "reconciled all things to Himself"—to Himself in the new and mysterious proceeding of government, whereby the doers of wrong were spared the effects of wrongdoing. "For it pleased the Father that in Him should all fullness dwell; and, having made peace through the blood of His cross, by Him to reconcile all things unto Himself; by Him, I say, whether they be things in earth, or things in heaven" (Col. 1:19–20). So that creatures "in heaven," all whose joy depended on their never doing wrong, had no murmur to raise, and no temptation to undergo, when they saw creatures "on earth," who had followed ways which would make any world sorrowful, received into the arms of eternal mercy.

The guilty He reconciled by forgiving their sin, and recovering their hearts; and the innocent He reconciled to see offenders exalted, by "setting forth" so conspicuously that all angels desired to look into it, "a propitiation," which fully "declared His righteousness," His strict care of right; which magnified law, magnified holiness, magnified obedience, and, in the act of saving the guilty, magnified beyond all previous conception the heinousness of guilt. What sense of the distinction between right and wrong could have been maintained among innocent creatures, had they seen transgressors raised to favor and honor without atonement?

O the joy of that first hour of praying *in the name* of Christ! Was not Martha there? As she met the Master on that mournful day, when Lazarus lay in the tomb, though despairing, she said, "But I know, that even now, whatsoever thou wilt ask of God, God will give it thee." If such was her confidence then, what would be her confidence now—He asking for her, and she asking in His name! How the souls of the disciples, following Him above the sky, would soar, with a new wing, a new eye, and a new song! What simple and glowing collects would they be which were uttered then! What words of joy and supplication would he pour forth who first bethought him of putting the Lord in remembrance of His own promises! What short and burning petitions would go up from the lips which first quoted, "Whatsoever ye shall ask the Father in My name, He shall give it you"! How would he plead who first remembered, "Ask what ye will, and it shall be done unto you"! How would tones of desire and triumph mingle in the first repetition of, "All things whatsoever ye ask in prayer believing, ye shall receive"! None of their prayers are recorded. We have ancient collects, and beautiful they are; but none of these most ancient are preserved. The Spirit has not seen it good to hand down the strong and tender collects of these ten, or of the following days. Then surely it is unlawful to impose good forms of prayer upon all men because ancient saints wrote them.

He who will never use a form in public prayer, casts away the wisdom of the past. He who will use only forms, casts away the hope of utterance to be given by the Spirit at present, and even shuts up the future in the stiff hand of the past. Whatever church forbids a Christian congregation, no matter what may be their fears, troubles, joys, or special and pressing need, ever to send up prayer to God, except in words framed by other men in other ages, uses an authority which was never delegated. To object to all forms is narrowness. To doom a Christian temple to be a place wherein a simple and impromptu cry may never arise to heaven, is superstition.

Does any one of the hundred and twenty, even in paradise, up to this moment forget the hour of prayer that Thursday night, after they had returned from Olivet?

Anticipating the Promise

The Friday morning dawns. It was on Friday the Lord had died. Would He not send His promised substitute today? O how His cross would all day long stand before the eye of every disciple! Now came back all His words about the death "which He should accomplish"; from the night when He told Nicodemus that, as the serpent had been lifted up, so must He, up to the night in which He said, "The hour is come"—words dark at the time, but pointed today as the steel of arrows. What had been mystery, was mystery no longer. Now the only mystery was, "What manner of love!" Was it on that day that John's fiery heart—the heart which had rebuked the man who followed not them, which wished to burn the inhospitable villagers, and to be, with his brother, head of all—was it then this heart fully embraced the meaning of the agony witnessed by him so close at hand, as compared with others, and written upon it forever? Was it then it first saw all the import of the words, "God so loved the world, that He gave His only begotten Son, that whosoever believeth in Him, should not perish, but have everlasting life"? and that the "son of thunder" was transformed into the child of charity?

Never before had the thought of man alternated between two such scenes, as those which divided the eye of every soul in that praying company: a cross, a drooping head, hands bleeding, feet bleeding, heaven black, thieves on either side, gibes below; and a preternatural sorrow on the soul of the sufferer, which cast over the whole an infinite dreadfulness. On this the eye looks one moment, and weeps. Then a throne, high and lifted up; the glory of the Lord; angels bowing; angels singing; saints with palm, and harp, and voice acclaiming; and in the center of all might, majesty, and dominion, the crucified body, living, but with its wounds "as slain." On this the same eye looks, and weeps again. O for the feeling of that day!

Yet the Friday wears away, and no "baptism of fire"! The Saturday sets in; its hours are filled up as before with prayer; but no answer. And now dawns the first day of the week, the day whereon He rose, the first Lord's day He had passed on His throne of glory. How did they spend that day? Surely they would fully expect that the blessing they sought would be delayed no longer. He said, "*Not many* days": this was the fourth day; it must come today! But the evening steals on, and all their prayers might have risen into a Heaven that could not hear. Monday, Tuesday, Wednesday pass. Their faith does not fail; still in the temple "praising and blessing God," or in the upper room in "prayer and supplication," they continue of one accord. Though He tarry, yet will they wait for Him.

A Unified Request

This *is* waiting. Some speak of waiting for salvation as if it meant making ourselves at ease, and dismissing both effort and anxiety. Who so waits for any person or any event? When waiting, your mind is set on a certain point; you can give yourself to nothing else. You are looking forward, and preparing; every moment of delay increases the sensitiveness of your mind as to that one thing. A servant waiting for his master, a wife waiting for the footstep of her husband, a mother waiting for her expected boy, a merchant waiting for his richly laden ship, a sailor waiting for the sight of land, a monarch waiting for tidings of the battle: all these are cases wherein the mind is set on one object, and cannot easily give attention to another.

"Tomorrow will be Thursday, a full week from the ascension: that *will* be the day, the term of the promise will not extend further. Tomorrow the Comforter will come; tomorrow we shall be baptized with fire, and fitted to do the works our Master did, 'yea, greater works than these.'" So they would probably settle it in their mind. The Thursday finds them, as before, "of one accord in one place"; no Thomas absent through unbelief.

How the scene of that day week would return to their view! How they would over and over again in mind repeat the walk from Jerusalem to Olivet; each recalling what he said to the Master, and what the Master said to him; each thinking he had got such a look as he never got before, and as he should not forget so long as he lived! How they would repeat the last words! "Ye shall receive *power*, after that the Holy Ghost is come upon you." In the repetition new faith would kindle. "Yes, we shall; let us wait on; we shall 'be endued with power from on high.'" Then another would repeat, "And ye shall be witnesses to Me in Jerusalem, and in all Judea, and in Samaria, and to the uttermost parts of the earth." This was vast language for them, whose thoughts were wont to move only in the sphere of Palestine.

Probably they did not so much weigh the import of the terms as look at the main promise. They should be endued with the power of the Holy Ghost—that power which had made psalmists and prophet; had rendered the words of Elijah stronger than the decrees of Ahab, the words of

Elisha stronger than the armies of Syria, the words of Isaiah as coals from the altar, and the words of Daniel mightier than the spirit of a king and "a thousand of his captains." Baptized with the same Spirit, they were to proclaim what these foretold, but never saw: the Child born, the Son given, the Prince cut off for sin, but not His own, the Lamb on whom were laid the iniquities of all.

All this they had seen fulfilled in the person of their glorious Lord. All this they had heard explained by His own lips before and after His death. They were to go and prove to others, as He had proved to them, that "thus it is written, and thus it behooved Christ to suffer, and to rise again the third day; and that repentance and remission of sins should be preached in His name among all nations, beginning at Jerusalem."

Here again they encountered the intimation that their message was for all, and their testimony to be borne to the uttermost parts of the earth. Yet still it seems that not the sphere, but the purport, of their commission now occupied their mind. They were to go, and as He had preached, so would they, far and wide, in cities and villages. In what tones would they tell the people that as He used to say to those who came to Him, "Be of good cheer, thy sins be forgiven thee," so would He now say from Heaven to all who lifted an eye to Him!

Did They Question His Delay?

But the day wears on, and no blessing. Is not the delay long? "*Not* many days!" Does the promise hold good? They must have felt disappointed as the evening fell, and no sign of an answer to their oft-repeated prayer. Now is the hour of trial. Will their faith fail? Will some begin to forsake the meetings which bring not the baptism they seek? Will some stay at home, or "go a fishing," saying that they will wait the Lord's time, and not be unwarrantably anxious about what, after all, does not depend on them, but on the Lord? Will no one say, "We have done our duty, and must leave results. We cannot command the fulfillment of the promise. We have asked for it, asked sincerely, fervently, repeatedly: we can do no more"?

Or, what is equally probable, will they begin to find out that the cause why they remain unblessed, and yet "orphans," lies in the unfaithfulness of their companions? Happily the spirit of faith and love abides upon them. John does not turn upon Peter, and say, "It is your fault; for you denied the Master." Philip does not turn to John, and say, "It is your fault; for you and James wanted to lord it over us all." Andrew does not turn to Thomas, and say, "It is your fault; for you *would* not believe, even when we had declared it to you." The Seventy do not say, "It is the fault of the Twelve; for, after the Lord had lifted them above us all, one of them sold Him, another denied Him, and a third disbelieved Him." The Marys do not say, "It is the fault of the whole company, a cold and unfaithful company, professing to love the Master to His face, but the moment He fell into the hands of His enemies, ye all forsook Him and fled!"

Well did they know that they had been slow of heart; been unworthy of such a Teacher; often grieved Him, and made Him ask, "How long shall I be with you?" John would never forget the rebuke, "Ye know not what manner of spirit ye are of." Peter would never forget, the third time, "Lovest Thou Me?" Philip would never forget, "Have I been so long time with you, and yet hast thou not known Me, Philip?" And surely Thomas would never forget, "Be not faithless, but believing."

Yet they knew He had not come to call the righteous, but sinners to repentance. His own lips had said, "He that is whole hath no need of a physician, but he that is sick." Had He not taken to His bosom the very head whose heats of ambition and of vindictiveness He had rebuked? Had He not said to Peter, "Feed My lambs"? Had he not said to Thomas, "Reach hither thy hand"? His promise was not made because they were a church without spot or wrinkle; but because they were feeble, and, deprived of His own presence, would be orphans indeed, did no other power cover them. He knew every fault with which either of them could charge the others; yet the promise had passed His lips, and the fire would fall even on them, unworthy as they were. Happy for them, that none fancied he could fix upon others the cause of their unanswered prayers!

The Thursday is gone; eight days! The Friday and the Saturday follow it, marked by the same persistency in union, in praise, in prayer, and by the same absence of encouragement. Ten days gone! The promise, "Not many days," is all but broken.

Peter was always warm and earnest. A thought of his had hardly time to become a thought before it turned into either word or action. When once his mind had embraced the glorious idea of standing up before the world a witness for his ascended Master, it would seem as if the whole plan was to be carried out in a day. One cannot help imagining how he bore the restraint of the ten days—the days of prayer, of belief, of waiting—in which they were not permitted to begin their work.

"Strange!" we almost hear him say, "Strange! The Lord has died that repentance and remission of sins should be preached in His name among all nations. He has finished the work, risen from the dead, and led captivity captive. The Heavens have received Him. The angels proclaim Him. Us He took from our homes; how He taught, and trained and practiced us; all, as we now see, for this work of proclaiming His love and the pardon it brings to all mankind! Here we are, unfitted for every other calling. His commission is to us as a Prophet's call, as a King's anointing. He said, 'Go into all the world, and preach the Gospel to every creature.' We want to go. Men stand in need: they are dying daily; dying in unbelief. Why does He not permit us to go? Why is the first command so long suspended by the other? 'Tarry ye in the city of Jerusalem until ye be endued with power from on high' We have tarried ten days. Why does our Master delay? The world needs the sound of His gospel; we are waiting to bear it forth. He is exalted at God's right hand, and all power is given unto Him in Heaven and in earth; yet does He look down upon the world sleeping a sleep unto death, and upon us waiting to blow the trumpet! Is not His instruction, His commission, enough? We are ordained, after much teaching: May we not go? No, we must abide by His word: 'Tarry until ye be endued with power from on high.'"

The final proof given by Peter that he was waiting indeed, making all preparations for the event, was in calling upon his brethren to fill up the number of the apostles. One had fallen. His place was vacant; and another was to take his "bishopric." Peter concluded that they were to fill up this vacancy, and called upon the company to select two men. No one objected that it remained to be seen whether they should be endued with power or not. All acted as feeling the certainty that the Holy Spirit was about to come, and the apostolic commission to be fulfilled to the ends of the earth.

CHAPTER 3

THE FULFILLMENT OF THE PROMISE

There was a day when death had struck a woeful stroke, and raised a nation's wail. "There was a great cry in the land of Egypt: for there was not a house where there was not one dead." That same day the Lord, by the sprinkling of a pure lamb's blood, averted death from the doors of Israel, and then led them away from yoke and taskmaster toward the goodly land. Fifty days afterward they reached the Mount of God, where He manifested Himself in the thunder of His power, with flame and trumpet, and a voice, whereat all the tribes did tremble. Then was the new dispensation formally inaugurated with the voice and the flame; its covenant sealed by sprinkling of blood, and its privileges opened to the sprinkled by the vision of glory, when the Elders "saw the God of Israel: and there was under His feet as it were a paved work of a sapphire stone, and as it were the body of heaven in his clearness" (Exod. 24:10).

This time of note was come, the fifty days were elapsed from the time when the Lamb was slain, and captivity broken. Forty days He had been with them after His resurrection; the rest He had passed within the veil. And was it not possible that in saying, "Not many days," He pointed them forward to the day which commemorated the opening of the new dispensation of God to Israel by the hand of His servant Moses? Was it not probable that the glorious dispensation of His Son would be opened at this time? Unbelief would have long ago ceased to expect; but faith would probably renew its anticipation, and look to this day.[1]

Not One Heart Has Failed!

On the morning of the resurrection, some—the women—were early at the tomb; but the others were sauntering into the country, or here and there, with nothing to wait for, as they thought; yet partly expecting something to come to their ears. Even late in the day, when they did meet to hear what some had seen and heard, Thomas was away. Now, however, after ten days have elapsed, their patience is not exhausted. They *do* expect, and therefore will not cease to wait. They have no attention for anything else.

The kingdom of God is at hand. Did He not say, "Not many days"? Ten are gone; and the conclusion is, not that of servants too idle to wait: "Our Lord delayeth His coming; we may as well sit still. He will come in His own good time." That is not waiting: it is idling. They said, in their believing hearts, "Ten days are gone; therefore the day of our Lord draweth nigh. This is the day of Pentecost; and as the fire appeared on Sinai, in the presence of our fathers, when God made His covenant by Moses, it may be that today He will seal His covenant by the hand of the Prophet whom

Moses foresaw, baptizing us with fire, according to the word wherein He hath made His servants to hope."

No Thomas is absent now! Not one heart has failed! "They are *all* in one place." No discord or doubt have they permitted to arise: "They are all *with one accord* in one place." Nor are they slow or late. We are not told at what hour they met, but it must have been very early; for after they had received the baptism, and filled all Jerusalem with the noise of their new powers, Peter reminded the multitude, who came together, that it was only the third hour of the day—nine o'clock in the morning.

A Mighty Rushing Wind and a Crown of Fire

Early, then, on the second Lord's day after the ascension, is the entire company met, with one heart, to renew their oft-repeated prayer. We cannot go to the house where was that upper room; nor to the site where it stood. These points are left unnoticed, after the mode of Christianity, which is in nothing a religion of circumstances, in everything a religion of principles.

We know not how long they had that morning urged their prayer, nor whose voice was then crying to Him who had promised, nor what word of the Master he was pleading, nor what feelings of closer expectation and more vivid faith were warming the breasts of the disciples. But "suddenly there came a sound from heaven as of a rushing mighty wind." Not, mark you, a wind; no gale sweeping over the city struck the sides of the house, and rustled round it. But "from heaven" directly downward fell "a sound," without shape, or step, or movement to account for it—a sound as if a mighty wind were rushing, not along the ground, but straight from on high, like showers in a dead calm. Yet no wind stirred. As to motion, the air of the room was still as death; as to sound, it was awful as a hurricane.

Mysterious sound, whence comest thou? Is it the Lord again breathing upon them, but this time from His throne? Is it the wind of Ezekiel preparing to blow? Shaken by this supernatural sign, we may see each head bow low. Then timidly turning upward, John sees Peter's head crowned with fire; Peter sees James crowned with fire; James sees Nathaniel crowned with fire; Nathaniel sees Mary crowned with fire; and round and round the fire sits "on each of them." The Lord has been mindful of His promise. The word of the Lord is tried. John was a faithful witness. Jesus was a faithful Redeemer. He is now glorified; for the Holy Ghost is given. Jesus "being by the right hand of God exalted, and having received of the Father the promise of the Holy Ghost, He hath shed forth this."

The instant effect of the descent of the Spirit on the first Gentile converts in the house of Cornelius was that they began to "magnify God."[2] The effect would be the same in this first case. That bosom has yet to learn what is the feeling of moral sublimity, which never has been suddenly heaved with an emotion of uncontrollable adoration to God and the Lamb—an emotion which, though no voice told whence it came, by its movement in the depths of the soul, farther down than ordinary feelings reach, did indicate somehow that the touch of the Creator was traceable in it. They only who have felt such unearthly joy need attempt to conceive the outburst of that burning moment. Body, soul, and spirit, glowing with one celestial fire, would blend and pour out their powers in a rapturous "Glory be to God!" or "Blessed be the Lord God!"

Modern believers—not those who never unite in simple and fervent supplications to the throne of grace, but those who meet and urge with long-repeated entreaty their requests to God—can recall times which help them to imagine what must have been the peal of praise that burst from the hearts of the hundred and twenty, when the baptism fell upon their souls; times when they and their friends have felt as if the place where they met was filled with the glory of the Lord.

What Is Baptism by Fire?

One word as to the mode of this baptism. In this case we have the one perfectly clear account contained in Scripture of the mode wherein the baptizing element was applied to the person of the baptized. The element here is fire; the mode is shedding down—"hath shed forth this." "It sat upon each of them." Did baptism mean immersion, they would have been plunged into the fire, not the fire shed upon them. The only other case in which the mode of contact between the baptizing element and the baptized persons is indicated, is this: "And were all baptized to Moses in the cloud and in the sea." They were not dipped in the cloud, but the cloud descended upon them; they were not plunged into the sea, but the sea sprinkled them as they passed. The Spirit signified by the water is *never once promised under the idea of dipping*. Such an expression as, "I will immerse you in my Spirit," "I will plunge you in my Spirit," or "I will dip you in clean water," is unknown to the Scripture. But, "I will pour out my Spirit upon you," "I will sprinkle clean water upon you," is language and thought familiar to all readers of the Bible. The word "dip," or "dipped," does not often occur in the New Testament; but when it does, the original is *never* "baptize," or "baptized."[3]

A Tongue of Fire: Man's Voice

The fire is not a shapeless flame. It is not Abram's lamp, nor the pillar of the desert, nor the coal of Isaiah, nor

the enfolding flame of Ezekiel. It is a tongue; yea, cloven
tongues. On each brow glows a sheet of flame, parted into
many tongues. Here was the symbol of the new dispensation.
Christianity was to be a Tongue of Fire. It was a symbol of
their "power," the power whereby the new kingdom was to
be built up; the power for which they had so long to tarry,
and so eagerly to pray, when all other things were prepared;
for which the whole arrangement for the world's conversion
was commanded to stand still. The appearance of this one
symbol was the signal that former ones had waxed old and
were ready to vanish away. Altar and cherubim, sacrifice and
incense, ephod and breastplate, Urim and Thummim—their
work was done. Even of the most sacred emblem of all, that
which was the "pattern of things in the heavens," the Ark
itself, it had been foretold, "They shall say no more, The
Ark of the Covenant of the Lord; neither shall it come to
mind; neither shall they remember it; neither shall they visit
it; neither shall it be magnified anymore." Of the temple
itself the Master had said, that not one stone should be left
upon another.

All the emblems of the old dispensation were now
forever suspended. In their room the Lord had appointed
only two; and they chosen with a singular aptness at once
to suggest ideas, and to avoid image representation: the
water, wherein the mind could see a symbol of the cleansing
Spirit, but the eye no attempted likeness; the bread and
wine, wherein the body and the blood are forcibly brought
to mind, but no personal similitude set before the eye.
These two only were the inartistic emblems which Christ
had ordained for His church. His was to be a religion of the
understanding and the heart; wholly resting on the convic-
tions and the principles, building nothing on sense, and
permitting nothing to fancy.

In strict keeping with this spiritual stamp of Christianity, was the symbol which, once for all, announced to the church the advent of her conquering power—the power by which she was to stand before kings, to confound synagogues, to silence councils, to still mobs, to confront the learned, to illuminate the senseless, and to inflame the cold—the power by which, beginning at Jerusalem, where the name of Jesus was a byword, she was to proclaim His glory through all Judea, throughout Samaria, and throughout the uttermost parts of the earth. The symbol is a tongue, the only instrument of the grandest war ever waged: a *tongue*—man's speech to his fellowman; a message in human words to human faculties, from the understanding to the understanding, from the heart to the heart. A tongue of *fire*—man's voice, God's truth; man's speech, the Holy Spirit's inspiration; a human organ, a superhuman power: not one tongue, but cloven tongues; as the speech of men is various, here we see the Creator taking to Himself the language of every man's mother; so that in the very words wherein he heard her say, "I love thee," he might also hear the Father of all say, "I love thee."

How does that fire-symbol, shining on the brow of the primitive church, rebuke that system which would force all men to worship God in one tongue, and that not a tongue of fire, but a dead tongue, wherein no man now on earth can hear his mother's tones! Cloven tongues sat on each of them; so that each had not only the fire-impulse to go and tell aloud the message of reconciliation, but also the fire-token that all mankind, of whatever nation, kindred, people, or tongue, were heirs alike of the gospel salvation, and of the word whereby that salvation is proclaimed.

Blessed be the hour when that Tongue of Fire descended from the Giver of speech into a cold world! Had it never come, my mother might have led me, when a child, to see slaughter for worship, and I should have taught my little ones that stones were gods. "Blessed be the Lord God, the God of Israel, who only doeth wondrous things! And blessed be His glorious name forever: and let the whole earth be filled with His glory! Amen and Amen!"

Notes

1. Among the many writers on the *temporal relation* between the Pentecost and the Passover, no one is more familiar or clearer than Kuinoel.

2. See Baumgarten.

3. It is always "bapto," never "baptidzo."

CHAPTER 4

EFFECTS WHICH IMMEDIATELY FOLLOWED THE BAPTISM OF FIRE

Section I. Spiritual Effects

The Promise of Boldness to Declare the Gospel

The first effect which followed this baptism of fire is thus described: "They were all filled with the Holy Ghost." This expression is so clearly joined with the record of the miracle, that we easily suppose that it is itself intended to express miraculous inspiration; but this is not its constant, nor even its most frequent, use in the New Testament. It is sometimes employed to describe an inspiration antecedent to a miraculous manifestation, and sometimes one antecedent to a purely moral manifestation. Examples of the latter occur in several cases of "speaking the word of God with boldness," when the circumstances were such that human nature unassisted would have shrunk from the danger.

John the Baptist wrought no miracle; yet of him it was said, that he should be "filled with the Holy Ghost from his mother's womb." Here the expression denotes some inward and spiritual operation, which may take place in the silence of an infant's heart, and show its fruit in the quiet ways of childhood. Had he been filled with the Holy Ghost immediately before commencing to preach, we should have connected the former with the latter, as an official, rather than as an inward and moral qualification.

When men were required to fill the office of deacons— not to work miracles, not to speak with tongues, but to promote the brotherhood and good feeling of the church, by a better regulation of its daily relief to the poor—the qualification demanded was, that they should be "men full of the Holy Ghost and wisdom." Again, Barnabas "was a good man and full of the Holy Ghost and of faith." This is said of him, not as accounting for any miracles or tongues, but in relation to the fact that, when he had seen the converts at Antioch, "he was glad, and exhorted them all that with purpose of heart they would cleave unto the Lord."

Again, when the apostles were first called to bear witness for Christ before the rulers, "Peter, filled with the Holy Ghost, said unto them . . ." Here we have no working of miracles, no speaking with foreign tongues; but we find the man who, when left to his own strength, denied his Master, now filled with a moral power which makes him bold to confess that Master's name, before the rulers of his people, and with a wisdom to speak according at once to the oracles of God, and the exigency of the moment.

After this first persecution was reported to the disciples generally, they, moved and distressed, appealed to the Lord in prayer, crying, "And now, Lord, behold their threatenings; and grant unto Thy servants, that with all boldness they may speak Thy word." The answer to this prayer is recorded in terms more striking than in any other case, except that of Pentecost: "And when they had prayed, the place was shaken where they were assembled together; and they were all *filled with the Holy Ghost*, and they spake the word of God with boldness." Here, being "filled with the Holy Ghost" was not followed by any miraculous effects whatever, but was an inspiration, the result of which is special moral strength— strength to confront danger and shame—strength to declare all the gospel, though, in so doing, they periled every interest dear to them.

Our Lord had promised to His disciples miraculous light and power by the Spirit; but it was not as a miracle-working power that He had chiefly foretold His coming. It was as a spiritual power, a comforter, a guide unto all truth, a revealer of the things of God, a remembrancer of the words of Christ; one who would convince the world of sin, of righteousness, and of judgment; one who would embolden the Lord's servants to bear witness before the most terrible adversaries, and would guide their lips to wise and convincing speech. Had it been His design that they should expect the Holy Spirit chiefly as a miraculous power, the leading promises would have had this aspect.

The Promise of the Indwelling of His Spirit

When He first clearly proclaims that the Comforter should come as a substitute for His own presence, He marks the classes who shall know Him, and those who shall not.

The distinction between them lies not in apostleship or ministry, not in gifts or powers, but in being of the world, and "not of the world." "Whom the world cannot receive, because it seeth Him not, neither knoweth Him: but ye know Him; for He dwelleth with you, and shall be in you" (John 14:17). Not, "For He will work miracles by you." That was not promised to all. Not, "He will prophesy by you." That He did not promise to all. But He did promise to all who are "not of the world," that He should dwell with them and be in them. Nor is this promise confined to the apostolic age, or to the times immediately succeeding. "That He may abide with you forever," gives an interest in the personal influences of the Comforter to the disciples of all ages, as well as to those of the first days.

This promised substitute for the personal presence of Christ was one whom the world should not see—who was to be invisible to the natural eye, indiscernible by the natural mind; yet known and discerned by believers, though not seen; known, not by outward sign, but by inward consciousness. Our Lord's expression is to be distinctly noted: "The world seeth Him not, neither knoweth Him; but ye *know* Him": not, "Ye *see* and know Him." In one respect the disciples and the world were to be alike; neither should see Him. Yet the disciple should "know" Him; for "He dwelleth with you, and shall be in you." Their knowledge of Him was to come not by sense, but by consciousness.

Was this "being in them" to be an ordinary grace of believers, or to be coupled only with office or supernatural endowments? The want of it is made by St. Paul conclusive against the claim of any man to be considered even a member of Christ: "Ye are not in the flesh, but in the Spirit, if so be that the Spirit of God dwell in you. Now if any man have not the Spirit of Christ, he is none of His." This passage, however, like many others, expresses only a participation of the Spirit in some degree, without indicating what that degree might be; leaving it open to doubt, were there no other passages bearing upon the point, whether some might not be blessed with the indwelling of the Spirit, who yet were to be debarred from the fuller privilege expressed in the strong words, "filled with the Holy Ghost."

What Is the Difference between Receiving the Spirit and Being Filled with the Spirit?

The apostles themselves had doubtless received the Spirit in some measure before the day of Pentecost; for our Lord had breathed upon them immediately after His resurrection, and said, "Receive ye the Holy Ghost." Yet in the time which intervened between that and Pentecost, whatever might have been the advancement of their spiritual condition beyond what it was before, it rested far behind that which immediately followed upon the baptism of fire. It was only then that they were "*filled* with the Holy Ghost." We find, however, that even the expression, "be filled," is applied broadly to ordinary believers; and that, too, not merely as describing the actual enjoyments of some individuals, but as a precept applicable to all: "Be not drunken with wine, wherein is excess, but *be filled with the Spirit*."

Whatever is meant by being "filled with the Holy Ghost" is, by these plain words, laid upon us as our duty. Looking at it in the aspect of a duty, and thinking of the moral height which the expression indicates above our ordinary life, we shrink. Can such an obligation lie upon us? Is it not commanding the purblind to gaze upon the sun? And yet, *whatever is the duty of man must be the will of God*. In this view, then, the commandment seems to carry even a stronger encouragement than the promise—seems, in fact, to sum up many promises in one conclusive appeal, saying: "ALL things are now ready. The Lord has provided; the fountain is open; the pure river of the water of life, clear as crystal, is proceeding out of the throne of God and of the Lamb; you are called to its banks, and with you it rests to drink and be filled with the Spirit."

He who has not received the Holy Ghost has not yet entered into the real Christian life, does not know the "peace which passeth understanding," has in no sense "Christ in Him the hope of glory." He is still "in the flesh," in his natural and carnal state; for the Spirit of God does not dwell in him. The difference between receiving the Spirit and being filled with the Spirit is a difference not of kind, but of degree. In the one case, the light of heaven has reached the dark chamber, disturbing night, but leaving some obscurity and some deep shadows. In the other, that light has filled the whole chamber and made every corner bright. This state of the soul—being "filled with the Holy Ghost"—is the normal antecedent of true prophetic or miraculous power, but may exist without it: without it, in individuals who are never endowed with the gift either of prophecy or of miracles; without it, in individuals who have such powers, but in whom they are not in action, as in John the Baptist before his ministry commenced.

Eyesight is the necessary basis of what is called a painter's or a poet's eye; the sense of hearing, the necessary basis of what is called a musical ear: yet eyesight may exist where there is no poet's or painter's eye, and hearing where there is no musical ear. So may the human soul be "filled with the Holy Ghost," having every faculty illuminated, and every affection purified, without any miraculous gift. On the other hand, the miraculous power does not necessarily imply the spiritual fullness; for Paul puts the supposition of speaking with tongues, prophesying, removing mountains, and yet lacking charity, that love which must be shed abroad in every heart that is full of the Holy Ghost.

Being Filled with the Fullness of God. "Filled with the Holy Ghost!" Thrice blessed word! Thanks be to God, that ever the tongues of men were taught it! It declares not only that the Lord has returned to His temple in the human soul, but that He has filled the house with His glory; pervaded every chamber, every court, by His manifested presence.

"That ye might be filled with all the fullness of God" is a prayer at which we falter. Is it not too much to ask? Is it not a sublime flight after the impossible? Let us remember it is not, "That ye might contain all the fullness of God." That would be more impossible than that your chamber should contain all the light of the sun. But it can be filled with the light of the sun—so filled that not a particle of unillumined air shall remain within it. When, therefore, the hand of the apostle leads you up toward the countenance of your Father; when you approach to see the light which outshines all lights, "the glory of God in the face of Christ Jesus," put away all thought of containing what the heavens cannot contain; but, humbly opening thy heart, say, "Infinite Light, fill this little chamber!"

Reason says, "It may be"; Scripture says, "It may be"; but a shrinking of the heart says, "It cannot be; we can never 'be filled with all the fullness of God.'" When Paul had uttered that prayer, perhaps this same shrinking of heart had almost come over him. How does he meet it? Glancing down at his wonderful petition, and up at his Almighty King, he breaks out, "Now unto Him that is able to do exceeding abundantly above all that we ask or think, according to the power that worketh in us; unto Him be glory in the church by Christ

Jesus throughout all ages, world without end. Amen." Yea, Amen, ten thousand thousand times. The words of this doxology had been holy and blessed in any connection; but they are doubly blessed, closely following, as they do, the prayer "That ye might be filled with all the fullness of God." Nor should we forget that the power which Paul here adores is not some abstract and unmoved power of Deity, but "the power which *worketh in us*." What is this power? The Holy Ghost—"might by His Spirit in the inner man."

Abounding in Love from God; Abounding in Love to Others. What a labor of expression do we find in 2 Corinthians 4:8, when Paul wants to convey his own idea of the power of grace, as practically enabling men to do the will of God! "And God is able to make all grace abound toward you; that ye, always having all sufficiency in all things, may abound to every good work." Here we have "abound" twice, and "all" four times, in one short sentence.[1] "Abound" means not only to fill, but to overflow. The double overflow, first of grace from God to us, then of the same grace from us to "every good work," is a glorious comment on our Lord's word: "He that believeth on Me, as the Scripture hath said, out of his belly shall flow rivers of living water. But this spake He of the Spirit which they that believe on Him should receive: for the Holy Ghost was not yet given, because that Jesus was not yet glorified."

The believer's heart, in itself incapable of holy living, as a marble cistern of yielding a constant stream, is placed, like the cistern, in communication with an invisible source; the source constantly overflows into the cistern, and it again overflows. Happy the heart thus filled, thus overflowing with the Holy Spirit! Where is the fountain of those living waters, that we may bring our hearts thither? "He showed me a pure river of water of life, clear as crystal, proceeding out of the throne of God and of the Lamb" (Rev. 22:1). There is the fount, there is the stream; the Spirit proceeding from the Father and the Son. To the throne of grace! To the mercy seat! And you are at the fountain of all life. Nor seek a scant supply at that source. "Be filled with the Spirit," sounds in your ears; and, if you believe, not only will a well "spring up within" you, but rivers shall flow out from you.

The Spirit, as replenishing the believer with actual virtues and practical holiness, is ever kept before our eye in the apostolic writings. "That we might walk worthy of the Lord unto all pleasing, being fruitful in every good work, and increasing in the knowledge of God; strengthened with all might, according to His glorious power, unto all patience and long-suffering with joyfulness."

Putting these various expressions together, what a view do they give of the riches of grace!—"all sufficiency," "in all things," "always," "abound to every good work," "fruitful in every good work," "strengthened with all might," "according to His glorious power," "according to the power which worketh in us," "filled with all the fullness of God." Eternal Spirit, proceeding from the Father and the Son, answer and disperse all our unbelief by filling our hearts with Thyself!

What Does It Mean to Be "Filled with the Holy Ghost"?

Restored to Our Highest Fellowship. The expression, "filled with the Holy Ghost," places before us the human spirit restored to its original and highest fellowship. In many respects that spirit is alone in this world. It finds here nothing that is its own equal. Everything upon which it can look is its inferior in both nature and powers. Earth and sky, beasts and birds, are the instruments of its comfort, or the subjects of its thoughts; but never can share in its cares or affections. The fields never say, "We enjoy thy presence," nor the stars, "We return thine admiration." The lower animals can take no part in its deep movements of hope and fear; can shed no light on its problems of justice, pardon, and the world to come. In the spirit of its fellowman alone can it find an equal; and communion with it, though it often solaces, often both wounds and defiles. Yet it is the nature of man to seek an object kindred to himself, but superior. Probably this is necessary to all natures which are at the same time rational and finite. But where can man find a being kindred to himself, and yet superior to him? Below the sky he is head, yet upward his instincts turn—upward toward some one brighter or greater than himself.

What can answer to those upward aspirations of the soul? Its Creator. After years spent in search of happiness, the human spirit penitently returns toward its God, and, trusting in the atonement of His Son, finds forgiveness for the past. Then does the great Comforter, the Witness of the Father's love, the Spirit of adoption, give the manifestation of the divine favor which David delighted to call "the light of Thy countenance."

This manifestation may be gentle, or it may be rapturous; but in any case it is comforting. When gentlest, it touches chords of satisfaction more delicate than were ever reached by the most subtle joy of intellect; when most rapturous, it carries with it an assent of the whole judgment such as no previous enjoyment, however tranquil, commanded. The thirst of the soul has no deeper seat than is now reached. Wisdom has no remonstrance, expectation no disappointment, fear no warning. It may be in a profound calm, it may be in an unspeakable joy; but it is with core-deep consciousness that the soul feels it has now touched, yea, tasted, its supreme good, and that, for time or for eternity, it needs no more than to abide in this blessedness, and improve this fellowship.

The gloomy chamber of which we spoke a little while ago was entered by the sunbeams noiselessly and impalpably; no hand could feel, no ear could hear them as they came; nothing but an eye within that chamber could discern the great change. It remains the same chamber, with the same contents; yet everything is changed, even to the very air. So it is with the soul of man when the Lord saith, "My Father will love him, and We will come unto him, and make Our abode with him." This is not only the presence of God with the spirit of man, but a special and manifested presence.

He Makes His Abode with Us. How can that be special which is universal? God is not far from every one of us; every man who moves upon the earth moves in Him. How then can He be specially present with one man more than with another? Strictly speaking, perhaps it is more a question of manifestation than of presence. Electric agency may be present everywhere, but it rarely makes itself visible in a flash. Heat may be present everywhere, but is not everywhere manifested by fire. Jude said, "Lord, how is it that Thou wilt manifest Thyself unto us, and not unto the world?" God is with all, but is unseen by any eye, and, alas! undiscerned by many a spirit. He does not withdraw His presence from any part of His universe, or His care from any of His creatures; but, as a human frame may be moving amid the light of the sun, and see no light, so may a soul be moving in that universe which is fuller of God than the atmosphere at noontide is of sunbeams, and yet discern no God.

All objects require a suitable faculty, or they are unperceived: sound exists not to the eye; light exists not to the ear; flavor exists not to the touch. It is of no avail that an object is, unless our nature has the special faculty whereby we can descry its presence. A strong magnetic power may be acting on the compass, whereon the steersman concentrates his attention; but eye, ear, hand, smell, taste, give no report of its presence to the mind; and he first learns that it was there, by the crash of the ship on a coast which he thought was far away.

Our Lord said, in reply to Jude, "If any man love Me, he will keep My word; and My Father will love him, and We will come unto him, and make our abode with him." This is more than mere presence. Presence may be unfelt, and therefore forgotten; may be with displeasure, and therefore joyless. But this is presence *manifested*—"We will come to him"; gracious—the coming is from "love"; *habitual* and *involving fellowship*—both of these ideas lie in, "Make our abode with him."

Two men are walking upon the same plain, and each turns his face toward the sky. The light of the sun is shining upon both, but one sees no sun, while the other sees not only light, but the face of the sun, and his eye is overpowered with its glory. What makes the difference between the two? Not that one is in darkness, and the other in light; not that one is near the sun, and the other far away; not that one has an eye differently constituted from the other; but simply that there is a thin cloud between heaven and the one, and no cloud between it and the other. The latter cannot only trace evidence that there is a sun, and that he is up, but has the presence of that sun before his face, and his glory filling his eye. So two men stand in relation to the universal and all-present God. One believes, infers, intellectually knows, that He is; ay, that He is present; yet he discerns Him not: it is a matter of inference, not of consciousness; and though believing that God is, and that He is present, he sins. Another spiritually discerns, feels His presence and he learns to "stand in awe, and sin not."

Suppose the case of a cripple who had spent his life in a room where the sun was never seen. He has heard of its existence, he believes in it, and, indeed, has seen enough of its light to give him high ideas of its glory. Wishing to see the sun, he is taken out at night into the streets of an illuminated city. At first, he is delighted, dazzled; but, after he has had time to reflect, he finds darkness spread amid the lights, and he asks, "Is this the sun?" He is taken out under the starry sky, and is enraptured; but on reflection finds that night covers the earth, and again asks, "Is this the sun?" He is carried out some bright day at noontide, and no sooner does his eye open on the sky than all question is at an end. There is but one sun. His eye is content; it has seen its highest object, and feels that there is nothing brighter. So with the soul: it enjoys all lights; yet, amid those of art and nature, is still inquiring for something greater. But when it is led by the reconciling Christ into the presence of the Father, and He lifts up upon it the light of His countenance, all thought of anything greater disappears. As there is but one sun, so there is but one God. The soul which once discerns and knows Him, feels that greater or brighter there is none, and that the only possibility of ever beholding more glory is by drawing nearer.

Our Bodies Are a Living Temple. The operation of the Holy Spirit implies a quickening of the nature of man by an impartation of the divine nature, and every increase of it implies a fuller communion of the Eternal Father with His adopted child. When the soul of man is "filled with the Holy Ghost," then has God that wherein He does rejoice, "a temple not made with hands," not reared by human art, of unconscious and insensible material; a temple created by

His own word, and living by His own breath. In that living temple He displays somewhat of His glory. In the Shekinah of the sanctuary He could manifest majesty only. In this living temple He can manifest truth, purity, tenderness, forgiveness, justice—the whole round of such attributes as His children below the sky are capable of comprehending.

Thus inhabited, not only is the soul of man unutterably blessed, but his body reaches dignity, the thought of which might make even flesh sing. "Your body is the temple of the Holy Ghost which is in you, which ye have of God; and ye are not your own." Not your own, for purchase has been made: "Ye are bought with a price"; not your own, for possession has been taken: "Know ye not that ye are the temple of God, and that the *Spirit of God dwelleth in you?*" (1 Cor. 3:16, etc.).

A holy man, whose presence breathes an unworldly air around him, whose name is identified with a constancy of godly actions, is a visible monument and remembrancer of God. Each member of his body is as a temple vessel. By it holy works are done, and the will of the parent Spirit on moral points expressed by material instruments. His spirit is led by the Spirit of God. His "mortal body" is quickened by the Spirit "that dwelleth in him." He not only "*lives* in the Spirit," but "*walks* in the Spirit"—his visible acts, as well as his hidden emotions, being "after the Spirit." The natural man has disappeared from his life and actions. Another creature lives. Thoughts, purposes, works, which his nature never prompted, which, when prompted by revelation, his nature could not attain to, now abound, as sweet grapes on a good vine. This precept is embodied in his life: "Neither yield ye your members as instruments of unrighteousness unto sin; but yield yourselves unto God as those that are alive from the dead, and your members as instruments of righteousness unto God" (Rom. 6:13).

In this the power of the Holy Ghost is practically manifested by a reversal of the relations of the human spirit and the flesh. To persons yet in the body, the apostle says, "Ye are not in the flesh, but in the Spirit, if so be the Spirit of God dwell in you." Not in the flesh, yet in the body! The unconverted man has a spirit, but it is carnalized; the play of its powers—the studies of the intellect, the flights of the imagination, the impulses of the heart, are dictated by motives which all range below the sky and halt on this side of the tomb. The spirit is the servant of the flesh; and man differs from perishing animals chiefly in this, that for carnal purposes and delights he commands the service of a spiritual agent—his own soul.

We Are an Instrument of God's Holy Spirit. The Holy Spirit, as man's regenerator, reverses this state of things. He quickens the spirit, and through it quickens the frame, so that instead of spiritual powers being carnalized, a mortal body is spiritualized; instead of soul and spirit being subjected by the flesh, flesh and blood become instruments of the Spirit. Limbs move on works of heavenly origin and intent. Thus a direct connection is established between the will of the Supreme Spirit and the material organs of man. A purpose originates in the mind of God; by His Spirit it is silently and swiftly transmitted to the spirit of His child; and by this to the "mortal body." Then, as an iron wire, on the shore of the Crimea, expresses the will of our queen in London, so do the earthly members of a mortal express, in the outward and physical world, the purpose of the Holy One.

This is redemption achieved; this is adoption in its issues; this is the new life; this is human nature restored, man walking in the light; "God dwelling in him, and he in

God." Then his life is a light, and a light so pure, that it gives those on whom it shines, not the idea of "good nature," but of something heavenly. They see his good works, and "*glorify his Father which is in Heaven*"; not extol his character, but feel that he is raised above his own character and is "*God's workmanship*, created anew in Christ Jesus unto good works."

A piece of iron is dark and cold; imbued with a certain degree of heat, it becomes almost burning without any change of appearance; imbued with a still greater degree, its very appearance changes to that of solid fire, and it sets fire to whatever it touches. A piece of water without heat is solid and brittle; gently warmed, it flows; further heated, it mounts to the sky. An organ filled with the ordinary degree of air which exists everywhere, is dumb; the touch of the player can elicit but a clicking of the keys. Throw in not another air, but an unsteady current of the same air, and sweet, but imperfect and uncertain, notes immediately respond to the player's touch: increase the current to a full supply, and every pipe swells with music. Such is the soul without the Holy Ghost; and such are the changes which pass upon it when it receives the Holy Ghost, and when it is "filled with the Holy Ghost." In the latter state only is it fully imbued with the divine nature, bearing in all its manifestations some plain resemblance to its God, conveying to all on whom it acts some impression of Him, mounting heavenward in all its movements, and harmoniously pouring forth, from all its faculties, the praises of the Lord.

The moral change wrought in the disciples, by the new baptism of the Spirit, is strikingly displayed in the case of one man. A difficult service was to be performed in Jerusalem that day. Had it been desired to find a man in London who would have gone down to Whitehall a few weeks after Charles was beheaded, and, addressing Cromwell's soldiers, have endeavored to persuade them that he whom they had executed was not only a king, and a good one, but a prophet of God, and that, therefore, they had been guilty of more than regicide—of sacrilege; although England had brave men then, it may be questioned whether any one could have been found to bear such a message to that audience.

The service which had then to be performed in Jerusalem was similar to this. It was needful that some one should stand up under the shadow of the temple, and braving chief priests and mobs alike, assert that He whom they had shamefully executed seven weeks ago, was Israel's long-looked-for Messiah; that they had been guilty of a sin which had no name; had raised their hands against "God manifest in the flesh"; had, in words strange to human ears, "*killed the Prince of Life.*" Who was thus to confront the rage of the mob, and the malice of the priests? We see a man rising, filled with a holy fire, so that he totally forgets his danger, and seems not even conscious that he is doing a heroic act. He casts back upon the mockers their charge, and proceeds to open and to press home his tremendous accusation, as if he were a king upon a throne, and each man before him a lonely and defenseless culprit.

Who is this man? Have we not seen him before? Is it possible that it can be Peter? We know him of old: he has a good deal of zeal, but little steadiness; he means well, and, when matters are smooth, can serve well; but when difficulties and adversaries rise before him, his moral courage fails. How short a time is it ago since we saw him tried! He had been resolving that, come what might, he would stand by his Master to the last. Others might flinch; he would stand. Soon the Master was in the hands of enemies. Yet his case was by no means lost. The governor was on his side; many of the people were secretly for Him; nothing could be proved against Him; and, above all, He who had saved others could save Himself.

Yet, as Peter saw scowling faces, his courage failed. A servant-maid looked into his eye, and his eye fell. She said she thought he belonged to Jesus of Nazareth; his heart sank, and he said, "No." Then another looked in his face, and repeated the same suspicion. Now, of course, he was more cowardly, and repeated his "No." A third looked upon him, and insisted that he belonged to the accused Prophet. How his poor heart was all fluttering; and, to make it plain that he had nothing to do with Jesus of Nazareth, he began to curse and swear.

Is it within the same breast where this pale and tremulous heart quaked, that we see glowing a brave heart which dreads neither the power of the authorities, nor the violence of the populace; which faces every prejudice and every vice of Jerusalem, every bitter Pharisee and every street brawler, as if they were no more than straying and troublesome sheep? Is the Peter of Pilate's hall the Peter of Pentecost, with the same natural powers, the same natural force of character, the same training, and the same resolutions? If so, what a difference is made in a man by the one circumstance of being filled with the Holy Ghost!

O for high examples of God's moral "workmanship"! O for men instinct with the Spirit; the countenance glowing as a transparency with a lamp behind it; the eye shining with a purer, truer light than any that genius or good-nature ever shed; limbs agile for any act of prayer, of praise, of zeal, for any errand of compassion; and a tongue of fire! O for men on whom the silent verdict of the observer would be, "He is a good man, and full of the Holy Ghost"! Never, perhaps, did earthly eyes see more frequently than we see, in our day, men with ordinary Christian excellences—men in private life whose walk is blameless—men in the ministry who are admirable, worthy, and useful.

But are not men "full of the Holy Ghost" a rare and diminished race? Are those whose entire spirit bespeaks a walk of prayer, such as we would ascribe to Enoch or to John; whose words fall with a demonstration of the Spirit, and a power such as we conceive attended Paul or Apollos; who make on believers the impression of being immediate and mighty instruments of God, and on unbelievers the impression of being dangerous to come near, lest they should convert them;—are such men often met with?

Do not even the good frequently speak as if we were not to look for such burning and shining lights? as if we must be content in our educated and intelligent age with a style of holiness more level and less startling? Do not many make up their minds never more to see men such as their fathers saw; men at whose prayer a wondrous power of God was ever ready to fall, whether upon two or three kneeling in a cabin, and wondering how the unlearned could find such wisdom, or on the great multitude, wondering how the learned could find such simplicity? Never more see such men! The Lord forbid! Return, O Power of Pentecost, return to Thy people! Shed down Thy flame on many heads! To us, as to our fathers, and to those of the old time before them, give fullness of grace! Without Thee we can do nothing; but filled with the Holy Ghost, the excellency of the power will be of Thee, O God! and not of us.

Section II. Miraculous Effects

The Mental Miracle

"They began to speak with other tongues, as the Spirit gave them utterance." It is not said, "with unknown tongues." In fact, the expression, "unknown tongues," was never used by an inspired writer. In the Epistle to the Corinthians, it is found in the English version; but the word "unknown" is in italics, showing that it is not taken from the original. Speaking unknown tongues was never heard of in the apostolic days. That *miracle* first occurred in London some years ago. On the day of Pentecost no man pretended to speak unknown tongues; but just as if we in London suddenly began to speak German, French, Spanish, Russian, Turkish, and other foreign languages, so it was with them. Not one tongue was spoken that day but a man was found in the streets of Jerusalem to turn round, and cry, "This is my own tongue, wherein I was born!" The miracle lay in the power of speaking the tongues of adjacent nations, from which individuals were in Jerusalem at that very time. This is not only miraculous, but a miracle in a very amazing form; perhaps, as to its form, the most amazing of all miracles.

Matter is a great and pregnant thing. To us its properties are not only wonderful, but exceedingly mysterious. When we see it flourishing while we fade, towering in hills, or careering in waves, or spread out in the firmament, we almost feel as if it were greater than we. Yet are we ever proving that, in spite of appearances, matter is less than mind. Mind searches out matter, wields it, molds it, makes it the servant of its will. Mind, then, being the superior, it follows that a work wrought in mind is greater than one wrought in matter. Miracles in seas, mountains, the firmament, or the human body, display a power which rules the frame of nature and the frame of man. Yet, as the sphere of these is matter, the whole order may be called the PHYSICAL MIRACLE—works above nature, wrought upon physical agents in attestation of the revelation of God. But beyond this lies a higher miracle, of which the sphere is mind; and which, therefore, we may call the MENTAL MIRACLE—works above nature wrought in mind in attestation of the revelation of God. Of this order two forms had been witnessed previously—inspiration and prophecy; but now a new miracle in mind was to challenge the belief of all Jerusalem.

This miracle, as to its moral impression, differed totally from all physical miracles; even from that complex and most peculiar miracle, the raising of the dead, wherein we see a power which matter and spirit, animal life and mental illumination, equally obey. That miracle stands alone; yet the chief impression which it makes, and certainly the impression which all purely physical miracles make, is that of power. They suggest, also, indeed, the idea of wisdom, else the power would not go so unerringly to its end; and of goodness, else power so irresistible would move, not to bless, but to destroy; yet the leading impression produced is undoubtedly that of power. In such miracles we recognize chiefly "the high hand, and the stretched-out arm."

In inspiration, we see the mind of man enabled to sit down among the morning mists of things, and to write a book which will stand while the world stands. In prophecy, we see the mind enabled to look through a thousand years, and describe what lies beyond so plainly, that, when it is unfolded to ordinary sight, it shall at once be recognized. Both these miracles bring us, not so much into the presence of a ruler, as into the presence of a Spirit.

In beholding a sea dried, or a wilderness strewn with food, we feel ourselves near the Lord of nature and the Stay of life. So here we feel ourselves near the Fount of all mind, whose own knowledge depends neither on material phenomena, nor on the lapse of time; whose mode of acting on the human mind is not by laws analogous to those whereby the latter acts on material organs, or on its kindred minds through them. As, however, we watch the miracle

of tongues, a strange solemnity falls upon us; we feel as if
we had left the region where mind slowly and dimly learns
through sense, had crossed some invisible line into the land
of spirits, and were standing before the Original Mind. What
knowledge of mind so minute as that which scans every sign
whereby every mind expresses its ideas? What power over
mind so unsearchable as that which can fill it in an instant
with new signs for all its ideas—signs never before present
to it, yet answering exactly to those which others had been
trained from childhood to use?

A number of Galilean peasants issue from an upper
room into the streets of Jerusalem. A strange fire is in every
eye, a strange light on every countenance. Each one looks
joyful and benignant, as if he felt that he was carrying the
balm for the world's sores in his breast. Each has plainly a
word to say, and wants listeners. Probably their steps turn
toward the temple, which during the ten days had divided
their presence with the upper room. One meets with an
Arab, and addresses him; another goes up to a Roman, and
in a moment they are deeply engaged; a third sees a Persian,
a fourth an African from Cyrene; and, as they go along, each
one attaches himself to some foreigner. He tells a strange
tale, strange in its substance, equally strange in its eloquence;
a new and unaccountable eloquence, wonderful not for grace,
expression, or sweet sound, but for power.

One hearer in Latin, another in Coptic, another in
Persian, another in Greek, exclaims first at the wonder of the
story, and then at the wonder of the narrator: "Art not thou
a Galilean? Whence then hast thou this fluency of Latin?"
He answers that he has received it today by gift from God. A
smile curls on the lip of the Roman, and he turns round to a
neighboring group. There an Egyptian has just been putting
the same question, and received the same answer. Yonder

is an excited little knot, where a Parthian declares that the tongue in which a man has told him of the death, resurrection, and ascension of Jesus, is his mother tongue. People from Jerusalem are mocking, and saying, "The men are full of new wine"; but the strangers, on speaking one to another, find that they have all been hearing precisely the same things in their "own tongues."

Those faces of different complexions, on comparing their opinions, express awe. They find that in all this diversity of tongues the same tidings are repeated, and thus see the unity of matter in the variety of language: they find that the men who speak are unschooled peasants, yet are all gifted with the same unheard-of power; and thus see in the variety of speakers the unity of inspiration. The tongues are the tongues of all mankind; but the impulse is one, and the message one! From what center do all these languages issue? The same instinct which leads back the thought from speech to a mind, leads it back from this universal speech till it stands awestruck in the presence of the Central Intellect of the Spirit which "formeth the spirit of man within him," of the Supreme Mind, to which all mind is common ground—of the Father of Thought!

Our Tongues Are the Instrument of God

It would be impossible to conceive any form of credential so well framed to certify that a doctrine was the immediate issue of the mind of God. The bare thought of such a miracle as that of tongues, had it only been a thought, would have made in itself an era in the history of man's intellect; and it may be fairly questioned whether such a thought could have originated in anything else than in the fact. The leading feature of the new religion was to be a divine teaching upon things invisible and spiritual—on points of which the unaided powers of man could give no conclusive solution. For such a teaching no attestation could be so apposite as one that accredited it as a message from the Spirit which "searcheth all things." The universal call to man was worthily issued into the world by a sign which showed that it came directly from the only wise God, who gives understanding, and holds the keys of thought. The command of all languages, by one consentaneous impulse, proclaimed the new message to be the WORD OF GOD.

The great question for humanity is, Hath God spoken? Are we poor wanderers each left here to his own light, and Heaven looking down in eternal silence on all our straying and perplexity? Hath the parent Spirit, whence these spirits of ours come, surrounded them with His infinite presence at every step of their stumbling and perilous journey, and never once, from the day of Adam to our day, signified that He saw, and heard, and felt? Has He dealt with the soul of man as with "the spirit of a beast," that could never bless Him, and never break His law? Are all words the words of erring man, and all lights those doubtful and deceptive lights, following which so many have miserably perished? Is all doctrine the guesses of thinkers, or the juggling of priests? Has God never, never spoken?

"God spake all these words, and said!" On the Pentecost of Israel, from out of the fire on Sinai, came "a mighty voice," which, sweeping down from the distant peak as if from a throne at hand, filled the ears of three millions of people, or more, as if they had been a little group. Ten times the Voice sounded mysteriously over all that awed and quivering host, till human nature, smitten to the core, cried out, "We die, we die." The Voice had uttered only gentle and wholesome laws, laws binding man to God, and man to man, laying sure paths to peace and blessedness; but human nature was already guilty under these laws, and the VOICE awoke only the response, "Let not God speak with us, lest we die" (Exod. 20:19).

Thus, in the old time, a whole nation could be appealed to, that all words were not uncertain, nor all questions open—"Ye came near and stood under the mountain: and the mountain burned with fire unto the midst of heaven, with darkness, clouds, and thick darkness. And the Lord spake unto you out of the midst of the fire: ye heard the voice of the words, but saw no similitude; only ye heard a voice. And He declared unto you His covenant which He commanded you to perform, even ten commandments; and He wrote them upon two tablets of stone."

As in the Pentecost of Israel, so in the Pentecost of Christianity, the Lord once more speaks "out of the midst of the fire." Now, however, the accompanying tokens are not physical, but mental; employing many human minds and human tongues as His instruments, yet manifesting the unity of that impulse whereby they are all moved, He makes not merely the people of one nation, but the representatives of all nations, feel that God hath spoken. Yes, tell it wherever there are ears to hear, tell it to the ends of the earth, *God hath spoken*; man has not been forgotten; guesses are not all our light; there is a *gospel*, a "speech of God"; questions affecting salvation are settled; and our way to holy living and happy dying traced by the Hand which rules both worlds.

Cloven Tongues or Manifest Ears? With regard to the gift of tongues, some curious questions have been raised, especially by the learned. One is whether the miracle was really in the speaker, and not in the hearer; so that although all that was spoken was in one language, the ordinary language of the disciples, yet the hearers of different nations each heard in his own tongue. For this opinion, as for all opinions, it is possible to cite some considerable names. But had it been as here supposed, the symbol of the miracle would not have been cloven tongues, but manifold ears. The double declaration of the narrative perfectly corresponds with the symbol. As regards the speakers, it says that they "spake with other tongues"; as regards the hearers, that they "heard every man in his own tongue."

When St. Paul finds fault with the use of the gift of tongues in Corinth, he does not blame the hearers for lacking an ear that would interpret their own tongue into foreign ones but blames the speakers for speaking "with the tongue words not easy to be understood" by the unlearned; and the only reason he ever assigns why the auditors could not understand is, that they were unlearned; clearly showing that a foreign language was employed, which education might have enabled them to understand, but for the understanding of which miraculous power does not seem ever to have been given. If the supposition of the miracle in hearing, instead of in speech, has been resorted to with a view to simplify the miracle, it defeats its own object; for, to sustain that supposition, the miraculous influence must have been exerted on a number of persons, as much greater than in the other case, as the hearers were more numerous than the speakers. At the same time, the nature of the miraculous operation would be in every respect equally extraordinary.

Another question is whether the speakers understood what they said in the foreign languages. The doubt as to this is not raised upon the narrative of the Pentecost, but on certain expressions used by St. Paul in writing to the Corinthians. There he says, "Let him that speaketh in an unknown tongue pray that he may interpret"; and again, "If one speak in an unknown tongue, let one interpret." Hence it would appear that some could speak with tongues, who could not render into their own language that which they had spoken. This, however, is not clear; for he also says, "Greater is he that prophesieth than he that speaketh with tongues, except he interpret, that the *church may receive edification.*" Here he supposes that the person who possesses the gift of tongues does also possess the power of interpreting into the common language that which he has uttered in a miraculous way.

But, even granting that some were unable to interpret, *so as to edify the church*, that which they had themselves spoken, it would appear that this did not at all arise from their not understanding what they had said, but from their being destitute of the gift of prophecy, whereby only they could edify believers. As to any doubt whether the person speaking really understood his own utterances, it is completely removed by the text, 1 Corinthians 14:14–19: "For if I pray in an unknown tongue, my spirit prayeth, but my understanding is unfruitful. What is it then? I will pray with the spirit, and I will pray with the understanding also: I will sing with the spirit, and I will sing with the understanding also. Else when thou shall bless with the spirit, how shall he that occupieth the room of the unlearned say Amen at thy giving of thanks, seeing he understandeth not what thou sayest? For thou verily givest thanks well, but the other is not edified. I thank my God, I speak with tongues more than ye all: yet in the church I had rather speak five words with my understanding, that by my voice I might teach others also, than ten thousand words in an unknown tongue."

Here, publicly praising "with the understanding" is taken to be, so praising that a common man may understand; and publicly preaching "with the understanding" is taken to be, so to speak as to "teach others also." To praise and to preach in public without these, is to act without understanding. The words, "He understandeth not what thou sayest," though "thou verily givest thanks well," settle the whole matter. They take it for granted—as, indeed, the apostle does all through—that the speaker clearly understands himself; but the fault is that he uses speech which was never given for the sake of intercourse with God, but for that of intercourse with man, in a way that defeats its own object. Speech is man's revelation of his own spirit to his fellowman; and when nothing is revealed, it becomes a mockery. Feelings and thoughts are the language which God listens to: man hearkens in the air, God in the soul within. To speak to Him we need no sounds; sounds are for human ears, and useful only when the ear can recognize the meaning. The fact that some who could not prophesy could yet speak with tongues is apparent in several parts of Scripture, and is a singular proof at once of the generality and the diversity of gifts. The lower gift, that of tongues, was more generally diffused than the higher, that of prophecy.

Divine Gift

The miracle indicated not only the origin of the new doctrine, but also its sphere. It was a message from the Father of men to *all men*. National diversities, instead of being a barrier before which it stood still, were opportunities to display its universal adaptation. Each various tongue was made an additional witness that it had come for "every people under heaven." Our Lord's last words, "the uttermost parts of the earth," had here a strange and multiplying echo. A force was set in motion, which claimed all humanity as its field; a voice was lifted up, which called upon every nation to join its audience.

Again, this manifestation met and answered all doubts which might have arisen as to the power of our Lord to gift

His servants with language and utterance needful for their coming contest with the whole world. He had told them that, when brought before rulers and kings for His name's sake, it would be given to them what they should say: "For it is not ye that speak, but the Spirit of your Father which speaketh in you" (Matt. 1:20). He had evidently referred to such divine aid *in speech*, when He told them that they should receive power after the Holy Ghost would come upon them, and that they should be *His witnesses*, even "to the uttermost parts of the earth." Moses had feared to plead before Pharaoh, from a dread that utterance equal to the gravity of the mission could not be given to him. Jeremiah had feared on a similar ground.

Nothing is more natural than that one who feels himself charged with a sublime truth, on the proper delivery of which infinite interests depend, should distrust his ability to frame suitable language. It is very probable that such thoughts had troubled the disciples in the contemplation of the great work which lay before them. If so, what an answer did they receive in the miracle of tongues! He who enabled their lips to pour forth the testimony in words they had never spoken, and never heard, could surely give them every measure of propriety, of clearness, of copiousness, of power, whereof human speech was capable. All questions as to how copious diction could be imparted to the unready, and force to the feeble, how the slow could be made impressive, and the tame eloquent, were here answered.

The old promise, "I will be with thy mouth," received an unlooked-for commentary. The effects which the Spirit of the Lord could produce upon the human tongue were shown to be illimitable by any natural impediment. The ground of confidence as to their success in preaching was conspicuously changed from talent, learning, office, or credentials, to the working of the Holy Ghost. Their power ceased to be a question of natural ability, and became one of divine gift. The measure of the former might be greater or less, without materially affecting the fruit of their work; but this would exactly correspond with the degree of the latter.

Andrew had heard the Baptist preach, had seen how his words had plowed up the rude feelings of the soldier, and at the same time commanded the subtle conscience of the scribe. He had heard the Lord Himself, when every word struck the ear as a wonder. Probably he had always thought it impossible that such sword-edged sentences should ever come from his lips, or from those of "his own brother Simon." He might conceive that he should be able to repeat the substance of the lessons which the Lord had taught them, and that, when he stood before counselors and magistrates, he should be enabled to assign a reason for his hope.

Perhaps he would think it possible that, when filled with that new Comforter, who had been so often promised to them, he could address a multitude with feeling. But, as to words like fire, melting and burning the spirits of men—words like hammers, breaking in pieces the hearts of stone—words that should rush on the congregation with a force too overwhelming to be called eloquence—should win a conquest too rapid and too complete to be called persuasion—should make the speaker not only a prodigy, but a power—his hearers not only an orator's audience, but a Master's disciples—as to such words as these, how was it possible that they should ever proceed from him, or Simon? So might he naturally reason; but when he finds himself fluently telling a man from the shores of Cyrene the whole story of the birth, and death, and resurrection, and ascension, in a tongue which he had never heard before; when the African assures him that it was the tongue of his native town, then, had you asked him, "Is it now impossible that you or Simon should speak with a voice mightier than the voice of a prophet, or that the least of your company should be greater than the thunder-tongued Baptist?" he had answered, "With God nothing is impossible."

Different Giftings Available to All

"And it sat upon each of them. And they were all filled with the Holy Ghost, and began to speak with other tongues, as the Spirit gave them utterance." The tongue of fire rested upon each disciple, and all spoke with a super-human utterance. Not the Twelve only, the Lord's chosen apostles; not the Seventy only, His commissioned evange-lists; but also the ordinary believers, and even the women. The baptism of the Spirit fell upon all, and spiritual gifts were imparted to all—not equally; for the expression, "As the Spirit gave them utterance," seems to indicate a diver-sity of gifts, which accords with other passages in the New Testament. It is not probable that each one could speak every language; for St. Paul says of himself, that he "spake with tongues more than they all," clearly implying a limit in that gift, and a different limit in different persons. And it is certain that all had not the gift of prophesying suited to address such congregations that they would meet, or even publicly to teach in ordinary assemblies.

As in His later operations, so now, the blessed Spirit would doubtless show "diversities of operations," giving to "one the word of wisdom, to another the word of knowl-edge, to another prophecy," etc. But the cloven tongues sat upon each of them, and, by the joint effect of spiritual life imparted and of spiritual gifts bestowed, all were instantly set upon spiritual services; all led to become active witnesses for Christ and for His cross.

The fire did not fall on the Twelve to be by them communicated to the Seventy, and by them again to the ordinary flock. It came as directly on the head of the disciple whose name we never heard, as on that of the beloved and honored John. It did not confound John the Apostle in the promiscuous mass, or place his office at the disposal of the multitude; but confirmed it, and fitted him by new gifts to adorn and make full proof of his ministry. But it did not, on the other hand, leave the ordinary believers as mere spectators to see the spiritual work of the Lord committed wholly to the selected ministry; their part being passively to receive spiritual influences and illumination from those who had direct access to Him with whom is the supply of the Spirit.

This original blessing meets beforehand the error, which was likely to spring up, from looking on the true religion in the light in which all false ones are ever regarded—as a mystery to be confined to an initiated few, on whose offices the multitude must depend for acceptance with the invisible Power. Here was a religion that did single out and lift up some above their fellows, investing them with a high and solemn ministry; but from their ministry it swept away all seeming priesthood.

The usual idea of priesthood is that of a power standing between man and God, through which alone we may draw near, and find mercy at His hands. But so far from any such characteristic belonging to the ministry of the gospel, it is distinguished as being an office, the special labor of which is to point each man *direct* to God, and to assure him that between him and the throne of grace there is no power, visible or invisible, and no mediator but One to whom alike apostle, evangelist, and the humblest penitent must look. True, all were not apostles, all were not evangelists, all were not prophets; but, in the only sense in which any were priests, all were priests. The one altar of the cross, the one sacrifice of the Lamb, the one High Priest within the veil, were alone to be named in any light of peacemaking with God. To all, the privilege of offering up the sacrifices of praise and of prayer, of living bodies and of worldly goods, was equally open. No man was made a depository or store-house wherein spiritual favors should be laid up for the use of those who might purchase or implore them at his hands. He was most honored who could most successfully turn the trust of men away from all other advocates and fix it upon the Son of God alone.

"*They all* began to speak." This shows that the testimony of Christ was not born by the ministry alone; that this chief work of the church was not confined to official hands. The multitude of believers were not mere adherents, but living, speaking, burning agents in the great movements for the universal diffusion of God's message.

Many feel as if religion, on the part of the ministry, was to be a matter of bold and public testimony; but on that of ordinary Christians, a heart-secret between themselves and God. Let such sit down in sight of that first Christian scene; let them behold every countenance lighted up with the common joy, and hear every tongue speak under the common impulse, and then ask Bartimeus, or Mary, if the private disciple has not just as much cause to be a witness that Jesus lives, and that Jesus saves, as either James or John? Let them ask if it is like their religion that one lonely minister shall, on the Lord's Day, bear witness before a thousand Christians, who decorously hear his testimony as worthy of acceptance by all, and then go away, and never repeat the strain in any human ear?

Looking at the universal movement of that Pentecostal day, who could think that the new religion was ever to come down to this? that speaking of its joys, its hopes, its pardon, its mercy for the wide world, was to be considered a professional work, for set solemnities alone, and not to be a daily joy and heart's-ease, to ever-growing multitudes of happy, simple men? Cheerless is the work of that Christian minister, who, at set times, raises his testimony in the ears of a people, all of whom make a practice of hiding it in their hearts! Blessed in his office is he who knows that, while he in his own sphere proclaims the glad tidings, hundreds around him are ready, each one in his sphere, to make them their boast and their song! Spiritual office and spiritual gifts vary greatly in degree, honor, and authority, and he who has the less ought to reverence him who has the greater, remembering who it is that dispenses them; but the greater should never attempt to extinguish the less, and to reduce the exercise of spiritual gifts within the limits of the public and ordained ministry. To do so is to depart from primitive Christianity.

Section III. Ministerial Effects

Imbued with Power from on High

In immediate connection with the gift of tongues was a gift less startling as a phenomenon, but more influential as an instrument for the recovery of mankind. Peter was soon called upon publicly to deliver the Lord's great message. Then, undoubtedly, he spoke not in any foreign tongue, but in his native dialect. He had often spoken before, yet nothing remarkable is recorded of his preaching, or its effects. He is now the same man, with the same natural intellect, and the same natural powers of speech; and yet a new utterance is given to him, the effects of which are instantly apparent.

Never was such an audience assembled as that before which this poor fisherman appeared: Jews, with all the prejudices of their race—inhabitants of Jerusalem, with the recollection of the part they had recently taken in the crucifixion of Jesus of Nazareth, met in the city of their solemnities, jealous for the honor of their temple and law: men of different nations, rapidly and earnestly speaking in their different tongues; one in Hebrew, mocking and saying, "These men are full of new wine"; another inquiring in Latin; another disputing in Greek; another wondering in Arabic; and an endless Babel beside expressing every variety of surprise, doubt, and curiosity.

Amid such a scene the fisherman stands up; his voice strikes across the hum which prevails all down the street. He has no tongue of silver; for they say, "He is an unlearned and ignorant man." The rudeness of his Galilean speech still remains with him; yet, though "unlearned and ignorant" in their sense—as to polite learning—in a higher sense he was a scribe well-instructed. As respected the word of God, he had been for three years under the constant tuition of the Prophet of Nazareth, hearing from His lips instruction in the law, in the Prophets, and in all the "deep things of God." On whatever other points, therefore, the learned of Jerusalem might have found Peter at fault, in the sacred writings he was more thoroughly furnished than they; for though Christ took His apostles from among the poor, He left us no example for those who have not well learned the Bible, to attempt to teach it.

Yet Peter had no tongue of silver, no tongue of honey, no soothing, flattering speech, to allay the prejudices and to captivate the passions of the multitude. Nor had he a tongue of thunder; no outbursts of native eloquence distinguished his discourse. Indeed, some, if they had heard that discourse from ordinary lips, would not have hesitated to pronounce it dry—some of a class, too numerous, who do not like preachers who put them to the trouble of thinking, but enjoy only those who regale their fancy, or move their feelings, without requiring any labor of thought. Peter's sermon is no more than quoting passages from the word of God, and reasoning upon them; yet, as in this strain he proceeds, the tongue of fire by degrees burns its way to the feelings of the multitude. The murmur gradually subsides; the mob becomes a congregation; the voice of the fisherman sweeps from end to end of that multitude, unbroken by a single sound; and, as the words rush on, they act like a stream of fire.

Now, one coating of prejudice which covered the feelings is burned, and starts aside; now, another and another; now, the fire touches the inmost covering of prejudice, which lay close upon the heart, and it too starts aside. Now, it touches the quick, and burns the very soul of the man! Presently, you might think that in that throng there was but one mind, that of the Preacher, which had multiplied itself, had possessed itself of thousands of hearts, and thousands of frames, and was pouring its own thoughts through them all. At length, shame, and tears, and sobs overspread that whole assembly. Here, a head bows; there, starts a groan; yonder, rises a deep sigh; here, tears are falling; and some stern old Jew, who will neither bow nor weep, trembles with the effort to keep himself still.

At length, from the depth of the crowd, the voice of the preacher is crossed by a cry, as if one was "mourning for his only son"; and it is answered by a cry, as if one was in "bitterness for his firstborn." At this cry the whole multitude is carried away, and forgetful of everything but the overwhelming feeling of the moment, they exclaim, "Men and brethren, what must we do?"

No part of the proceedings of the day strikes us with a deeper or more lasting impression than the amazing change in Peter, which is here manifest. We are continually prone to consider the power of a minister as a natural power, simply intellectual. Here was a man who, in all probability, had passed the period of life when eloquence is most forcible, without having distinguished himself by any such power. He comes forward with a most unwelcome message, to address an unfavorable audience, himself unskilled in the arts of oratory; and yet, such is the power of utterance given to him, that he produces an effect, the like of which had never been known before in the history of mankind. Never has it been recorded in any other instance that three thousand men were in an hour persuaded by one of their own nation, of obscure origin and uninfluential position, to forego the prejudices of their youth, the favor of their people, and the religion of their fathers. "I will be with thy mouth," is more strikingly fulfilled here, in those extraordinary effects of the speaking of an ordinary man, than in any other form in which the power of God could be displayed, through the instrumentality of a human tongue. There is no part of the whole series of events which has a more direct bearing upon the permanent work of the Christian church.

The Gift of Prophecy Even Greater

This is the first example of prophesying in the New Testament sense; not the limited sense of foretelling, but the more comprehensive sense of delivering a message from God, under the impulse of the Spirit of God, and by His aid. In this the speaker has the double advantage of ascertained truth to declare—truth which his own understanding has received, which he can enforce by citing the word of God—and of aid direct from the Spirit in uttering it. This gift is conspicuously placed by St. Paul above that of tongues: "Greater is he that prophesieth than he that speaketh with tongues." The gift of tongues was "for a sign to them that believe not"; and even to them only under certain circumstances, when they were addressed in a tongue which they understood, and that by one of whom they had proof, or what amounted to strong probability, that he had not learned it in a natural mode. For the union of these two requisites nothing was so favorable as the meeting of a number of foreigners in one city, and hearing natives of the country speak all their different languages. A foreigner appearing in a city, and professing to speak its language by miracle, would lie under the suspicion of having learned it before he came; and persons speaking foreign tongues in the presence of their own unlearned countrymen, would seem to utter gibberish. This Paul puts strongly to the Corinthians: "If the whole church be come together into one place, and all speak with tongues, and there come in those that are *unlearned*, or *unbelievers*, will they not say that ye are mad?"

If a number of persons in Corinth had a gift in Hebrew, or in Latin, and their fellow-townsmen, who knew only Greek, came and heard a rush of unmeaning sounds, and were told that it was a miracle, it might be, but it was no miracle to them. If they saw an African peasant speaking fluently in Greek, then, indeed, they would be startled; and if *once assured* by any means that he had not learned it, they would recognize a miracle.

But the effect of persons resident in a place using the gift of tongues could only be to satisfy the learned of a miracle. For the unlearned it would be simply bewildering. Suppose that, in the city of Oxford, the stonemasons, joiners, and shoemakers heard a few of their own number uttering something in Latin, they would only be impressed with a belief that they had gone mad, or were amusing themselves with gibberish. But did the learned men of the university find these groups discoursing on the doctrines of the gospel in the language of ancient Rome, which it had been the study and the labor of their lives to acquire perfectly, they would be overwhelmed with a sense of the prodigy. All through the fourteenth chapter of the First Epistle to the Corinthians, St. Paul admits that upon the learned the gift of tongues would make an impression; but that the unlearned, if believers, would be unedified, and, if unbelievers, would be led to mock.

To the higher gift of prophecy he assigns two offices which that of tongues could never fulfill. One is the edifying of believers; and on this score he much argues the Corinthians to seek for that gift. The other is its effect upon the unlearned unbeliever. "If all prophesy, and there come in one that believeth not, or one unlearned, he is convinced of all, he is judged of all: and thus are the secrets of his heart made manifest; and so falling down on his face he will worship God, and report that God is in you of a truth."

Here is a man who knows no language but one, and who has no faith in the divine mission of the Christians; yet he enters an assembly where men are speaking in his own tongue: that tongue, as to its words, is familiar to him from his childhood; but its words now convey new ideas, and those ideas are accompanied by a strange power which pierces, lays open, and searches his heart. He seems as if God had found him out, and told another man all about him, his hidden sins, his bosom pollutions, and covered deeds which had been even forgotten, but which now are brought strangely to his view again. An unaccountable impression of God's presence, of a message, a warning, a call from God, sinks down into his soul. He feels, as he never felt before, "God is in this place"; and, falling down upon his face, forgetful of appearances, and heedless of consequences, periling his temporal peace, and exposing himself to every manner of remark, he worships, in bitterness of penitence, an offended, but a forgiving God, and goes forth to tell those with whom he comes in contact that the people whose words had searched his heart and made manifest its secrets must have God in the midst of them.

This was the gift of prophecy, as the term is generally employed in the New Testament. It differs from prophecy in the ordinary sense in this, that the gift conveys no "revelation," either as to truth hitherto unrevealed, or as to future events. It differs from the gift of tongues in this, that the intellect and organs act according to natural laws, though under a supernatural influence. It is that gift through which the whole of man's nature works in cooperation with the Holy Spirit, the intellect illuminated with divine light, the moral powers quickened by divine feeling, and the physical organs speaking with divine power. This is placed by the apostle as the highest gift—the one wherein man stands closest in communion with God as His intelligent instrument for His most hallowed work—the work of calling prodigal sons back to His arms, and of training feeble children into strength and steadfastness.

This gift was that which had the most direct utility, was capable of the most universal application, and was destined to be permanent; equally needful for the converting of sinners and the edifying of the church; and therefore to be ever kept in view by the church as a special subject of prayer: for, let this cease, and Christianity dwindles into a natural agency for social improvement, blessed with superhuman doctrines, but destitute of a superhuman power.

If the preaching of the gospel is to exercise a great power over mankind, it must be either by enlisting extraordinary men, or by the endowing of ordinary men with extraordinary power. It does often happen that men whose eloquence would affect and sway, whatever might have been their theme, give all their talents to the gospel; yet in such cases it ever proves that the religious impression produced upon mankind is never regulated by the brilliancy or natural force of the eloquence, but always by the extent to which the preacher is imbued with that indescribable something commonly called the "unction," or the operation and power of the Spirit. On the other hand, it often happens that a man in whose natural gifts nothing extraordinary can be discovered, produces moral effects which, for depth at the moment, and for permanency, are totally disproportioned to his natural powers. In hearing such a man, and afterward discovering the effects of his preaching, people often ask, "What is there in Mr. _____ to account for such effects? We hear many who are abler, profounder, better theologians, more eloquent, more persuasive; yet this man's preaching brings people to repentance and to God." They cannot discover the source of his power; and it is precisely this fact which intimates that it is spiritual.

The Power of Utterance: The Tongue of Fire

On the day of Pentecost, Christianity faced the world, a new religion, and a poor one, without a history, without a priesthood, without a college, without a people, and without a patron. She had only her two sacraments and her tongue of fire. The latter was her sole instrument of aggression. All that was ancient and venerable rose up before her in solid opposition. No passions of the mob, no theories of the learned, no interests of the politic favored her; nor did she flatter or conciliate any one of them. With her tongue of fire she assailed every existing system, and every evil habit; and by that tongue of fire she burned her way through innumerable forms of opposition. In asking what was her power, we can find no other answer than this one: "The tongue of fire."

With regard to one of her deacons, Stephen, it is said that his enemies could not resist the wisdom and the power with which he spoke. It was not every disciple who had the gift of prophecy, like him, to pour out in clear and copious utterance the testimony which could command the attention of national councils, and confound the sophisms of a college of disputers; but, each in his own sphere and style, the Christians of that happy day were distinguished among their fellowmen by a strange power of declaring the deep things of God. Many of them would go, like Andrew, who went first to "his own brother Simon," and tell their kinsmen of Jesus, and forgiveness, and the resurrection of the dead, and the world to come, in strains which, by some unaccountable power, fixed the attention and entered the heart.

Others of them would go, as did the brothers of Nathanael, telling the neighbors and friends whom they met the great things of redemption, so that prejudices, even the strongest, were often melted in the fire of their speech. True, they did not always succeed, but how marvelous their success was notwithstanding! Had Christians of the present day, in addressing those whose conscience, creed, early impressions, all favor every word they say, but that strange influence which bore down the most rooted aversion, how rapid and how glorious would be the spread of living religion in the land!

This power of utterance is ordinarily referred to throughout the New Testament as at once the gift of God and the great weapon of the church. We have already noticed how, when opposition first threatened them, they went in earnest prayer to God, and asked for power, that they might speak His word with boldness. So when any one of them, in critical circumstances, is enabled specially to declare and magnify the truth, we are told that he does so, "being filled with the Holy Ghost"; and Paul, who, though he was not present on the day of Pentecost, received the tongue of fire in a very remarkable degree, did not hold that gift as being constitutional, like natural talents and aptitude of speech.

Among the subjects with regard to which he entreats the prayers of his Christian brethren, he specially mentions "utterance." "Praying always with all prayer and supplication in the Spirit, and watching thereunto with all perseverance and supplication for all saints; and *for me, that utterance may be given unto me*, that I may open my mouth boldly to make known the mystery of the Gospel." Again and again have we brought before us the fact, that this utterance is the direct gift of God; nor are we without traces of the same fact in earlier times than those of Christianity. In the cases of Mary and Elizabeth, we hear them, under the influence of the Divine Spirit, uttering great and glorious things. In the cases of Jeremiah and Isaiah, we find the Lord making Himself their strength in regard to the message wherewith He charged them; and in the case of Moses, the gift of speech was especially promised to him, but his faith failed, and consequently another had to exercise that power which, had he believed, he himself would have fully possessed.

In all the history of the primitive Christians, we find traces of the effect produced upon men by the testimony they bore, even when bearing it under the constraint of public persecution, and in the face of impending danger. Without a press, without a literature, without any of our modern means of influencing masses of men; cast solely on the one instrument of the tongue, and in that destitute of the wisdom of the Greek, and of the skill of the scribe; seldom favored with the opportunity of repeatedly addressing numerous assemblies of the same individuals; destitute of prestige, contemptible in numbers, rustic in manners, and thwarted by circumstances; strong only in the one particular attribute—the unseen fire which filled them; on they went, and on, turning the hearts of their enemies, and advancing the name of the Lord.

Religion has never, in any period, sustained itself except by the instrumentality of the tongue of fire. Only where some men, more or less imbued with this primitive power, have spoken the words of the Lord, not with "the words which man's wisdom teacheth, but which the Holy Ghost teacheth," have sinners been converted, and saints prompted to a saintlier life. In many periods of the history of the church, as this gift has waned, every natural advantage has come to replace it—more learning, more system, more calmness, more profoundness of reflection, everything, in fact, which, according to the ordinary rules of human thought, would ensure to the Christian church a greater command over the intellect of mankind, and would give her arguments in favor of a holy life a more potent efficacy. Yet it has ever proved that the gain of all this, when accompanied with an abatement of the "fire," has left the church less efficient; and her elaborate and weighty lessons have transformed few into saints, though her simple tongue of fire had continually reared up its monuments of wonder. This has been not less the case in modern times than in ancient.

If the amazing revival which characterized the last century be viewed merely as a natural progress of mental influence, no analysis can find elements of power greater than have often existed in a corrupting and falling church, or than are found at many periods when no blessed effects are produced. Men equally learned, eloquent, orthodox, instructive, may be found in many ages of Christianity. It is utterly impossible to assign a natural reason why Whitfield should have been the means of converting so many more sinners than other men. Without one trace of logic, philosophy, or anything worthy to be called systematic theology, his sermons, viewed intellectually, take a humble place among humble efforts.

Turning again to his friend, Wesley, we find calmness, clearness, logic, theology, discussion, definition, point, appeal, but none of that prodigious and unaccountable power which the human intellect would naturally connect with movements so amazing as those which took place under his word. Neither the logic of the one, nor the declamation of the other, furnishes us with the secret of his success. There is enough to account for men being affected, excited, or convinced; but that does not account for their living holy lives ever after. Thousands of pulpit orators have swayed their audience, as a wind sways standing corn; but, in the result, those who were most affected differed nothing from their former selves. An effect of eloquence is sufficient to account for a vast amount of feeling at the moment; but to trace to this a moral power, by which a man, for his life long, overcomes his besetting sins, and adorns his name with Christian virtues, is to make sport of human nature.

Why should these men have done what many equally learned and able, as divines and orators, never did? There must have been an element of power in them which criticism cannot discover. What was that power? It must be judged of by its sphere and its effects. Where did it act? and what did it produce? Every power has its own sphere.

The strongest arm will never convince the understanding, the most forcible reasoning will never lift a weight, the brightest sunbeam will never pierce a plate of iron, nor the most powerful magnet move a pane of glass. The soul of man has separate regions, and that which merely convinces the intellect may leave the emotions untouched, that which merely operates on the emotions may leave the understanding unsatisfied, and that which affects both may yet leave the moral powers uninspired.

The crowning power of the messenger of God is power over the moral man; power which, whether it approaches the soul through the avenue of the intellect or of the affections, *does* reach into the soul. The sphere of true Christian power is the heart—the moral man; and the result of its action is not to be surely distinguished from that of mere eloquence by instantaneous emotion, but by subsequent moral fruit. Power which cleanses the heart, and produces holy living, is the power of the Holy Ghost. It may be through the logic of Wesley, the declamation of Whitfield, or the simple commonsense of a plain servant-woman or laboring man; but whenever this power is in action, it strikes deeper into human nature than any mere reasoning or pathos. Possibly it does not so soon bring a tear to the eye, or throw the judgment into a posture of acquiescence; but it raises in the breast thoughts of God, eternity, sin, death, heaven, and hell; raises them, not as mere ideas, opinions, or articles of faith, but as the images and echoes of real things.

We may find in many parts of the country, where much has been done to dispel darkness and diffuse true religion, that some of the first triumphs of grace were entirely due to the wonderful effects produced by the private and fireside talking of some humble Christians, who had themselves gone to the throne of grace, and waited there until they had received the baptism of fire.

In proportion as the power of this one instrument is overlooked, and other means are trusted in to supply its place, does the true force of Christian agency decline; and it may without hesitation be said, that when men holding the Christian ministry, habitually and constantly manifest their distrust in the power of the Holy Ghost to give them utterance, they publicly abjure the true theory of Christian preaching. It is, according to the authority of its Author, delivering a message from God—a message through man, it is true; but delivered not with the excellency of man's speech, not under the guidance of man's natural wisdom; a message, the effect of which does not rest upon the artistic arrangement, choice, and order of words, but upon the extent to which its utterance is pervaded by the Holy Ghost.

Section IV. Effects Upon the World

The Gospel Spread Despite Ignorance of the Messiah

When the promise of the Spirit was given, our Lord expressly intimated that His influence should not be confined to the church, but that He should "convince the world of sin, and of righteousness, and of judgment." It was only thus that the church could be extended beyond the number of the original disciples. Through the gifts bestowed upon Peter, the Spirit moved to the fulfillment of His great office in the hearts of worldly men.

Both the miraculous and the ministerial gifts were made subservient to this end. The former was a wonder which raised curiosity and then amazement, which brought together a multitude, first excited, finally awed. This, however, was all it did. Had the events of the day ended with the pure effect of the miracle, perhaps no Jew would have become a Christian, and certainly no sinner would have become a saint. The miracle prepared an audience for the preacher; but it did not convert, and did not even instruct them: no one there knew the doctrine of the incarnation, and its glorious concomitants, when Peter stood up to preach. All that the gift of tongues did was to produce an impression that these men were messengers of God. And even this it did not produce on all; for some mocked; probably people of the place, on whom the effect of the foreign tongues was lost.

The entire advantage which Peter, as a preacher of Christianity, derived from the evidences of his religion, when he stood up on the day of Pentecost, amounted to this: a large number of men were congregated in a state of much agitation, fresh from the impression of a prodigy before unimagined, and with a strong suspicion that the preacher and his coadjutors were probably teachers from God. His advantage, as compared with a modern preacher, lay in the freshness of this feeling—in the opened state of the mind just after an indisputable marvel had forced a passage through all its prejudices. His disadvantages lay in the comparative ignorance of his hearers, in their disbelief of most of the points wherewith he wished to impress them, in the amount of religious and national prejudice which fortified this belief, in the array of temporal interests which stood up against his appeal, in the discredit attached to his position, the obscurity of his person, and the rustic stamp of his speech.

Putting his single advantage on the one side, and his many disadvantages on the other, we naturally raise the question, Had he more advantage from the miracle of tongues than the modern preacher has from the Christian evidences generally? It would be hard to exaggerate the value of that freshness of impression under which he found his hearers; yet, taking the whole course of human nature, the miracle, whether in the hand of Moses, the Prophets, or the Lord Himself—however mighty as an instrument of impression, as a credential of a divine mission, never proved an instrument of moral regeneration to the people.

From the Pentecostal and other miracles, from the whole array of the Christian evidences, the modern preacher derives the advantage of an audience who believe that every doctrine he propounds is truly the word of God. Within their conscience he has far more on his side than Peter had in the consciences of his auditory. Peter had the advantage of a fresh and excited feeling: the modern preacher has that of standing closer home upon the conscience. The latter often thinks how much might be effected had he only some such supernatural sign as arrested the multitude on the day of Pentecost: what would Peter have thought of his prospects, if, instead of such an audience as he had, one had been offered to him where all believed that his Master was the Son of God, and that there was "no other name given under heaven among men whereby we must be saved"?

The effect of the miracle was a general impression in favor of the divine origin of the message. At this point the ministerial gift came into operation. By an ability clearly to state and argue the truth, Peter was enabled to put the understanding of his hearers into possession of the great revelation, that God had sent His Son to redeem them. By a sacred pathos, he was enabled to engage their sympathies in favor of each truth, as he presented it. Clear and feeling utterance of the gospel was his ministerial gift: understanding and impression were its effects.

The Gospel Spread Despite Human Nature

The united effect of the miraculous and ministerial gift amounted to favorable attention, understanding of the truth, and inclination to embrace it. But had no power beyond the testimony of the miracle, and the appeal of the sermon, touched the souls of the auditors, what single

individual would have embraced truth so dangerous to his
respectability and comfort, however convinced that it was of
heavenly origin, and fraught with eternal advantages? The
indignation toward such a step, raised by Peter's warmth,
would have been counteracted by many and potent inclinations of interest and of nature. Nothing is more common
than for the human mind to turn its back upon a truth, firmly
believed to be from God, deeply felt to carry eternal hopes,
but demanding the sacrifice of present gratifications, or of
the friendship of the world. Mere conviction never carries a
point of practical moral conduct.

Deeper than the judgment, deeper than the feelings, lies
the seat of human character, in that which is the mystery
of all beings and all things, in what we call their "nature,"
without knowing where it lies, what it is, or how it wields
its power. All we know is that it does exert a power over
external circumstances, bending them all in its own direction, or breaking its instruments against what it cannot
bend. The nature of an acorn turns dew, air, soils, and
sunbeams to oak; and though circumstances may destroy its
power, they cannot divert it while it survives. It defies man,
beast, earth, and sky, to make it produce elm. Cultivation
may affect its quality, and training its form; but whether it
shall produce oak, ash, or elm, is a matter into which no
force from without can enter, a matter not of circumstances,
but purely of nature. To turn nature belongs to the Power
which originally fixed nature.

In man, feelings and intellect are related to nature, as in
a plant tissues and juices: they derive their character from
nature, and manifest its bent; but are not nature, though the
means by which it acts on the external world, and is reacted
upon by it. Nature does not decide the comparative excellence of character in the different members of the same

species: one oak may be much stronger than another, one rose much sweeter; one man much wiser, or more generous.

The nature of man is essentially moral; and when intellect shoots up to eminence, it depends on the moral nature whether it is a blessing or a curse to the species, a joy or a trouble to the individual. According to the moral nature are the intellectual powers directed; and in man often wastefully, often hurtfully—as to the great majority, in ways far below their capability. Just as in all other objects, so in man, his nature eludes our analysis, lies out of sight, and defies our direct influence. We approach it through the intellect, or the feelings; but always with uncertainty, never knowing what unseen power may counterwork our most careful endeavors.

It is the nature of fallen man to prefer present pleasure to the prospect of eternal happiness, the favor of the world to the favor of the Almighty; to love himself, and forget his Creator. In adults this nature is fortified by its own developments; by habits and connections which all tend in its own direction. When a man's nature in boyhood produced fruits of vice and trouble, when his advancing years have steadily answered the impulse of the same nature, and his present associations are all based upon an alienation from heavenly ties; to bring him into immediate and permanent conformity to a divine ideal of life requires the ultimate Power of the universe, the Power which rules nature, and through nature circumstances. Set before all the wise and good of the world one man of thirty years, or upward, whose life has been wicked or worldly; and tell them by a word, a warning, or an appeal, infallibly to change him then and there to a pure man, or to a pious man; and they will each be ready to exclaim, "Am I God, that I should do this?"

To say that man is the creature of circumstances is as much as to say that he is destitute of a nature; for, where a nature is, there is a power, a power of which circumstances are often the mere effect, but are never the masters. Let all the circumstances under heaven conspire against the force of nature, as embodied in a seed of thorn, and they can never defeat it: all the gardeners, manures, heats, and waterings possible, would fail to make it produce fir. Heap upon it every advantage which art and creation can give, and it will steadily turn all to thorn, hopelessly incapable of rising above its nature.

Change your treatment, and endeavor to debase it, and the same superiority of nature to circumstances continues to manifest itself. You may starve it to death, you may stunt or blight it, but by no adversity will it degenerate to brier; thorn in spite of allurements upward, thorn in spite of repulses downward: as it can never rise above, so it can never sink below its nature. Circumstances are the creatures of natures, not natures of circumstances.

Human nature is said by many to be good: if so, where have social evils come from? For human nature is the only moral nature in that corrupting thing called "society." Every evil example set before the child of today is the fruit of human nature. It has been planted on every possible field— among the snows that never melt; in temperate regions, and under the line; in crowded cities, in lonely forests; in ancient seats of civilization, in new colonies; and in all these fields it has, without once failing, brought forth a crop of sins and troubles. This is absolute and inexpugnable proof that human nature, in the aggregate, is a seed which produces sins and troubles.

But a proof lies nearer the breast of each man. When you meant to do a wrong, and had made up your mind upon it, did any instinct within you tell you that you were unable, and must seek supernatural help to carry out your intention?

Never. You felt that to go forward was not only easy, but almost irresistible; was, in fact, yielding to nature.

When you had made up your mind to overcome wrong inclinations, and to do right, and only right, did not an instinct as unfailing as that whereby an infant searches for the breast of a mother, teach you to seek help, inward help, help against yourself? A decision to do wrong finds you strong in your own strength; a decision to conquer wrong, and do right, sends you to your knees, or makes you cry, "God help me!" If that be so, you need consult no man's books as to what side your nature is inclined to.

Man is the only being coming within our knowledge who has a nature that is plainly unnatural. This language is not paradoxical for the sake of paradox, but for the sake of strictly describing a mournful fact. Is a nature natural which can be changed without destroying the identity? That of man can be changed, and not only leave his identity perfect, but restore the course of a higher, and evidently an older, nature than the one which had previously reigned. Is a nature natural which urges toward courses which blight and ruin?

Human nature, when least affected by culture, in the loneliest and loveliest islands of unfrequented seas, urges to courses of headlong ruin and destruction. In the highest seats of civilization, it urges men to neglect the God of all, though they believe that to Him they are indebted for being, reason, and joy, and on Him are dependent for their continuance; urges them to neglect objects which they believe to be truly noble and of eternal utility, for pleasures which they cannot help despising, and for gains which they know are neither honorable nor lasting. In proof of this more than enough is said by the simple words, London, Paris, Rome. Yet, while their nature is thus overriding their true dignity, true happiness, and true interest, a voice within, as if of a friend who has survived from better days, is ever protesting against this monstrous condition of things, and averring that this nature is not nature.

There is not a beast of the field but may trust his nature and follow it; certain that it will lead him to the best of which he is capable. But as for us, our only invincible enemy is our nature; were it sound, we could hold circumstances as lightly as Samson's withes; but it is evermore betraying us. Often, when we honestly meant to be good and noble, our miserable nature, at the first favorable juncture of circumstances, betrayed us again, and we found ourselves falling by our own hands, and bitterly felt that we were our own enemies. Heal us at the heart, and then let the world come on! We are ready for the conflict. Make us sound within, and we will stand in the evil day. We can defy circumstances, and resist the devil, if only our own breast become not a hold of traitors; if inclinations, silent, subtle, and strong as nature, do not arise to beguile us into captivity to evil.

You tell us to withstand these inclinations, not to yield to our impulses, but to subject them to reason; that is, not to follow nature which is inward and impulsive, but to be guided by external indexes which observation notes, reason interprets, and will may apply to the control of nature. That, in fact, is saying, "Do not live by your nature, but resist your nature." What a world of appalling truth comes in with that one admonition! My nature not a nature to live by! Self-regard putting me on the watch against nature! A nature, and that the highest nature in this terrestrial system, self-injurious! This is not Thy handiwork, O Eternal Parent, Author of order, beauty, and love; Creator of natures, each of which is in unison with itself, and in harmony with all Thy other creatures! What has happened since man first left Thy hand?

It was strange to see three thousand men, after one hearing of a new and untried religion, accept it as their faith, and publicly enroll themselves as its disciples. It was especially strange, since the men at whose hands they, with docility, took the sacramental pledge of their conversion, were men without repute, whom they had themselves previously despised. But it is not till after some weeks have elapsed that the highest wonder of this phenomenon breaks upon us.

Raised into Saintship. Human nature is liable to unaccountable illusions, and multitudes to ungovernable impulses. It may be that in a week or two we shall find those thousands of a thousand different views, as to what they had heard from Peter on the day of Pentecost, and as to the pardon and grace which he had professed to declare to them. But, as day by day we watch that throng, moral marvels come continually into view. What was so rare in human nature is now ordinary—a holy man. Persons who were as commonplace in character as can be conceived, now live before us, saints. The vile have become noble, the churl self-denying, the bitter gentle, the sensual wonderfully pure. A community drawn from Jews of the ordinary standard, from persons of every variety of character and of sinfulness, is a community so pure, so far beyond what human eyes ever have seen before, that it seems as a commencement of heaven upon earth. Raised suddenly into saintship, they steadily maintain their moral deviation: first astonishing and captivating those who look on, and then withstanding all the opposition which prejudice and power can bring to crush them.

Day after day, month after month, year after year, this new and glorious life goes on. These men, lifted up from the ordinary level of sinners, continue "steadfast in the apostles' fellowship, and in breaking of bread and prayers," "filled with the Holy Ghost," rich in faith, overflowing with inward consolation; not seeing their glorified Redeemer with the eye, but more than seeing with the heart—feeling, embracing Him, they "rejoice with joy unspeakable and full of glory." Their close prospect is immortality; their citizenship is in heaven, their wealth lies where change can never reduce it, nor moth corrupt, nor thief steal.

Happy upon earth, and inheritors of heaven, it is naught to them that all mankind frown upon them; they know that they "are of God, and the whole world lieth in wickedness." Their saintliness spreads its fame to the ends of the earth—a fame that has never died until our day; and even upon our homes and our hearts are now descending the mild and holy influences of the first community called into existence by the tongue of fire.

Three thousand men permanently raised from death in sin to a life of holiness! Three thousand sinners converted into saints! Three thousand new-made saints enabled day by day to walk in the fear of God, and in the comfort of the Holy Ghost! Three thousand of our brethren, weak, sinful by nature, open to the temptings of Satan even as we are, maintaining a life in the body which almost surpasses belief, so is it marked with goodness and with purity!

This, of all the spectacles of Pentecost, is the one that speaks in deepest tones to the heart. On those three thousand we gaze; and our souls break out with adoration. Glory, honor, salvation!—for now the word "salvation" may be boldly uttered by human lips—salvation is come, is come to the race of Adam! Here, we see it, not in word, not in promise, but in practical demonstration; in human beings redeemed; in our nature recovered from sin, and that not in a solitary convert, not in one ardent youth, or in one exhausted worldling, but in hundreds and thousands of men with ordinary hearts, and wants, and employments, to whom human life has become a fellowship with God, and a straight road to eternal joy.

A Moral Miracle. We have already said that we may speak of a *physical miracle* and of a *mental miracle*; and to this we may add a *moral miracle*. Mind, we have said, is greater than matter, and therefore a work wrought in mind is greater than one wrought in matter; it bespeaks not merely a power, but a spirit. Just as intellect sways matter, so does that for which it is hard to find a name—the moral nature, the self and substance of a man, the heart—sway the intellect. We will use the word "heart," not to signify the emotional nature, represented in Scripture by the "bowels," but the moral nature; that is, so far as man is concerned, nature.

The heart commands the man. Give me a heart, and you give me a man; it carries both a mind and a body with it. Heart is the greatest thing below the sky; the nearest to the government above, that which sways intellect, and sways all things human. A work, then, wrought upon heart, is the highest order of operation to which human nature can afford a sphere. Christianity professes to be a system for that which has never been otherwise professed—the renewing of bad hearts in the image of the God of heaven. To this all its powers are directed; and until this is done, Christianity is but a theory. All previous to this is but as the verbal explanation of principles by a physical philosopher, lacking his ocular demonstration. The problem of our nature is how to make the bad good; that is, how to change nature, which, by natural power, is absolutely impossible.

In the physical miracle we see the God of nature accrediting revelation; in the mental miracle we see the God of mind accrediting revelation. In both these, nature is counterworked, and a power above nature manifested. It is a grand and memorable thing to see the sea dried up, or to see the human mind illuminated with the lights of prophecy or the gift of tongues; but the highest manifestation of a power above nature, of a power acting against and contrary to nature, is, when the bad suddenly becomes good; the impure, pure; when a clean thing is brought out of an unclean; when the earthly becomes heavenly; the sensual, spiritual; the devilish, like God; when the Ethiopian changes his skin, and the leopard his spots; when instead of the thorn comes up the fir-tree, and, instead of the brier comes up the myrtle-tree. Here is the Ruler, not of the physical universe overruling physical nature, or of the mental universe overruling mental nature, but the Ruler of the moral universe overruling moral nature, in attestation of the gospel of His own grace.

This, though not in the technical language of theology a miracle, is so in common sense. Is it nature? Is it reducible to natural law? True, it is what is to be ordinarily expected in Christianity but expected as what? as a fruit of natural agency? or of supernatural power accompanying that agency, and attesting it as from God? Has any system of religion ever embodied such a conception as an evidence that God was in it, and working through it, which would admit of constant application, and, at the same time, would strike deeper into the human soul than any other imaginable demonstration? This is the singular glory of the gospel. The recovery of nature from her fearful fall, the creating anew of man in the image of God, the presenting the fir instead of the thorn, the myrtle instead of the brier, is the "EVERLASTING SIGN, WHICH SHALL NOT BE CUT OFF."

Other modes whereby the Lord attests and seals His messengers, whereby His operation accredits His word, have had their occasional and their glorious field; but this sign is equally adapted to all time, claims as its sphere all humanity, and addresses not the judgment merely, but the conscience of man, proclaiming to him the presence in the earth of a Power that heals human nature, and restores the like of himself to the image of God.

Each sinner transformed into a saint is a new token of a redeeming power among men. That token declares to observers, not that there is a King in heaven, not that there is a "Father of lights," but that there is a Savior. And this is the testimony which the world especially needs. There are few things in religion which men doubt more than whether it is possible for them, as individuals, to escape from their sins. No declaration of that possibility goes so far to convince them, as seeing those whom they have known as weak as themselves, as addicted to evil as themselves, suddenly changed, and enabled all their life long to walk "as seeing Him who is invisible." This at once says to them, "There is One who has power on earth to save from sin"; and when they know that their neighbor ascribes all to the cross of Christ, they feel that in that cross must lie an efficacy by which, if ever they are to find salvation, that salvation must come.

The regeneration of a sinner is an evidence of power in the highest sphere—moral nature; with the highest prerogative—to change nature; and operating to the highest result—not to create originally, which is great; but to create anew, which is greater: for, when nature has once become evil, how infinite the glory of the act whereby again it takes its place in the eye of the universe, "very good!" The creation of saints out of sinners is the demonstration whereby the divinity of the gospel is most shortly and most convincingly displayed. Of all the Christian evidences it alone proves that our religion does save from sin.

Again we look back to those three thousand, and in the sight we glory. Our nature is not hopelessly lost! Redemption is wrought out! Humanity may be sanctified! Communities of men may be reared who shall dwell in peace and love, and earth may become a mirror of heaven! Never, below the skies—never, until the tragic history of Adam's sons is ended, can we escape the death which sin has brought upon us, and its correlative woes.

But sin itself has found a conqueror; not sin in the abstract, not sin in some philosophical impersonation, not sin in the great prince of the powers of darkness; but sin in human hearts, sin in my nature, sin girt round with flesh of my flesh, and bone of my bone, flowing in veins like mine, and appealed to by temptations of the mind and of the body, just such as my own. Sin in living man has been conquered, its Conqueror reigns, His redeeming power is nigh; and in those converts at Jerusalem I see a pledge of my own deliverance, and can shout, "I, too, shall be made free from the law of sin and death!"

We see a pledge of the deliverance not only of individuals, but of multitudes, not only of families, but of thousands and tens of thousands. It has been too much the fashion for Christians to look upon pure and elevated religion as applicable only to a few.

At a time when Christianity and holiness became different things, and true religion was looked upon as something not for life, but for a condition secluded from life, amounting, for practical purposes, to a burial before the time; a style of thinking crept in, which has never disappeared to this day. In the Church of Rome we still find it maintained, that deep holiness finds its best place away from human life, in retreat and celibacy. Among Protestants this error is rejected, yet practical religion is looked upon as something not to be expected to gain thousands at a time, and to renew communities by its sacred power, but rather to be a select blessing for a few, scattered here and there, and everywhere little discerned.

Look back to Pentecost. See Christianity at her first step raising up her army by thousands. She seeks not the wilderness; she seeks not the few; she affects not little, dispersed, and hidden groups. In the sight of Jerusalem, in the sight of the world, she starts as the religion of the multitude; the religion of fathers and mothers, of traders, landowners, widows, persons of all classes and of all occupations. She takes in her hand, at the very first moment, an earnest of every nation, and kindred, and people, and tongue, of every grade and age, as if to expand forever the expectations of her disciples, and impress us with the joyful faith that her practical redemption was for the multitudes of men.

Fallen into the Hands of God. In the case of the converts of Pentecost we are struck first with the suddenness of their conviction, then with the sharpness of it, and then with the permanence of the result.

When the humble fishermen began to preach, many who had witnessed the miracle were mocking; none had become saints; perhaps not a man in the crowd believed in the mediation of Christ, or in any other of the great doctrines of the gospel. They were adverse—not to say dogged, and on system, enemies. His words were strangely edged: a sword went through the very souls of these men—a sword which told to the consciousness, that He who wielded it was the Unseen and the Almighty.

As if the whole of life were recalled, as if eternity had pressed itself with all its weight into one moment; processes of thought that would have required long, long meditation, and yet longer description, flashed and reflashed across the soul; and the man found himself a sinner in the midst of his own sins, accused by the past, menaced by the future, overwhelmed, confounded, discovered, and unable to wrestle against the one thought, "What must I do to be saved?"

The sharpness of this conviction is equally amazing with its suddenness. Why could not the men control themselves? Why not go to their homes and think? Why not take time to deliberate? Why not avoid exposure to the public eye? Because, wounded to the very quick, they forgot all other considerations, and wanted to be healed? They saw, they felt themselves fallen into the hands of God; and, for the moment, the eye, the voice, the opinion of man was shut out from their thoughts.

If a man really saw an angel, or one "risen from the dead," we should expect that all consideration of bystanders would forsake him in the awe of the moment. And so, if in an instant a supernatural power opens the unseen world to the soul, with its one eternal Light, its heaven and its hell, although the view of these must be imperfect and confused, yet if it is a *view*, a sudden view, it must shoot fear, wonder, awe, through and through the soul, till man and man's opinion are as little thought of, as fashion by a woman fallen into a steamer's foaming wake.

We find those who were affected by these sudden impressions, going on and on, month after month, sustaining in the ordinary walks of life the profession of saints, walking worthy, not only of themselves, not only of their teachers, but even *of the Lord*, leading such a life that "He that sanctifieth, and they which are sanctified, are all of one: for which cause He is not ashamed to call them brethren." This steadfastness in purity and piety, "in the apostles' doctrine and fellowship, and in breaking of bread, and in prayers," in liberality such as no community had ever practiced, in "gladness and single-ness of heart, praising God, and having favor with all the people"; shows that the fountains of life had been sweetened, the depths of the soul reached; that, in a word, nature had been touched, changed, renewed.

The permanence of the change shows that it is one of nature; its suddenness, that it is effected by supernatural means. Indeed, natural means can never change a nature, though they may greatly modify its manifestations. When we want to produce any moral impression on human nature that shall be permanent, we trust to slow and lengthened training. To turn a man from his ways, to turn him against his own interests, to lead him to place all he holds dear in continual jeopardy, purely for the sake of goodness here and happiness hereafter, is what, in any natural scheme, we must attempt by beginning early and by laboring long.

But if we are to depend not on natural processes, but on the power of God, then time ceases to be a matter of account; the Infinite One declares His presence by accomplishing in a moment that upon which we had gladly spent a life. Whatever reasons may be advanced in favor of gradual awakenings rather than sudden ones, this at least stands on the other side, that the sudden conversion conveys to all bystanders a much more striking impression of a power above that of man. What is gradual may be readily ascribed, by the ignorant or the unbelieving, to the natural results of human processes. They may say, "The wonder would be if, with so much teaching, so many homilies, directed to the one end of bringing man to consideration for his soul, he was not gradually brought to it." But when, by some single, and, perhaps simple message, the work of conversion is done in an instant, it looks like the raising of the dead. As to bystanding sinners, it first stirs their wonder, then moves their conscience; and if they see such cases multiplied, the feeling falls upon them—"It is the mighty power of God!"

Christianity was established by the creation of Christians.

The Gospel Changed the Community from Within

In the words, "Continued steadfast in the apostles' doctrine and fellowship, and in breaking of bread, and in prayers," we see the effect of the regeneration of individuals on the character of a community. From a number of good men at once arose a united and fraternal society. Statesmen and philanthropists, occupied with the idea of forming happy nations, frequently look to good institutions as the means of doing so; but find that when institutions are more than a certain distance in advance of the people, instead of being a blessing, they become a snare and a confusion. The reason of this is obvious: good institutions to a certain extent presuppose a good people. Where the degree of goodness existing in the people does not, in some measure, correspond with that presupposed in the institutions, the latter can never be sustained. As the organ, embodiment, and conservators of individual goodness, the value of good institutions is incalculable; and he is one of man's greatest benefactors, who makes any improvement in the joinings and bearings of the social machine; but as a means of regeneration, political instruments are impotent.

Good institutions given to a depraved and unprincipled people end in bringing that which is good into disrepute. In fact, it would be more correct to say that institutions which are good for a people of good principles, are bad for a people destitute of principle. The only way to the effectual regeneration of society is the regeneration of individuals; make the tree good, and the fruit will be good; make good men, and you will easily found and sustain good institutions. Here is the fault of statesmen—they forget the heart of the individual.

On the other hand, have not those who see and feel the importance of first seeking the regeneration of individuals, too often insufficiently studied the application of Christianity to social evils? When the result of Christian teaching long addressed to a people has raised the tone of conscience, when a large number of persons embodying true Christianity in their own lives are diffused among all ranks, a foundation is laid for social advancement; but it does not follow that, by spontaneous development, the principles implanted in the minds of the people make to themselves the most fitting and Christian embodiment. Fearful social evils may coexist with a state of society wherein many are holy, and all have a large amount of Christian light.

The most disgusting slave-system, base usages fostering intemperance, alienation of class from class in feeling and interest, systematic frauds in commerce, neglect of workmen by masters, neglect of children by their own parents, whole classes living by sin, usages checking marriage and encouraging licentiousness, human dwellings which make the idea of home odious, and the existence of modesty impossible, are but specimens of the evils which may be left age after age, cursing a people among whom Christianity is the recognized standard of society. To be indifferent to these things is as unfaithful to Christian morals on the one hand, as hoping to remedy them without spreading practical holiness among individuals, is astray from truth on the other.

The most dangerous perversion of the gospel, viewed as affecting individuals, is, when it is looked upon as a salvation for the soul after it leaves the body, but no salvation from sin while here. The most dangerous perversion of it, viewed as affecting the community, is when it is looked upon as a means of forming a holy community in the world to come, but never in this.

Nothing short of the general renewal of society ought to satisfy any soldier of Christ; and all who aim at that triumph should draw much inspiration from the King's own words: "All power is given unto Me in heaven and in earth." Much as Satan glories in his power over an individual, how much greater must be his glorying over a nation embodying, in its laws and usages, disobedience to God, wrong to man, and contamination to morals! To destroy all national holds of evil, to root sin out of institutions, to hold up to view the gospel ideal of a righteous nation, to confront all unwholesome public usages with mild, genial, and ardent advocacy of what is purer, is one of the first duties of those whose position or mode of thought gives them an influence on general questions. In so doing they are at once glorifying the Redeemer—by displaying the benignity of His influence over human society—and removing hindrances to individual conversion, some of which act by direct incentive to vice, others by upholding a state of things the acknowledged basis of which is, "Forget God."

Satan might be content to let Christianity turn over the subsoil, if he is in perpetuity to sow the surface with thorns and briers; but the gospel is come to renew the face of the earth. Among the wheat, the tares, barely distinguishable from it, may be permitted to grow to the last: but the field is to be wheat, not tares; wheat, not briers; a fair, fenced, plowed, sowed, and fruitful field, albeit weeds, resembling the crop, be interspersed.

The Importance of the Praying Church in Primitive Christianity. The same words, "The apostles' doctrine and fellowship, and breaking of bread, and prayers," indicate the various exercises of religion, in which all churches and individual Christians ought to "continue steadfast." It was not a "preaching Church," or a "praying Church," the one in opposition to the other: they had both "doctrine," teaching, and "prayers."

The idea of separating these two, or of setting the one up above the other, is foreign to the religion of the New Testament. They are no ministers sent of God who have not the gift of being "apt to teach." They may be good and useful men; but the proof that anyone never was designed by the Head of all for a certain position, is, that He never qualified him for it. All the authorities in the universe cannot make him an ambassador for Christ, to whom Christ Himself has given no power to beseech men to be reconciled to God, no power to warn every man, and teach every man, that he may present every man perfect. The pretense of a Christianity without ministers, served by priesthood who can manipulate, read prayers that others wrote, organize solemnities, and keep times and seasons, but who cannot "rightly divide the word of truth"; cannot "preach the Gospel with demonstration of the Spirit, and with power"; cannot do anything but what the most senseless, or the most wicked, of men could do, if drilled to it; is one of those marvels of imposition before which we are at once abashed and indignant—indignant that, with the New Testament still living, men dare palm this upon us for Christianity; and abashed, that human nature is ready to accept such a travesty.

On the other hand, the gift of teaching was not exercised to the exclusion, or even to the repression, of that of prayer. The disciples did not come together only when someone was prepared with a deep and weighty discourse on points of essential doctrine. Prayer was one of their habitual exercises; not merely hearkening to the solitary prayer of one gifted preacher, in the great congregation, before or after his sermon; but prayers in frequent and familiar fellowship, prayers prompted then and there, without book, and without study; prayers of private disciples who had no higher gift, but who could pour out their requests to God; prayers by men with provincial speech, and all the marks of being "unlearned and ignorant"; but also with clear signs that the Spirit was helping their infirmities, and teaching them what they should pray for as they ought.

Suppose that Peter had some day stood up, and said, "Brethren, all things must be done in order. The use of vulgar tones and uneducated language is unseemly. Henceforth none shall pray in our assemblies but those who can do so without exposing us to the ridicule of the respectable. Indeed, to secure propriety, we have prepared proper forms, and all our future praying shall be from these Litanies and Collects written here, the language of which is the most beautiful of human compositions, and may, indeed, be called faultless."

Would not this have altered the history of the primitive church? Were not prayers simple, unpremeditated, united; prayers of the well-taught apostle; prayers of the accomplished scholar; prayers of the rough but fervent peasant; prayers of the new but zealous convert; prayers which importuned and wrestled with an instant and irrepressible urgency;—were they not an essential part of that religion, which holy fire had kindled, and which daily supplications alone could fan?

Surely no church can be entitled to call herself a praying church because, by a trained priesthood, she often reads old and admirable forms of prayer. Against such forms, suitably mingled with the public services of the church, we mean to say no word. We use, admire, and enjoy them: but, with the Acts of the apostles open, it is impossible to repress astonishment, that any man should imagine that frequent and formal reading of the best forms ever written, unmixed even by one outburst of spontaneous supplication from minister or people, has any pretense to be looked on as the interceding grace, the gift of supplication bestowed upon the primitive church.

That in such modes holy and prayerful hearts may and do pour themselves out to God, we not only concede, but would maintain against all who questioned it. That such prayers are in many ways preferable to the one set prayer of one dry man, long, stiff, and meager, wherewith congregations are often visited, is too plain to need acknowledgment.

But gifts of prayer are part of the work and prerogative of the Holy Ghost; are of the very essence of a church; and to deliberately shut the door against them, or so to frame ecclesiastical arrangements that they are practically buried except when possessed by the minister, the well-educated, or the influential, is a plain departure from apostolic Christianity. In no form is the tongue of fire more impressive, more calculated to convince men that a power above nature is working, than when poor men, who could no more preach than they could fly, and could not suitably frame a paragraph on any secular topic, lift up a reverent voice, amid a few fellow-Christians, and in strains of earnest trust, perhaps of glorious emotion, and even of sublime conception as to things divine, plead in prayer with their Redeemer.

The Pentecostal Christianity was not framed on the ideal of an accomplished circle; but on that of a church, a church including learned and unlearned, the refined and the rustic, the honored evangelist, prophet, or apostle, and the humble member without public gifts; but all rejoicing as members of one brotherhood, and each, in fitting time and mode, taking his share according to his gifts in the active work of mutual edification. A church, to be apostolic, must have ministers powerful in preaching, and members mighty in prayer.

The Importance of Fellowship in Primitive Christianity.
They continued steadfast "in breaking of bread"; hence it is
plain, that it was not a purely spiritual system of worship, too
spiritual to stoop to our Lord's ordained symbols, or by the
breaking of bread to show forth His death.

Besides breaking of bread, and doctrine, and prayers,
"fellowship" is distinctly named. It was then not a church
where the "teaching" of the minister was taken for his
fellowship with the people, and their "breaking of bread" for
their fellowship one with another; but where, in addition to
public teaching, sacraments, and prayers, was another beauty
of primitive Christianity, "fellowship."

Fellowship is family life, forming a circle, smaller or
larger, to the members of which joys, sorrows, interests, and
undertakings are of common concern and matter of common
conversation. Between the life of man as an individual, and
as a member of a great community, lies a vast region of affections, which can be filled up only by family relations. In public,
an individual does not indulge his affections: the greater the
multitude, the more is the heart in privacy. The citizen who
stands honorably with the public, and yet has no wife, child,
or friend to partake of his life, is lonely: his place in the town
council, or the national legislature, may be filled, and all the
relations therein involved well sustained to him by others; but
he lives without fellowship: if from bereavement, men have
compassion for; if from choice, they turn cold at the thought
of him.

It would have been strange, had a church meant for
man, in all his aspects—individual, domestic, national—left
the space between the individual and the public unoccupied;
so that Christian life must have been divided into secret
and solitary intercourse with God, and public solemnities,

wherein each was a stranger to each; no family life, no circles of interwoven hearts, no unbosoming of joys, sorrows, and cares, no communication "one to another" as to the soul's health or progress. Had such a cardinal omission been traceable in Christianity, it might have raised many a question as to how the tenderest elements of our nature—the social ones—had been disregarded in forming a bond designed to unite all men in one loving brotherhood.

But the spiritual life of the primitive church is redolent of family feeling. You have not there the solemn and solitary man, who has things passing between himself and his Creator, of which he never breathes a word, though he will take his place in public assemblies, where his own heart is as effectually concealed as if he were in a desert; who regards any approach toward fellowship of spirit as an inroad on privacy; any inquiry for his soul's health as a stranger's intermeddling; any opening of hearts as weakness; who can live his religious life alone, and loves to do so, except when he comes into public; who wants no friends, fellow-helpers, or inner circle of companions; and, indeed, who loftily doubts whether sociality in religious life is a very good thing. That man who can find fellow-citizens among the children of God, but not family friends, may be a very good Christian, but not of the primitive stamp.

What a glow of family heartiness runs through the New Testament! Instead of stiff souls always either dressed for the public eye, or shut up in solitude, you have brothers, sisters, friends, lovers, who cling to each other by mutual attraction, and between whom the common talk often runs on their conversion, their conflicts, and their glorious foretaste of eternal joy. In writing to them, the apostles are manifestly addressing persons to whom one great event has occurred, the surpassing interest of which keeps it in continual remembrance.

Once they were foolish, dark, wicked; carried away by evil passions, without God, and without hope. But a wonderful change has passed upon them—a deliverance from the power of darkness, and a translation into the kingdom of God's dear Son; a change as if from being aliens to be of the household of God; as from darkness to light, as from life to death. To this great salvation, accomplished for and in them, the allusions made by their apostolic teachers are so free, incidental, and frequent, as clearly to show that it was a theme of unreserved and joyful thanksgiving and wonder in their communications with one another.

The dignity of the apostolic office does not prevent frank and touching allusions to personal conversion and to previous character, as also to present attainments; and, on the other hand, even the babe in Christ is one whose happy experience is matter of open congratulation: "I write unto you, little children, because your sins are forgiven you, for His name's sake."

The incidental proofs of the spirit which animated the first Christians, as to fellowship with one another, would be perfectly conclusive if they stood alone; but some important passages of the apostolic letters are plainly meant to preserve this spirit forever in the church. "Let the word of Christ dwell in you richly in all wisdom; teaching and admonishing one another in psalms, and hymns, and spiritual songs, singing with grace in your hearts to the Lord" (Col. 3:16). Here is an injunction, not to the ministry, but to ordinary Christians, to be well-acquainted with the word of God, with a view to the edification of one another, by teaching and admonition; but teaching and admonition which, so far from having the regularity of preaching, may even be, and ought frequently to be, in "psalms, and hymns, and spiritual songs."

Such counsel could never be given, had a system been adopted wherein every word of teaching or admonition must fall from the lips of the minister. Throughout the New Testament the system of the church is assumed to be such as to call forth the gift of every member, no matter of what order it might be; and the active cooperation of each one is enjoined to promote the edification of all. "From whom [Christ] the whole body fitly joined together and compacted by that which every joint supplieth, according to the effectual working in the measure of every part, maketh increase of the body unto the edifying of itself in love" (Eph. 4:16). Here "every joint" is to *supply* somewhat, "every part" to perform its "effectual working"; and by this means the body is to increase, "edifying itself" in love.

No system can be made to accord with this passage, any more than with the general spirit of the New Testament, wherein the pulpit is the sole provision for instruction, admonition, and exhortation; the great bulk of the members of the church being merely recipients, each living a stranger to the spiritual concerns of the others, and no "effectual working" of every joint and every part for mutual strengthening being looked for. It is not enough that arrangements to promote mutual edification be permitted, at the discretion of individual pastors or officers: means of grace, wherein fellow-Christians shall on set purpose have "fellowship" one with another, "speak often one to another, exhort one another, confess their faults one to another," and "pray one for another," shall teach and "admonish one another in psalms, and hymns, and spiritual songs," are not dispensable appendages, but of the essence of a Church of Christ.

Some make light of any "teaching" which could be gained by the mutual exercise of the gifts of private members of the church—not always either educated or wise—and think that only well-prepared addresses from the pulpit are instructive. The regular ministry of the word is undoubtedly the prime source of teaching, and on its vigor and clearness the life of all auxiliary agency will ever depend; but those who would reject the practical and home teaching of free-hearted "fellowship," little consider that to persons of simple mind, or slow heart—that is, to the majority of mankind—the great problems, "What must I do to be saved? What is believing? Whereby shall I know that I inherit glory? Am I, or am I not, deceiving myself? How can I overcome this temptation, the sorest that ever beset a man? How can I grow in grace?" and such like, have often more light shed upon them by the plain statement of an individual as to how divine mercy solved them in his own case than by any general explanation.

In practical religion, as in all things practical, instruction is miserably incomplete, even though correct as far as it goes, if it does not bring before the student or inquirer actual examples of the process he hears described. A minister surrounded by bands of lively members, who with glad and single heart say as the psalmist, "Come and hear, all ye that fear God, and I will tell you what He hath done for my soul," has at hand "living epistles" which he may send any inquirer to read, has practical demonstrations of his pulpit doctrines, by which he may at once convince and enlighten the doubter. One who seeks no such auxiliaries, who permits or encourages the frigid habit of walking each one with a sealed bosom, rests all his hopes of success on the words of his own lips, and that without scriptural sanction.

Some defend a plain departure from scriptural religion by openly questioning the utility of Christian fellowship.

One writer of note is so bold as to say that the spiritual experience of believers is "better never spoken about." Though this sentiment is completely alien to the spirit of both Old and New Testament piety, it is the natural fruit of the constitution of too many of our Protestant churches.

In them the social element of religion has been woefully overlooked. Provision is made for doctrine, for prayers, for breaking of bread; but none for fellowship. A Christian may be a member of a church, and yet walk all his way alone, no one knowing or caring to know of his conflicts or his joys. If he is tempted, he may stand; if overcome, he may get restored; if happy, he may hide his peace among his secrets, and ask no one to rejoice with him; if he had lost his pearl, and has found it again, he may be silent, for his neighbors are not wont to be called together to take share in another's cares and joys.

There is something fearfully chilling in a state of things of which this is too fair a description. Religion is a life to be lived in fellowship; a conflict to be sustained, not singly, but in bands; a redemption, of which we are to impart the joy; a hope, an anticipation, of which the comforts are to be gladly told to those who "fear the Lord." We once heard a contrite inquirer after spiritual comfort, "It is ten years since I was received a member of such a church, and during all that time no one has ever said a word to me about my soul." And this is the case with tens of thousands who are members of churches which provide only for public instruction and ordinances, not for the social fellowship of saints. It is a mournful example of the effect of overlooking any one of the essential features of vital Christianity; and a fair comment on the ungenial notion that religious experience had better never be spoken about.

How would the Psalms be altered, could we reconstruct them on the principle that all about the state of the soul—its

joys, sorrows, temptations, wanderings, and deliverances—
had better be kept in prudent reserve from the knowledge of
our brethren! How would the apostolic letters lose in dignity,
tenderness, and power, as well as in instruction, could this
frigid law of isolation once stiffen them!

If we turn from religion in her own person, as viewed
in holy writ, to look at a reflection of her in one of the best
mirrors, *The Pilgrim's Progress*, how would Bunyan have
handled pilgrims who would stiffly or prudently close up their
bosom? A Christian, a Faithful, a Hopeful, who had nothing
to say "one to another," as they traveled on, respecting the
beginning of God's work in their heart, their escapes, solaces,
temptations, and slips; a Christian, a Mercy, a Great-Heart,
an Honest, a Ready-to-Halt, who would interchange no
experience; holy damsels and genial Gaiuses who would have
no questions to ask on such matters, would be a set of people
whom Bunyan would not know, and whom, we suspect, he
would castigate with good will. Indeed, he has given such
some cutting stripes, as it is, in the person of Mr. Talkative,
who, though fluent on doctrines and such points, was very
reserved on experimental religion. Faithful, wishing to know
how he was to bring him to a point, said to Christian, "What
would you have me to do?"

"Why, go to him, and enter into some serious discourse
on the power of religion; and ask him plainly, when he has
approved of it (for that he will), whether this thing be set up
in his heart, house, or conversation?"

Faithful having described how a work of grace "discovers
itself when it is in the heart of a man," puts the plain question,
"Do you experience this first part of the description of it?"

Talkative at first began to blush, but, recovering himself,
thus replied, "You come now to experience, to conscience,
and God; and to appeal to Him for justification of what is

spoken. This kind of discourse I did not expect; nor am I disposed to give an answer to such questions: because I count not myself bound thereto, unless you take upon you to be a catechizer; and though you should do so, yet I refuse to make you my judge." How many professedly religious men, who think themselves very different people from Mr. Talkative, and in many respects are so, would, nevertheless, feel much as he did, if any Faithful came as abruptly close home on the question of personal experience!

Banish from *The Pilgrim's Progress* the social element, the fellowship of hearts, the free recital of the Lord's dealings with each pilgrim, and you would cool its interest down to a point which, doubtless, would be decorous in the eyes of some, but would never touch the many.

"But is not what you call 'fellowship,' the meeting of the lay members of the church for prayer, praise, and recital of experience, liable to be abused?" Most certainly; and that in several ways. But is not preaching the gospel liable to be abused, so as to be merely the means of displaying a man's talent, or of diffusing error? And baptism, so as to be put instead of the "renewing of the Holy Ghost"? And the Lord's Supper, so as to be put instead of holy living? When we want to learn what is Christian, we never ask what is incapable of being abused; for we should find no answer: but, what accords with the Word of God?

And it does accord with the Word of God, spirit and letter, that "they who fear the Lord" should "speak often one to another"; that the forgiven and happy sinner should have companions around him, before whom he may celebrate the mercies of his Redeemer; that the weak should not droop unknown, nor those whose love is waxing cold be left to grow cold unwarned. A church wherein, from the minister in the pulpit down, every man in his own order, "according to the grace that is given to" him, is called to exercise his gift, and every member to lend his "effectual working" toward the general life and strength; wherein hearts are open, and fellowship is free; can alone answer to the New Testament ideal of a church. How much of the failure of the various Protestant churches to maintain religion at a high point of vitality for any great length of time consecutively, or to diffuse it generally among the nations which have come under their spiritual care, is to be ascribed to their neglect of the social element of scriptural piety, we do not profess to determine. But let those churches who, as to this point, have been taught to seek after primitive spirit and usage, faithfully and immovably guard the inestimable treasure which has been committed to them.

Notes

1. In the Greek "padz" occurs five times, the last time being "pan ergon anathon," rendered, "*every* good work."

CHAPTER 5

PERMANENT BENEFITS RESULTING TO THE CHURCH

Among the permanent benefits resulting from Pentecost, we cannot include the visible flame. Of it we never again find any mention in the course of the apostolical history; it appears to stand related to the Christian dispensation as the fires of Sinai did to the Mosaic—the solemn token of supernatural power upon its inaugural day.

Neither are we warranted in looking upon the "gift of tongues" as one of the permanent privileges of the church. Only twice, throughout the Acts of the Apostles, do we find any record that it accompanied the first introduction of Christianity to a place; and both these instances are very peculiar. The first was in the house of Cornelius, when Peter, preaching to his Italian auditory, felt some misgiving whether he might not by possibility be doing wrong, should he include them within the fold of the church; but he saw a great change pass upon the men before him, and heard them begin to speak with other tongues, and thus saw that, as to themselves at the first, the Lord had now given a Pentecost to the Gentiles.

The other case is that wherein the disciples at Ephesus, who had been instructed in the baptism of John, but had not so much as "heard whether there was any Holy Ghost," received the word at the hands of Paul, and began to speak with other tongues. These two cases excepted, we never read of this miraculous gift immediately attending conversions effected under the preaching of the apostles. It would not be just, from this circumstance, to infer that these were the only cases in which the gift was bestowed; but we may at least infer, that it was not an invariable accompaniment of the first appearance of Christianity, even in the apostolic days.

The Gift of Tongues as a Permanent Gift?

Considerable question, as to whether it was designed to be a permanent gift of the church, is raised by St. Paul's discourse on this particular gift, in his letter to the Corinthians. It has been already remarked, that he shows it to be destitute of any power of edification for the church, and therefore not to be a gift likely to continue, where all were convinced of the truth of Christianity. "Tongues are for a sign, not to them that believe, but to them that believe not." The only specific use assigned to the miracle is that it is a sign to them who believe not. In any community, then, in which the whole population had become believers, this sign ceased to be called for.

It seems to be frequently taken for granted, that the chief value of the gift of tongues was to enable the possessors of it to preach the gospel to the natives of countries, whose language they did not otherwise understand. But this is never set forward, in the Acts of the Apostles, as a reason for the gift.

A solitary stranger, possessing the gift of tongues, and passing into a country, the language of which was to him otherwise unknown, would have a great advantage in that gift; but, as has been already noted, not the advantage of thereby impressing the people of the country with a sense of the miracle—for they would probably believe that he had been taught their tongue—but of ability at once to proceed with his work and mission.

It is, however, to be remarked that we never find this advantage quoted as one of the results of the gift. Except in the case wherein the gift of tongues was used as a sign to the disciples, that the Gentiles were admitted into the dispensation and community of the Spirit; the gift was no sign "to those who believe." Its one use was "a sign" to unbelievers, and even to them not in ordinary circumstances; for them prophecy, and not tongues, was the profitable gift. Not adapted to edify the church, or to bring ignorant unbelievers to repentance, and fitted only to be a sign under exceptionable circumstances, this gift does not seem clearly designed to be either universal or perpetual.

We are not called upon to say that it will never be restored to the church; for that is never said in the Word of God; nor should we ridicule or talk disrespectfully of the faith of any Christian who devoutly expects its restoration. We do not have scriptural ground to claim it as one of the permanent gifts of the Spirit; and, if it ever returns to the church, it will be, not a mystification, but a miracle, a real speaking with "other tongues," not a speaking in some unheard-of, unknown tongue.

Having premised thus far, we come to the serious question whether the Christian church derives any advantage whatever from the dispensation of the Spirit, beyond that of looking back to a glorious period of miracle and power at her origin—a period which she may not regard as the dawn of a long and brightening day, but as a wonderful time of mysteries and portents, which were to have no permanent place in the church. It may seem strange thus plainly to put the question, whether Christianity really has any benefits permanently resulting from Pentecost; but it is necessary to do so, in order honestly to meet, not so much well-digested and formally expressed opinions, as a habit of feeling, often prevailing among professed branches and members of the Christian church.

Nothing is more common than to find the whole system of Christianity as an organization for recovering mankind from their sinful condition, spoken of, treated, and trusted in, as if it had been clearly ascertained that it was neither more nor less than a deposit of divine doctrine cast upon the earth, forsaken by the Divine Power, and left to make such way among men as it might by the inherent force of truth, and the permission of auspicious circumstances.

Cases are stated in which it is taken for granted that Christianity can make no way, simply because natural difficulties exist, such as natural agency cannot in reason be expected to overcome. Anything like a consistent counting upon a superior power acting with the truth, and making it triumph over difficulties, such as on natural grounds are unconquerable, is jauntily dealt with, as pertaining to those whose religion is not entitled to the veneration which Christianity has, by the lapse of ages, gained from mankind.

In every thing practice is in danger, if theory be falsified; and after the right theory has been abandoned, the maintenance of right practice is always precarious, and never long continued. If the true theory of Christianity, that the living power of the Holy Ghost, additional to pastoral agency, additional to scriptural truth, additional to every doctrine and every ordinance—a power by which the truth is applied and the agent quickened for his work, is not to be expected as continually resident and active in the church; that theory ought to be clearly stated and formally recognized on the part of all Christians. If it is not the true theory, we should take care that it does not color any of our habits of thought.

No Christianity without the Holy Ghost

A religion without the Holy Ghost, though it had all the ordinances and all the doctrines of the New Testament, would certainly not be Christianity. In it the presence and power of the Spirit are ever taken to be the vital element. Our world without its atmosphere, though the same globe, with the same physical characteristics, would be another world; and, if inhabited at all, must be inhabited by a race governed by laws altogether dissimilar to those under which human life is sustained. The change from the church of the New Testament to a church without the Holy Ghost, would certainly not be less in its kind than this.

All who seriously handle Christianity must recognize the presence of the Spirit as an integral part of its system and power; but if this presence is to be in some occult and inconceivable manner resident in an abstract church; not in the hearts of individual believers, not in the living temple of animated bodies and sanctified souls, but in a holy church made up of unholy members, in a sacred ministry made up of secular persons, in holy houses where worldly multitudes gather, and in holy books which ungodly ecclesiastics handle; if this is to be the presence of the Spirit, then the debate as to whether it is to be expected in perpetuity or not, need excite little interest.

If His presence is to entitle men to promulgate new doctrines contradictory to those already revealed in His own Word, and even to withhold that Word from the mass of their fellowmen, on the plea of denying them a deceptive guide and substituting an infallible one, then would His presence become a self-contradiction and a danger. In none of these lights have we the slightest reason given in the Word of God to expect the presence of the Spirit. We hear not of Him there as dwelling elsewhere than in the bodies of believers, or ever yielding to future ages the right to depart from the ancient ways and the clear revelation of the Son of God.

Neither do we find the promise of His presence so given that all action and effort on the part of Christians is to be made at every moment dependent on each person's own impression of the Spirit's movement within him.

But while on the one hand, we do not expect the permanent presence of the Spirit with the Church in the Romish sense, or in the sense maintained by estimable Christians of the Society of Friends, we must, on the other hand, maintain, as we have said, that without His presence and operation in the hearts of believers, and in Christian agents, we cannot have the Christian religion. We do not expect visible signs or miraculous gifts: for these were not the substantial blessing and grace imparted at Pentecost; but were to them only as heralds and ushers.

The real grace and blessing lay in what we have called the spiritual influence of the Holy Ghost, acting on the believer's heart; His ministerial influence, acting on the church; His converting influence, acting on the world. These, we contend, are necessary to the identity of the Christian religion, and were bestowed for all ages, and will to the end of the world be shed on those who perseveringly "wait" for the baptism of fire.

The Unseen Soul

Whence arises a persuasion which we seldom find formally stated, but constantly trace in the words of thoughtful men—that our mind is cut off from communion with the Father Mind, and, though able to draw knowledge from physical objects and from the minds of men, is without any access to the Source of Spirit, or any recognizable lights from Him? On what inch of ground in all the realm of reason can we rest the notion, that the Spirit of God does not communicate actively and directly with the spirit of men? Is it that we are so completely outcasts that, though without doubt capable of being acted upon by the Divine Being for divine intents, He will not touch subjects so mean? This would be the death knell of intellect and morals; for, if thus cut off from the Source of Light, our souls must be lost in the dark at last. The sense of sin gives to the conscience a feeling of banishment; the only answer to which lies in redemption. It is vain to answer it by mere reason; for reason offers no footing for the feeling, except on ground which revelation first discovers, and then bridges over by the cross.

Is it that our mental perceptions are all derived through physical organs, and that, none such existing as channels between God and the soul, no communication can take place? Few would be so bold as to say this; many are bold enough to assume it. What! no communication but through physical organs? They never explain communication, but only increase the mystery. Physical organs, it is true, are only acted upon *from without,* by physical objects; and all our

sensations come through such organs. But they never have
sensations. The organ receives an impulse from the light,
the air, or other outward object, and transmits that impulse
to the brain, producing a vibration there; but what a gulf
between a vibration in a brain and a sensation of a soul, or an
idea of heaven, or an emotion of joy!

It seems no mystery that two men should be able to
communicate, but a great one that they should be able to
do so through an iron wire, when they are a thousand miles
apart. One makes a secret fire carry a thought from his mind
through a wire toward the mind of the other; a sensation
is given, and both an idea and an emotion follow; but the
wire feels none of them. The impulse passes along it; and
the mind interprets that impulse, and turns it into the image
of a dying father, a newborn babe, a ruined fortune, or a
Sovereign saying, "Well done!" All the sensation, perception,
emotion, lie within the mind, none of them in the wire.

It is just so with organs; they transmit impulses, but
they know nothing, feel nothing, and explain nothing. The
power of communication is a mental power. Spirit knows,
and gives knowledge. The wonder is not that a mind can
impart its ideas to a mind such as itself, but that, being shut
up in a silent chamber whence branch out wires incapable of
one thought or feeling, it can pour along these a vivid and
changeful fire which conveys its feeling to another.

"No man," says Paul, touching on these things,
"knoweth the things of a man, save the spirit of man which
is in him." To you all minds are invisible. True, the mind of
your neighbor is in all respects the fellow of your own; yet
you cannot tell what is within it. It may be forming plans
for your ruin or for your good; but this is beyond your eye,
or ear, or heart's divining. *Every man dwells in the invisible*,
and often rejoices to look out upon a race, no one of which

can look in upon him. Yet oftener does he rejoice to pour himself into others, and multiply his own feelings in the spirits around him. When the invisible "spirit of man" wills to make known "the things of the man," it has easy, though mysterious, means at command.

The Means of Expression and Perception

A man is seated in his chamber, and deep things are passing in his mind. His mother sees that he is thinking; but ask her to tell his thoughts, and she is at a loss. His wife looks into his eye, and knows that he is feeling; but ask her what is the spring and course of his emotion, and she is in the dark. His little daughter sees something lofty on her father's brow, but what it is she knows not. Presently a thousand people are before him, and "the spirit of the man" is opening itself. A stream of thought is pouring from it; thought which ranges from the most familiar objects at hand, to those which are hidden in the bosom of eternity. Yet all these thoughts, mingled with suitable emotion, pass straight from his unseen soul into the souls of the thousand people. How is this accomplished?

Between him and them is floating a something which we call "sound." The keenest eye cannot see it; the most delicate touch, or smell, or taste, can find no trace of it. As it is rushing upon the ear, both eye and hand search in vain for it. Yet is it carrying invisible thought, from a soul invisible, by channels invisible, into the silent places of many souls, where the thoughts it raises are invisible to the nearest neighbor, till expressed in looks or words. The mind of the speaker pours a succession of impulses through hidden chords to his tongue and lips: these strike the air, in which the stroke makes a wave; that strikes on the drum of the ear, which causes a quivering of a nerve behind, that a quivering of the brain;

and then the soul inside sees an image of Stephen dying, or Paul falling on the high-road, or Elijah ascending, or Jesus at the right hand of the Father! What connection is there between a wave of air, a quiver of the brain, and an idea of heaven or hell, of sin or holiness? That the connection exists, is plain; but HOW? Make it plain *how* "the spirit of man," which "knoweth the things of a man" can reveal them within other spirits. All we can say is, God has appointed a channel of communication, given to the spirit means of EXPRESSION, and to its fellows means of PERCEPTION.

With this fact before us, illustrated not only in the one form just cited, but in a thousand forms every day, upon what pretext do we set up a cry of mystery as to the communication of the Spirit of God with man? Absurdity can reach no limit greater than that of supposing that the central intellect knows no avenue to all intellect; that is, is defective in means of expression. Despair can hurl humanity no lower than to say that God, able to commune with it, enlighten, renew, and impel it, yet distantly stands away. For, if no communication exists, the reason lies in Him. To say that the defect is not in His power of expression, but in our power of perception, changes nothing: if He cannot "reveal the things of God" to man, with such powers of perception as man has, He cannot adapt the expression of His own will to our state.

Many who shun the extreme of denying that God does hold communion with human souls, yet cover the truth with a soft but cold cloak—a cloak of snow—by always speaking loudly of the mystery. What is the way of the Spirit? How can man recognize the voice, the eye, the countenance of God? How is it possible to feel His anger or His favor, His presence or His withdrawal? Is it not a mystery?

Yes, it is a mystery; but it is nothing more. A mystery is a thing we are most accustomed to. I know no one thing which I perfectly know. I know ten thousand which are full of mysteries. The nail of my finger is a mystery; the fact is manifest, the mode undiscoverable; about my hand I can ask more questions than all mankind can answer; wrist, arm, shoulder, all have mysteries; as I approach the heart, the brain, what crowds of questions rise and are checked by the known impossibility of an answer! If "the way of the Spirit" were capable of perfect explanation, the whole universe would be a riddle; for why should that which was so high be fully known, and every common thing under our eye contain mysteries? The mystery involved in the Lord's communicating with any of His creatures is far less than that of our communicating one with another. He is of infinite intelligence; He planted the ear; He gave man speech; for Him, therefore, to communicate with any spirit existing, must be easier than for the sun to shine.

"Eye hath not seen, nor ear heard, neither have entered into the heart of man the things which God hath prepared for them that love Him." The apostle does not say this of heaven: he is not even alluding to it; for it is "the glory that *is to be* revealed"; whereas he says of the "good things" here in view, "God hath revealed them unto us by His Spirit." These good things, then, are not teachings, for of them eye, ear, and mind take cognizance; nor heaven, for it is not yet revealed but those blessings which "are prepared" for those who come at the Lord's call—pardon, adoption, and the favor of God.

Anticipating the inquiry, "How can those things be? How can acts of mercy, which pass in the invisible world, be revealed to us?" The apostle gives this simple illustration: "What man knoweth the things of a man, save the spirit of man which is in him? Even so the things of God knoweth no man, save the Spirit." If the things of God are beyond our eye, ear, or discernment, so are those of a man: and if man can make his mind known, how much more the All-wise! "Now we have not received the spirit that is of the world, but the Spirit that is of God, *that we might know* the things that are freely given to us of God." Adoption is an act seen by no man; and were no communication of it made to him in whose favor it hath passed, he could never by his senses or reason discover it. Though adopted, he would lie in the spirit of bondage. But that we may not be ignorant of this essential change in our relation to our heavenly Father, not ignorant of the things which His grace has bestowed, He has provided a Comforter, whose benign work it is to solace our hearts by letting us "know" what the Lord hath done for us.

The belief that God does not commune with man, is no result of reason. Reason has no footing for it. It is, indeed, hardly a belief; it is a feeling, followed by a sort of half-seen mental conclusion. A boy, conscious of deserving his father's anger, somehow thinks he will not be received at home. Men, conscious that they are aliens from God, recoil from the thought that the very breast, wherein they have caged things unclean, may be a shrine of His presence. A feeling of moral improbability, of unfitness, leads the mind to shrink from such a hope. Hope, indeed, it does not seem at first; the boy forgets the hopefulness of standing by his father's side in the dread of coming under his eye; forgets the joy of regaining his favor in the heat of enmity to his rule and restraints.

A natural difficulty to the Creator's communion with His rational creatures never existed. A moral one did; and never was problem so deep as, How could the Holy One take the impure to His arms, and yet continue the Holy One? That problem has been solved. The Holy meets the unholy over the blood of atonement. There is death for evildoing, wrath against iniquity—yet mercy for the repenting. Sin is not encouraged, innocence is not confounded with guilt, and yet the fallen are lifted up. This moral difficulty being met, and no natural one ever having existed, did the Lord not commune with the soul of man as with His own "offspring," the only reason must be that He pleased to cut him off from such fellowship. To affirm this would be to run into downright opposition to the whole scope of revelation.

No Christianity without Power from on High

Not a few of those who, if formally expressing their belief, would maintain that the Spirit is to abide with the church in all ages; that the idea of impossibility in His communing with man is absurd, and the cry of mystery unmeaning; nevertheless, in practice, effectually shut out His agency from their own view, and that of those who may be under their influence, by continually speaking of the truth, the truth only, as the power to renew this sinful world.

Far be it from us to undervalue holy truth, and, above all, that truth which flows untainted from the fount of inspiration; but a truth, even when divine, is never more than *a declaration of what is*. It is not the power which renews the human soul, but the instrument of that power; not the electric current, but the conductor along which the current flows. It is necessary, as necessary as the metal wire to the telegraph; but, alone, it is as inefficient as the wire when the hidden power does not pervade it.

You may teach a man the holiest truths, and yet leave him a wretched man. Many who learn in childhood that "GOD IS LOVE," live disregarding, and die blaspheming, God. Thousands who are carefully taught, "Believe on the Lord Jesus Christ, and thou shalt be saved," neglect so great salvation all their days. Some of the most wicked and miserable beings that walk the earth are men into whose conscience, when yet youthful and unsophisticated, the truth was carefully instilled. Did the mere truth suffice to renew, there are towns, districts, ay, countries, where all would be saints.

Unmindful of this, and not considering the danger of diverting faith from the power to the instrument, however beautiful and perfect the instrument may be, many good men, by a culpable inadvertence, constantly speak as if the truth had an inherent ascendency over man, and would certainly prevail when justly presented. We have heard this done till we have been ready to ask, "Do they take men for angels, that mere truth is to captivate them so certainly?" ay, and even to ask, "Have they ever heard whether there be any Holy Ghost?"

On one occasion it was our lot to hear a preacher of name, preaching before a great Missionary Society, from the text, "I am come to send fire upon earth." Choosing to interpret the fire referred to in this passage as the power which would purify and renew the earth, he at once declared the truth to be that power, and most consistently pursued his theme, without ever glancing at anything but the instrument. Afterward, hearing the merits of the sermon discussed by some of the most eminent ministers of his own denomination, and finding no allusion to its theology, we asked, "Did you not remark any theological defect?" No one remarked any, till the minister of some obscure country congregation broke silence, for the first time, by saying, "Yes; there was not one word in it about the Holy Spirit."

The belief that truth is mighty, and *by reason of its might* must prevail, is equally fallacious in the abstract, as it is opposed to the facts of human history, and to the Word of God. We should take the maxim, that truth must prevail, as perfectly sound, did you only give us a community of angels on whom to try the truth. With every intellect clear, and every heart upright, doubtless truth would soon be discerned, and, when discerned, cordially embraced. But truth, in descending among us, does not come among friends.

The human heart offers ground whereon it meets error at an immeasurable disadvantage. Passions, habits, interests, ay, nature itself, lean to the side of error; and though the judgment may assent to the truth, which, however, is not always the case, still error may gain a conquest only the more notable because of this impediment. Truth is mighty in pure natures, error in depraved ones.

Those who compliment truth upon her might have need of much self-possession. What world do they dwell in, that they can utter such flattery under the gaze of her clear and sober eye? What are these nations yet neglecting commercial and political truth, though all their interests invite them to embrace it? What these "enlightened" populations that have had religious truth again and again held up in their view, but have angrily rejected it, though to the entailing upon themselves innumerable social disadvantages? Where is the town where truth always prevails, or the village where error wins no victories? Do they who know human nature best, when they have a political object to carry, trust most of all to the power of truth over a constituency? or would they not have far more confidence in corruption and revelry? The whole history of man is a melancholy reproof to those who mouth about the mightiness of truth. "But," they say, "truth will prevail in the long run." Yes, blessed be God, it will; but not because of its own power over human nature, but because the Spirit will be poured out from on high, opening the blind eyes, and unstopping the deaf ears.

The sacred writings, while ever leading us to regard the truth as the one instrument of the sinner's conversion and the believer's sanctification, are very far from proclaiming its power over human nature, merely because it is truth. On the contrary, they often show us that this very fact will enlist the passions of mankind against it, and awaken enmity instead of approbation. We are ever pointed beyond the truth, to Him who is the Source and Giver of truth; and, though we had apostles to deliver the gospel, are ever led not to deem it enough that it should be "in word only, but in demonstration of the Spirit and in power."

We well know that many who speak of the truth as accomplishing all, do not mean the truth without the Spirit to apply it; but what is meant ought to be said. Hold fast the truth as an instrument divinely adapted and altogether necessary; but, in magnifying the instrument, never forget or pass by the agent. The Spirit in the truth, in the preacher, in the hearer; the Spirit first, the Spirit last, ought to be remembered, trusted in, exalted, and not set aside for any more captivating name. There should never be even the distant appearance of wishing to avoid avowing a belief in the supernatural, or to reduce Christianity to a system capable, at all points, of metaphysical analysis. If no supernatural power is expected to attend the gospel, its promulgation is both insincere and futile.

In their reluctance to acknowledge any supernatural element in religion, many take refuge in the idea that, after all, we are not to expect what the primitive Christians enjoyed. If this means that we are not to expect miracles, to it we have no possible objection. If it means that we are to expect less grace, we can give it no kind of credit. Nothing can be more contrary to the whole spirit and genius of revealed religion, than that the progress of years and events should be coupled with a diminishing amount of divine life and grace among men. All things promise us progress, not retrogression. No principle of Christianity, and no passage of the Christian Scriptures, warrant the expectation that the system is to decline with age, and to grow dim before its day ends. The mode of thinking to which we now refer, seems to be closely connected with the favorite idea of unbelief in the world—that of the Almighty "leaving," as men express it, one and another province of His territories to the care of secondary principles and powers.

Limited as the human mind is, the idea of combining attention to the general and to the particular always presents to it an extreme difficulty. In its own experience, when taking a general view, it necessarily overlooks particulars; when minutely attending to particulars, it necessarily overlooks generals. Unconsciously transferring the idea of its own limitation to the Supreme Power, it would ease Him of the incomprehensible task of at once minutely caring for every atom, and gloriously ruling the universe.

But in the presence of the universal, the distinction between the particular and the general fades away. Artificial lights either shine in one particular apartment, leaving the street dim, or shine upon the street generally, leaving each particular apartment dim. But when the Universal Light arises, he knows no distinction between general illumination and particular. Every little casement in the world is equally lighted as the broad valley of the Ganges, and every solitary daisy as well shone upon as if there was no other thing upon earth to lighten.

His Power Has Not Left Us

"He leaves, He leaves, He creates and leaves, leaves to the course of nature, leaves to general laws." Such is the crude language we continually hear from men who would transfer the small ideas of human sense to the infinite sphere of the

Godhead. The idea of the Omnipresent leaving, forsaking any part of His own dominions; putting a limit to Himself, creating in fact the most incomprehensible of all incomprehensible things, a place where there was not a Creator—the idea of His presence being an effort, or His embrace and superintendence of nature being a task, is unworthy even of the dignity of physical science, much more of the sweep of human thoughts.

On the wings of the wind, on the universal flow of electric power, on the swift sunbeams, filling up with a finite infinity the whole expanse of the solar system at once—on the light of a fixed star present with our eye, and at the same moment present through space inconceivably immense at every point from our eye to the star, and then away as far beyond, and round and round again at all conceivable points of the circumference on every side—on these confessedly finite objects our thought may rest, and rise step by step, till it easily springs to the idea of a complete and consistent Infinite, a presence literally everywhere, a power constant as eternity, an activity to which inaction would be effort, an eye to which attention is but nature, and slumber would be an interruption of repose.

Those who would exclude the Divine Being from His own universe, have been often exclaimed against, and justly; but how much more may *they* be exclaimed against who would exclude Him from His own church, and from communion with His children? Had His power been exhausted by the act of creating and establishing the church, and then had He committed its future course to the development of natural laws and the inherent power of the truth, Himself retiring from all action in the great battle whereupon He had set His servants, we might reasonably look upon Christianity as a religion which, perhaps, was better than others, more serviceable to the social interests of those who embrace it, and more genial in its influence upon the destiny of mankind; but higher motives than these for its propagation, or greater strength for the men who undertake the task, could not be calculated on. So far, however, from this being the case, the express promise with regard to the Spirit was, "He shall abide with you forever"; and when about to leave the disciples as to his bodily presence, the Savior said, "And, lo, I am with you always, even unto the end of the world."

A presence this, better than a bodily presence; a presence by His Spirit and His power, whereby the souls of His children are made glad, and their hearts made strong, not in some solitary village of Galilee for the evening, but at the same hour all over the earth, wherever two or three are gathered together in His name. That presence will never be withdrawn while there is a believer whose heart embraces the promise; and such believers will not fail while the world stands.

So far from anything in Scripture countenancing the idea that Christians of all subsequent ages were to be deprived of that divine help which constituted the strength and holiness of the primitive disciples, we have no intimation that they were to be even inferior in spiritual attainments. On the contrary, everything countenances the expectation that, as generation succeeds generation, the influence of holy faith and holy example will steadily tend to the elevation of the standard.

As Christianity makes progress among a population, every new household which becomes imbued with it is an additional power toward elevating the standard of character in that neighborhood. It is impossible to calculate the influence exerted, even in a country like our own, where religion has yet so much to do, upon those who are still ungodly. In many points their consciences have been trained, by force of example and precept, to a tenderness and activity which

Christian doctrine alone could give; and, as age after age rolls on, and the proportion between the saints and sinners becomes altered, the latter diminishing, the former growing, the image of God in man will be yet more and more brightly seen, if not more conspicuously, in some rare and blessed individuals, yet much more generally, as a common ornament and glory of human nature.

For a Christian now to expect to be made as holy by the grace of God as the saints of the New Testament, so far from being presumption, is scarcely a worthy measure of faith. It may be fairly said that, if we are not better than those who went before us, we are not so good; for the very light of their example sheds upon us an influence to which nothing corresponding was shed upon them, and thereby gives us a clear advantage, by which, with a similar measure of grace, we ought to present a character more complete.

Were it once proved that our moral strength in the present day was natural, then, indeed, might we reasonably limit our expectations, but not to partial attainments and incomplete holiness; for on that ground the reasonable limitation would be, not, "We shall attain to much, though not as much as the early Christians," but, "We shall attain to nothing." Our Lord's word is not, "Without Me ye can do *little*," but, "Without Me ye can do *nothing*." If it then be settled that in this age, as in the first, our strength is not of nature, but of the Lord, the reasonable range of our expectation, now as then, is to be measured by His glorious power. The question no longer is: Of what are we capable in ourselves or by ourselves? but, What can He perform? and to what extent can He manifest forth His glory by making us monuments of His power, and mirrors to display His image?

That grace of His which was shed so plentifully on the believers of the first days, is not an intermittent radiance, like the flash of a human eye, but is steady as the glory which streams from the face of the sun. Waning or exhaustion it does not know; and from age to age, from generation to generation, His saints will grow more and more mature, human life will increasingly reflect the glory of the Lord, and display His power to make weak mortals, beset with temptations, meet to be partakers of the inheritance of the saints in light.

No Christians without the Spirit of Christ

Some who gladly admit that the church, generally, may advance in Christian virtues, yet hesitate to believe that individual Christians in our day are to enjoy the same comforts of the Spirit as were so conspicuous in the primitive Christians. Among these latter nothing is more noticeable than filial confidence and joy: their reconciliation to the Lord, their interest in the death and intercession of Christ, their consciousness of regeneration, of deliverance from sins once reigning over them, their clear foretaste of heaven, and their peace in the prospect of death, shine throughout the New Testament, and all the early records of the church. This was the natural "fruit of the Spirit," the natural effect of such a Comforter as the Redeemer had promised dwelling in the heart. Take this characteristic away, and they would at once fall from the level of "children of light," of "heirs of God and joint heirs with Christ," down to the admirers of other religions, among whom personal "joy in God," and prospects of immortal bliss, are things unknown.

As we said before, that a religion without the Holy Spirit would not be Christianity, so we may say that religionists without the Spirit in their hearts would not be Christians. "Ye are in the Spirit, *if so be* that the Spirit of God dwell in you. Now if *any man have not the Spirit of Christ, he is none of His.*" It requires much of that cold daring which men may acquire as to things spiritual, for anyone who even respects, though he should not study, the record of Christianity at its source, to teach that it is not a common privilege of believers to enjoy a sense of their salvation, and to walk in the light of God's forgiving countenance. No scrap of holy writ even seems to favor this attempt to sink modern Christians to a point almost infinitely below that of ancient ones; for who can measure the distance between a soul which is singing, "We know that we have passed from death unto life," and one that is saying, "I cannot hope to know, till death strikes me, whether or not I shall escape dying forever"?

A change more serious can hardly be imagined in the relations of the Lord to His people, than would take place under the Christian dispensation, if, beginning by enabling believers to say, "We have a building of God, a house not made with hands, eternal in the heavens." He ended by leaving them in utter doubt as to their future destiny; if, beginning by giving them a sense of His favor, clear as day, unspeakably joyful, He ended by leaving them to serve Him throughout life, without ever feeling conscious that He smiled upon them; if, beginning by holding communion with them, He ended by leaving them to doubt whether He was even reconciled.

It is trifling at once with a man's common sense, and with his most sacred hopes and fears, to tell him that he is called with the same calling as the early believers, by the voice of the same Redeemer, under the same covenant of grace, and with the same promise of adoption; but that, while his brother, ages ago, had "peace with God," and "joy unspeakable and full of glory," knew himself to be a child and then an heir of God, and daily felt that heaven was his home, he is to proceed on his pilgrimage without any of these comforts, and learn at the end whether or not his soul is to perish. Who has given any man the right to assert that such a change has taken place in the relation of the adopting Father to His adopted children, affirming Him to have grown, in our age, too indifferent to soothe their hearts, and make them partakers of the joy which He spreads among the angels when He declares that the "lost is found"?

The change which the supposition we are combating would require in the office, or, at least, in the operation, of the Spirit Himself, under the very dispensation of the Spirit, is sufficiently grave, one might imagine, to make the least careful pause, ere he assumed that it had taken place. The act wherein the Everlasting Father absolves a guilty being from his offenses, and recognizes him before the angels as an heir of His glory must ever be of deep importance in the government of God. Of old time, when that great act took place, heaven rejoiced; but the deed did not remain without effect upon earth.

The King had proclaimed a pardon, and that proclamation must have effect. The Comforter sped to the mourner's heart. "Where the Spirit of the Lord is, there is liberty." With the presence of the Comforter, the captive found "deliverance," and he that was bound, an "opening of the prison"; and, tasting the liberty of the children of God, he sang, "O Lord, I will praise Thee: though Thou wast angry with me, Thine anger is turned away, and Thou comfortedst me."

Are we, then, on the word of some men, without one intimation of Scripture to support them, to believe that the Spirit has so essentially changed His mode of dealing with a forgiven sinner, that now the decree of pardon promulgated above, and hailed by angels, receives no effect in the soul of him whom it absolves? that the Comforter abstains from comforting, leaving the ransomed captive still to mourn his captivity, without relieving him of his load or of his chain? O Dove of Peace, ancient Comforter of the pilgrims who traveled this heavenward road before us, they say that Thy wing has grown weary with the lapse of time!

Unchanging Grace

How great a change would take place also in the privilege of believers! "We are of God," "born of God," "heirs of God," "followers of God, as dear children," "fellow-citizens with the saints, and of the household of God"; "once darkness, now light in the Lord." Such was the sense of adoption enjoyed in apostolic times. Of all the privileges wherewith the soul of man ever has been blessed, or ever can be blessed in this life, by far the most consoling and elevating is the sense of adoption into the family of God. No man can read the New Testament, and deny that this was an ordinary characteristic of the believers then living, or that it was a main element of their strength, kindling in them a joy which made them ready to face reproach, and emulate high service. Where is the intimation that this privilege was to be denied to Christians in succeeding ages?

When Paul says, "But I obtained mercy, that in me first Jesus Christ might show forth all long-suffering, *for a pattern to them which should hereafter believe on Him* to life everlasting," does he give any intimation that the believers of following ages, though they should be believers just as he, and should obtain "life everlasting" just as he, and should have his case and his mercies before their eyes, as "a pattern" whereby to measure their expectations from Jesus Christ's "long-suffering" were yet to lose an essential portion of the believer's joy; namely, the power of saying, "But I obtained mercy"?

Even the psalmist, under a dispensation lower than our own, could say, "I said, I will confess my transgressions unto the Lord, and Thou forgavest the iniquity of my sin." Does he hint that this is a privilege to which only a few can attain, and from which the children of God, in the better days to come, shall be ordinarily debarred? "For this shall *every one that is godly* pray unto Thee, in a time when Thou mayest be found"—conveying a clear intimation, that, just as he, on confession of his sins, found forgiveness—such forgiveness as healed the grief of soul which he describes a moment before, and enabled him to sing, as he here does, "Blessed is he whose transgression is forgiven" (Psalm 32), so would every godly disposed person find an acceptable time, if he prayed to the same merciful Lord for like forgiveness.

No godly man, no one whose heart was seeking after God, in the day of David, could read this without feeling that the "blessedness" of absolution was held out to him as his privilege. Indeed, all through the Psalms it is taken for granted that the righteous man rejoices in his forgiving God. And does the grace of our blessed Redeemer grow narrower as time advances? Does He gradually withdraw the light of His countenance till upon us of the latter days complete darkness settles, and we are doomed to grope our way through life's temptations without the encouragement of one smile from Him, and at the end to set a doubtful foot on the threshold of eternity?

The idea of any such deterioration in the privilege of believers is totally groundless; without one prop in Scripture or in reason. In a structure of ice, formed in cold seasons, and melts away when brought either into the sunlight of Scripture, or the warmth of living Christian society. We could not easily believe in any accession to our privileges, beyond those of our brethren in early times, unless it were clearly taught in the word of God; but if, without Scripture proof, we must believe either in an increase or in a diminution of them, we should choose the former, as far more supported by the analogy of the Lord's dealings with men.

"PEACE" was the Savior's legacy to His followers; peace to be imparted by the Comforter; peace which the world cannot give, and which passeth understanding. He leaves no hint that this legacy was to be recalled before "the end of the world." Indeed, in both the Old Testament and the New, happiness is an essential part of religion; that kind of happiness which is called "joy in God through our Lord Jesus Christ." The reigning of such joy in any human bosom clearly presupposes that the individual is satisfied of the reconciliation of God to him, notwithstanding his sins. Wherever this is doubtful, distrust, fear, and gloom must ever accompany the contemplation of the Most High; and this gloom would settle most densely on the most contrite spirit.

Happiness is to be a feature of religion to the last. That odious caricature of Christianity, which offers to the view of the world a man with all the doctrines of the gospel on his lips, but gloom on his brow, disquiet in his eye, and sourness in his bearing, has done infinite injustice to our benign religion, and infinite harm to those who never knew its worth.

Now, as in the days of Solomon, "her ways are ways of pleasantness, and all her paths are peace." Now, as in the days of David, she "puts gladness into the heart, more than in the time that their corn and their wine increased." Now, as in the days of Paul, she gives "joy and peace in believing." Happiness is not a separable appendage of true piety; it is part of it, and an essential part: "The joy of the Lord is your strength." Some would regard happiness as if it were to religion what a fine complexion is to the human countenance—a great addition to its beauties, if present; but if not, no feature is wanting. In the sacred writings, from first to last, it is regarded as a feature, which we cannot remove without both wounding and defacing. The kingdom of God is not only "righteousness," but "righteousness and peace and joy in the Holy Ghost."

While that kingdom stands, this "joy in the Holy Ghost" will be the privilege of the children of God; and let no man stand between the humblest believer of this our day, and the full light of his Redeemer's countenance. Let none take it for granted, that the work of God in the soul of man has degenerated; that the merciful Father no more gladdens the prodigal He accepts, by letting him know He loves him; that Jesus no longer says, "Be of good cheer, thy sins be forgiven thee"; or that when a penitent is accepted as a son, the gracious Comforter does not now, as in the old time, hasten on His dove-like message to diffuse heavenly peace in another troubled bosom.

The assertion sometimes confidently made, that the witness of the Spirit to our adoption is given to some believers, years after their conversion, as the reward of special holiness, has not even a pretext of scriptural footing. The witness of the Spirit, so far from being the reward of sanctification, is one of its chief springs; for without love there is no holiness, and we only love because we *feel* that God first loved us. "*Because ye are sons*, God hath sent forth the Spirit of His Son into your hearts, crying, Abba, Father." Not because you are old and eminent among the sons of God, but because you are sons: it is not a good-service reward, but a birthright; not a crown of distinction, but a joy of adoption. "In whom ye also trusted, after that ye heard the word of truth, the Gospel of your salvation; in whom after that ye believed, ye were sealed with that Holy Spirit of promise." Here the order is, "Ye heard, believed, were sealed": no long period of doubt and labor intervenes between the believing and the sealing. The father of the prodigal does not keep him for years, working "as one of his hired servants," before he prints the fatherly kiss of reconciliation on his cheek and on his heart.

The hackneyed objection, that it is presumption for anyone to say that he is a child of God, takes too much for granted. It never is presumption to acknowledge what you are. Had David never been taken from the sheepcote and made king it would have been presumption in him to say that he had; but, when it was the case, he was in gratitude bound to own and to commemorate the mercy shown to him. So, if a man has not been delivered from the dominion of sin, and adopted into the family of God, for him to say that such is the case is presumption; but if he has, then not to praise his Redeemer for it, would be ingratitude. Saying that it is presumption for *anyone* to call himself the child of God, takes it for granted that no one is; or else it is absurd. Presumption has many forms; and it is worth considering, whether a great and good Being would most disapprove the presumption which expected too much from His goodness, or the presumption which dared positively to disbelieve His promise.

Because He First Loved Us

Many who readily admit that, to some extent at least, the church in all ages will enjoy the gifts and graces of the Holy Spirit; and who would not deny that the first believers were favored with direct manifestations of the favor of God, yet make a difficulty of believing that, when sinners are forgiven in the present age, they are comforted by the Spirit *manifesting Himself* in their hearts, and crying, "Abba, Father." They do not deny that, even in our day, forgiven sinners are solaced with a confidence that they are forgiven; but they see prudential reasons against admitting that this is imparted by the direct witness of the Spirit, and would arrive at it by a process which, however unwittingly on their part, removes the office of sealing the adopted children of God from the Spirit, and gives it to the reason of man. They teach the seeker of salvation that, instead of looking to the cross for mercy, *till* the Spirit, as the Comforter, "reveals the Son of God in his heart"; he is certainly to look to the cross, but not to expect that to bring any such manifestation; on the contrary, he is only to learn what are the marks of a child of God, to compare his life with them, and, if it and they agree, his mind will arrive at the comfortable persuasion that he is a child of God.

This is one instance of the common error of taking part of a process for the whole. On the part of the Christian, the comparison of the scriptural marks of the regenerated with his own character, is not only good, but absolutely necessary; for, no matter what may be his supposed comforts, joys, or revelations, if, in his life, he is not led by the Spirit of God, he is not a son of God.

But because certain evidence is essential as a corroboration, it does not follow that it is the chief evidence of the fact, the first ground of conviction. As a guard against delusion, a strengthening of our confidence, and a constant stimulus to press forward to the things which are before, a sober judgment passed upon our own progress in grace is scriptural, rational, and indispensable. As the mode of binding up the broken heart of a penitent, of imparting to him the first feeling of filial confidence in the Lord, it is neither scriptural nor rational. It never can be the *original ground* of consciousness in any soul, that, through the abundance of grace, I, even I, am an adopted child of God.

Yet this is the consciousness to be given, and that not to the heart of one who is "whole," but of one who is "sick"; not

of a man who thinks that he is good, who is ready to interpret everything in his own favor, and has no feeling that he is
vile, or that the Lord is angry with him; but of one who now
feels what probably he believed all his life—that he is a sinner,
covered with dark and filthy spots, the displeasure of the Lord
hanging over him for many unholy deeds, and his poor soul
both fitted for destruction and exposed to it. Until painfully
sensible of his need of Christ, no man flees to Him for refuge;
and one in this state of feeling is soberly told, that his burden
is to be removed, and the sense of his salvation to be originated, by his being satisfied of the agreement of his own life
with the fruits of the Spirit, as stated in the word of God.

What are those fruits? "Love, joy, peace," etc., or
"righteousness and peace and joy in the Holy Ghost." No
enumeration of the fruits of the Spirit will be found which
excludes peace and joy, much less love; and from these
graces, if, indeed, not from the last named alone, spring the
various fruits which unitedly constitute "righteousness." The
poor penitent, then, is not to be first relieved of his load, and
given to feel that God loves him; but, previous to obtaining
such divine comfort, he is to become satisfied that his love,
joy, peace, and other graces, are such as to mark the children
of God! that is, while yet feeling that the Lord is angry with
him, he is to love the Lord; while yet feeling that his soul is
unsaved, he is to feel joy in the Holy Ghost.

If it be said that the feeling of the Lord's wrath and
his own danger is removed before the filial affections appear,
then a direct action of the Comforter, antecedent to his
satisfaction with his own graces, is admitted; and if that be
denied, there is no alternative but to conclude that, at the
same time and in the same heart, one can both feel that he is
under God's anger, and love God as a forgiving Father; can
feel that he is in danger of hell, and enjoy spiritual peace. If

the sense of wrath and danger is removed before the fruits of the Spirit appear, there is a direct witness of the Spirit Himself; if not till after, the totally incompatible states of mind just mentioned must coexist.

The relation of the fruit of the Spirit to the witness of the Spirit is clearly indicated to us. John says, "We love Him because He first loved us." Here the fruit, "We love," is made consequent on our *sense of the fact*, "He first loved us." To say that we first know that God loves us, because we feel that we love Him, is to make the fruit of the Spirit the foundation of the witness of the Spirit, a relation totally repugnant to the principle announced in this text, and pervading the New Testament, as, indeed, also the Old. "Bless the Lord, O my soul, and forget not all His benefits; who forgiveth all thine iniquities." The fact of forgiveness ascertained is the ground of filial gratitude; not filial gratitude the ground from which the fact of forgiveness is inferred.

Mental conclusions, as to spiritual truths, do not govern the feelings. The marks of "a child of wrath" are plainly laid down. Thousands know that they bear them; and yet this produces no contrition or distress, till the coming Spirit pierces their hearts. As it is with convincing, so would it be with comforting. A mental conclusion as to my own spiritual attainments would never dispel a sense of guilt from my conscience, or make my trembling heart "rejoice in the Lord." Did an awakened sinner conclude a hundred times that the marks in the Bible and the traits in his character agreed, his wounded spirit having no other balm, all this concluding would never heal his sore. The same voice which spoke condemnation into his conscience must speak justification; the same hand which broke his hard heart must bind it up.

The deeper the penitence of anyone, the slower would he be to take comfort from any good in himself; therefore, on a theory which makes this the *foundation* of comfort, the further would he be from finding rest; while, on the more evangelical view, the very depth of his penitence would drive him the more speedily to bring his burden to the cross, when it would fall off.

This allusion brings Bunyan and his Pilgrim once more to our view. He does not set Christian to undo his own burden by arguing, "I have fled from the City of Destruction; I have forsaken house and friends, wife and children; have resisted temptations to return; have knocked at the gate and entered in, and am in the narrow path": but, with all this done, he brings him to "a place somewhat ascending," where stands a cross, and, "just as Christian *came up with the cross*, his burden loosed from off his shoulders, and fell from off his back." He did not cast off the burden by a process which could easily be explained; but, when he set his eye on the cross, it fell off itself; and "it was very surprising to him that the sight of the cross should thus ease him of his burden." And so it is to others; but, however surprising, do thou, my penitent brother, heed no other direction than that which points thine eye straight to the cross; for pardon, for escape from hell, for rest, and hope, and purity, look thither, thither, only thither! If thy burden fall not at once, yet still look, look to the cross; and fall it will, far sooner, and far more surely, than if thou attempt to untie it by thy arguments!

As Christian thus stood before the cross, wondering, the "Three Shining Ones came to him. The first said, 'Thy sins be forgiven thee'; the second stripped him of his rags, and clothed him with change of raiment; the third, also, set a mark on his forehead, and gave him a roll with a seal upon it, which he bid him look on as he ran, and that he should give it in at the celestial gate."

This is unsophisticated Christianity. A burdened sinner, after discouragements and wanderings, comes, at last, to the foot of the cross. He looks, and is healed; his pardon, freely given, is tenderly manifested to him. The Father, Son, and Spirit unite to assure his heart, and give him present and abiding peace. He receives an evidence of acceptance, where he may always

> Read his title clear
> To mansions in the skies.

After this, the more he "searches" his own self, "and proves" his own self, "whether he be in the faith," the better for his vigilance and progress. But no such examining before would have unloosed his burden, or given him the roll.

Spiritually Discerned

The theory of an inferential comforting of believers, as a substitute for the scriptural mode of a "witness" of the Spirit, is singularly hopeless; for, at every step, it is obliged to lean upon that which it professes to dispense with and replace. It rests all "quietness and assurance" for penitent hearts on the fruits of the Spirit; and the very chief of those fruits, "love," etc., presupposes the witness of the Spirit by a necessity as clear as that by which repentance presupposes His convincing operation.

No; the sealing and solacing of penitent believers is not left to mere reasoning, especially with a foundation so liable to be misapprehended as our own attainments in grace. It is the work and office of that "other Comforter" whom our dying Lord promised; and let no man take it out of His hand. He it is who "cries" in the heart, "Abba, Father!" He who seals, He who bears witness, He who sheds abroad the love of God, He who enables us to know the things that are freely given to us of God. Any attempts to escape the mystery involved in the Holy Spirit revealing the mercy of God to a human soul only leads to contradictions and perplexities. To the old question, "How can these things be?" the one sufficient answer is, "They are spiritually discerned." What the Lord spiritually reveals, the soul can spiritually discern; and a divine presence, or a divine communication, may be assumed always to carry its own evidence with it, first to the consciousness, and then, by its fruits, to the reason. "One thing I *know*: whereas I was blind, now I see."

It is not to be wondered at that many who are sincere, and even earnest, pass the days of their pilgrimage in gloom, having no roll in their bosom which they know can be presented "at the celestial gate"; no conscious title to enter into the city; no permanent "joy or peace in believing." Nothing is more dangerous than to divert the eye from the one object of faith. And if persons are not taught to look, and look upon the cross, until their sins are blotted out, and the comforting Spirit Himself heals their wounds, but to seek rest by noting their own progress in the Christian graces, and are at the same time left without any fellowship of saints, through which they might learn by what steps of fear and doubt, of despair, and hope, and faith, others, whose whole spirit savors of the peace of God, obtained that blessing; is it not natural that they should walk in dim moonlight instead of walking in the sun? Yet, even amid those so dealt with, the Lord oftentimes breaks up man's theories by converting a sinner with such manifestation of the Spirit that it would be equally impossible to persuade him that his peace first came by contemplating his graces, and to keep him from telling what the Lord had done for his soul.

The Privileges of the Adopted

The character of the Christian church, as a whole, must always be ruled by the character of individual Christians; for the church is but the assembly and aggregate of individuals. If, then, as the ages advance, the individual Christian degenerate, the church must gradually degenerate also, her ministry be debilitated, and her efforts upon the world be less fruitful. All Christian character depends on the relations of the soul with its Creator: if these be cold instead of being joyous, if they be governed by the feeling of a doubtful reconciliation instead of that of a happy sonship, then, of necessity, the life is overcast with the shadows of not improbable perdition instead of being sunned with cloudless hopes of glory, and service is rendered as to an austere Master instead of to a most forgiving and loving Father. Strike from the language of the Christian the words, "Our fellowship is with the Father and the Son," and at once we have a race whose religion is not the religion of John, whose heart-strength is not drawn from the same sources as his.

Whether it be in comforts, in sensible communion with the reconciled Deity, or in practical sanctification of life, we contend that all Scripture holds out to us disciples of this actual hour, poor and undeserving though we be, the same sources and the same measure of grace as were open to our brethren of former times. There has been no recall of the Spirit, no curtailing of the "abundant pardon," no abridging of the privileges of the adopted.

The promise of the Holy Spirit was not only to the first converts; but, as Peter, addressing them, said, "to us, and to *our children, and to all that are afar off* even *to as many as the Lord our God shall call.*" However distant from that spot in Jerusalem, and however distant from that moment of time,

the call might sound, it would carry with it the PROMISE—
even that promise, the fulfillment of which made the early
church so holy and so victorious. The flames, the tongues,
the outward signs, were not the saving grace of the Spirit.
That was "within you," in the soul of man, and was shown in
"new creatures." That saving grace of the Spirit, working in
Christians now, constitutes their identity with those of old.
Without this, in apostolic times, though one spoke with "the
tongues of angels and of men," and could "work all miracles,"
he was not a true disciple. With this, in our times, though
one work no miracle, and speak not with tongues, he is a true
disciple; for, "as many as are led by the Spirit of God, they are
the sons of God." Miraculous gifts were not of the essence,
but separable attendants, of a real Christian; and all that was
then essential remains to us, unimpaired and free as ever it
was to them.

Father, Son, and Spirit, pardon the unbelief which has
imagined that Thou didst repent of the exceeding abundance of grace once given to Thy ransomed church! Afflict
us not, on account of it, by a real withdrawal of Thy presence!
Manifest forth Thy glory anew, by filling Thy children with
joy and light, that the world may see that Thine ancient love
and grace remain our heritage!

Call and Qualification

Next to the question, whether the privileges of the
modern Christian, as respects grace, are to be equal with
those of the primitive one, comes the question, whether the
Christian ministry is now essentially the same institution
as at first. If believers are not now the same as formerly, it
is impossible that the same religion should be preserved in
the world; and if the ministers be not the same, it is highly
improbable that the ordinary members of the church will be

so. Few would take the ground that our Lord founded His ministry on an unstable basis, requiring essential changes to render it capable of perpetuation in any age or country to which Christianity might extend: and all would admit the high probability that the principles on which He established it were those best adapted for its success under every future change of circumstances.

No Christian Ministers without the Holy Spirit

When we look at the example of the New Testament, in spirit, usages, and principles, it is too manifest to need more than assertion, that the anointing of the Holy Spirit was the one thing essential in the minister of the gospel. As we have before said that a religion without the Holy Spirit would not be Christianity, and that religionists without the Holy Spirit would not be Christians, so we may strongly say that teachers without the Holy Spirit would not be Christian ministers, according to the original sense of that term, the only sense in which we find it employed in the sacred writings.

Every arrangement respecting the training, or labors, of Christian ministers, which does not proceed upon the ground that they are certainly to be men first regenerated, then gifted for the ministry, and moved to it, by the operation of the Holy Spirit—an operation not to be assumed without proof, but to be tested by its fruits—must be as faulty in theory, and as inefficient in practice, as any arrangement for the employment of firearms, which did not proceed on the ground that explosion is the source of power.

The bow was a mighty weapon, and its combination of steel and timber, of cord and arm, of the strength of the vegetable, the mineral, the animal, entitled it to the admiration and confidence of many a host; and, as all its forces were mechanical, no question ever needed to be raised but one lying within the limits of mechanical inquiry. But the moment you adopt powder as your impeller, the elasticity of yew, or the strength of muscle, are considerations out of place. You have left mechanics, and cast yourself upon chemistry; and all your calculations must proceed on the ground that you have but to provide an instrument which will cooperate with an explosive agent.

The New Testament ministry rests not on mental, emotional, or educational strength, but, using each of these as occasion may serve, finds its own power in a spiritual influence; and all reasoning applied to it, without being founded on this fact, is reasoning on the rifle upon principles belonging to the bow.

The Ranking of Spiritual Gifts

The miraculous gifts imparted to many in the early church are carefully ranked and marked by the hand of the apostle as inferior to those gifts which were "for edification, and exhortation, and comfort." "And God hath set some in the church, first apostles, secondarily prophets, thirdly teachers, *after that* miracles, then gifts of healing, helps, governments, diversities of tongues" (1 Cor. 12:28). Here miracle-working, healing, and speaking with diverse tongues are set as inferior gifts to those whereby men were constituted teachers or prophets.

A similar design is observed in Ephesians 4:11: "And he gave some, apostles; and some, prophets; and some, evangelist; and some, pastors and teachers." Here we *do not find any miraculous gifts even mentioned as part of the institution of Christ* "for the perfecting of the saints, for the work of the ministry, for the edifying of the body of Christ": to this—the true end of the ministry—the effects produced by miraculous gifts were only auxiliary.

True, the apostles, prophets, and evangelists, as well as the pastors and teachers, possessed, and often exercised, miraculous gifts; but it was not by these they effected the "perfecting of the saints, the work of the ministry, or the edifying of the body of Christ." The essential point with regard to every one proposed for the sacred office is to ascertain whether or not he is "a man sent of God."

As the gift of the Spirit Himself is represented as consequent upon the ascension of our Lord, so, in the passage in Ephesians to which we have just alluded, the institution of the ministry also is represented as the result of His triumphant ascension. "He ascended up on high, He led captivity captive, and gave gifts unto men"; and "*He gave* some, apostles; and some, prophets," etc. These were the gifts which He, from His throne of mediation, bestowed on His church—men endued with power by His Spirit, and also moved by the same Spirit to spend their lives in the work of the ministry for the edifying of the body of Christ.

Whether we take the prophets under the old dispensation, or the Lord's messengers under the new, we find that the distinctive characteristics of a true minister of God lay in a call and a qualification. The qualification involved a gift, a power, and a training. He who had a call from God, a gift from God, and a power from God, and he only, was ever prophet, evangelist, or pastor and teacher, in any scriptural sense. The training varied with the age, dispensation, and circumstances; but no training ever did, or ever can, make him a minister who has no call, no gifts, and no power sent upon his soul by the anointing of the Eternal Spirit.

The call presupposed grace, or the moral qualification, and implied a gift, or what may be called the mental
qualification; for to call without imparting a gift, would be
leading an unarmed soldier into battle; and to call and gift
an unregenerate man, would be to commission and arm a
rebel. These two, call and qualification, can never be looked
upon as separable. "The love of Christ constraineth us," is
the language in which the apostle expresses that which is
essential in the internal working of a call from God to spend
and to be spent for the salvation of men; and he who, thus
constrained by the love of Christ, finds himself possessed of
a gift to speak to edification, or exhortation, or comfort, has,
in that motion and in that faculty, strong evidence that the
Lord is calling him into His vineyard. What he feels is not a
mere desire to enter the ministry as a good and useful office,
or to spend life in an honorable and happy vocation; but is
a constraining movement of the love of Christ, as if issuing
from His heart into the heart of His servant, and working
there a strong impulse to cry out and labor for the recovery
of Adam's lost children to the favor of their God and the rest
of heaven.

But, however strongly this desire may exist, if it is not
accompanied with a gift for public teaching, that alone
proves that the Lord has not constrained this particular
individual to the public labors of the ministry, but to other
efforts for the same end. Whom God sends to any work, He
qualifies for that work.

Loyalty to the King

A person feeling a true impulse to labor for Christ, and
misjudging his own gift, may conceive himself to be called
for the ministry when he is far from being qualified for it.
The *onus* of judgment cannot properly be laid upon him, but

must rest upon the church. He only can judge as to the inward motive of his soul whether or not his heart is moved by the Holy Ghost to undertake this work. The responsibility of declaring that he believes himself to be so moved is thrown upon the candidate for the ministry by most churches, if not by all, is a public and solemn testimony that the operation of the Holy Spirit in the heart is recognized as continuing to be the one basis of qualification for the ministry of the gospel. Only one's own self can tell what has passed between the soul and its Savior. No stranger can meddle with the question whether the Spirit has, or has not, in holy promptings, moved one to consecrate his life to the sole work of edifying and multiplying the flock of Christ. If any come to offer his hand to the church for this high service, on his own soul it lies to say whether or not he is led by an impulse from on high, or by ordinary professional motives.

The church, nevertheless, has her responsibility, and before she seals the credentials of any, she is bound to take note whether the Lord Himself has sealed them by the gifts of His Holy Spirit. As much as the responsibility lies on the individual of making or not making a solemn profession that he is inwardly moved by the Holy Ghost, does the responsibility lie upon the church to see that he has all the corroborative marks of such a call. Those marks are grace, gifts, fruit. Does his whole life testify that he has felt the repentance to which he is to call sinners, exercised the faith to which he is to encourage penitents, and experienced, in some degree, that sanctification to which he is to lead on believers? If the evidence of this is not clear, the church sins a grievous sin in accrediting him to the world as one qualified to "warn every man, and teach every man, that he may present every man perfect."

No circumstance of time, age, or nation can authorize any church to dispense with the essential qualification that he who is to be a minister of God shall first be a child of God. Any credentials given without full proof of this are presumptuous and null. When our Lord was about to restore to His beloved disciple Peter the commission which his fall had seemed to forfeit, He puts to him the question, "Lovest thou Me?" and thrice repeats it, searching him to the soul; and, on the ground that he does love Him, intrusts him anew with the commission, "Feed My sheep." No man whose true love to the Savior is doubtful, who cannot appeal to Him who knoweth all things as witness that he does love Him, has that qualification for a commission which is most indispensable of all—loyalty to the King.

"The same commit thou to *faithful* men." "Who is that *faithful* and wise steward whom the Lord will set over His house, to give to every man a portion of meat in due season?" In both of these passages, as all through the Word of God, the spiritual qualification is set as a consideration antecedent to that of gifts: first of all "faithful"; but not merely "faithful." "The same commit thou to faithful men, who *shall be able to teach others also.*" The steward is to be not only "faithful," but "wise," able to distribute to everyone in due season. He who is not apt to teach should never be commissioned as a teacher. The gifts of the Spirit are various. "To one is given the word of wisdom, to another the word of knowledge, to another prophecy." With reward to the servants of the Lord Christ, according to the gift of each, so let his sphere be. If "prophecy, let him prophesy according to the proportion of faith; or teaching, let him wait on his teaching; or he that exhorteth, on exhortation."

When, therefore, anyone comes forward to offer himself as a laborer in the vineyard of the Lord, before he can be rightly assigned to any sphere, the question as to spiritual character must be favorably decided, and then his sphere should be determined by his gifts. Which of the various gifts of the Holy Spirit have been conferred upon him? If none of them, who will say that he is to be a minister of God and a teacher of the souls of men? Surely this is not the church of Christ, that is going to lay hands upon a man, of whom no one knows whether he has any gift whatever from God—a man whose voice has never been raised in exhortation, teaching, preaching, or public prayer, who has given no more evidence of gifts and fitness than a thousand others who make no pretensions to be fit—going to set such a one over hundreds of professed Christians as their teacher and pastor, as the leader of their devotions, and the only instructor of their souls!

It is a manifest inversion of Christian order, when the commission of the church is taken to be the authority to *commence the exercise of spiritual gifts*. In the New Testament the church's only warrant for issuing her commission is the known possession of such gifts; and this can only be proved by their previous exercise. Her work was not to create gifts, but from among the gifted brethren to select those whom the Lord had, by His own will and act, previously fitted for special offices. The ordination of the church to the ministry was not a Christian's first authority to preach Christ—for that, opportunity and ability were authority enough; but the special eminence and usefulness of some among the company of preachers was the church's warrant for separating them to the sole work of the ministry.

If a commission from the church is held to supply the place either of the Spirit's constraining call, or of His qualifying gift, His office in perpetuating the ministry is superseded. To do this effectually, it is not necessary to blot from creeds the expressions of right belief, but only to adopt in practice such regulations as will enable men without grace, or without gifts, by the use of ordinary professional preparations, to obtain a commission, and stand up as accredited stewards of the mysteries of God.

The Gift of Prophecy

The operation of the Spirit in fitting the minister for the work of God is seen in the Old Testament in connection not with the priestly office, but with that of the prophet. The former was a typical and temporary office, existing only as the precursor and type of the great High Priest, and terminating at once and forever when He whom it foreshadowed had made His offering, and passed within the veil.

The work of the priest was not to teach, edify, warn, and forewarn, but to be the medium of access to the presence of God on His mercy-seat. As such, he has no earthly successor in Christianity: his office, we repeat, ended forever with the atonement and ascension of our Lord. Then came a change of the priesthood, that of Levi giving place to that of Melchisedec, which was vested, not in a succession of mutable men, but all in the Unchanging One, whose sacrifice should never need repetition, whose years should never fail, and whose infinite tenderness should feel every infirmity of every suppliant.

The office of the prophet was to warn, to reprove, to rebuke, to exhort, as well as to foreshow. That office is not repeated in all its features in the Christian "pastor and teacher," but as to its essentials it is. Foretelling is the one function wherein the two differ; and that was appropriately the gift of an age in which revelation was incomplete, and all the hopes of believers turned to a light yet unrisen. Indeed, it may be worth considering whether the perpetuation of the foretelling gift would not suppose an incomplete revelation, and whether the closing of the canon of revealed truth does not naturally carry with it the termination of that wonderful gift by which, from age to age, additions had been made to the previous stores of truth.

When St. Paul urges upon us to desire, and to follow after, the "spiritual gift" of prophecy, and holds out the inducement which should lead us to covet it above all other gifts, he has not in his eye, and does not present to ours, the honor or the profit of foretelling. The only inducements he assigns are these: "He that prophesieth speaketh unto men to edification, and exhortation, and comfort." "I would that ye all spake with tongues, but rather that ye prophesied: for greater is he that prophesieth than he that speaketh with tongues, except he interpret, that the church may receive edifying. . . . But if all prophesy, and there come in one that believeth not, or one unlearned, he is convinced of all, he is judged of all: and thus are the secrets of his heart made manifest; and so, falling down on his face, he will worship God, and report that God is in you of a truth."

Thus, in the passages where the apostle speaks most upon the Christian gift of prophecy, he makes no allusion to foretelling; and in the Acts of the Apostles we read that "Judas and Silas, being prophets also themselves, *exhorted* the brethren with many words, and *confirmed* them." We have no record anywhere of Silas foretelling, nor is there the least allusion to the exercise of such a gift; yet his exhortation and that of Jude, with their confirming arguments or appeals, are at once set down as the exercise of the prophetic gift.

The highest office of the Spirit in the prophet of the old dispensation was to enable him to see and to depict "the sufferings of Christ, and the glory that should follow," as though they were before his eye; and the highest office of the same Spirit in God's minister, in our day, is to enable him to descry, by an inner eye, the glories and the grace of a Lord whom he has never seen; and to descant upon them as though his eye beheld Him, and his ear were tingling with His voice. The same spiritual light which made a future Redeemer present to Isaiah, is needful to make a past Redeemer present to the Christian preacher. Without it, the one might have had an expectation, and the other might have a belief; but neither could burn and melt as in the presence of a living, loving, redeeming Prince of Peace. The spirit of prophecy illuminated the future to the one, and illuminates the past to the other—gave that which was a promise the force of a thing done, and gives that which is a record the force of a thing now doing.

The difference, within the soul of a man, between merely cherishing an expectation or a belief, and seeing, feeling, thrilling under the impression of a present Friend and Deliverer, makes in his utterance the difference between a tame declaration which disturbs neither prejudice nor indifference, and an overpowering force of speech that bears men's hearts away. So far was the gift whereby the Spirit enabled the servants of Christ to speak as the oracles of God (respecting the Master whom, though "not having seen, they loved") from being considered essentially different from that with which He had endued the ancient prophets, that the same name is freely applied to it, even when, as we have seen, the idea of foretelling is not included.

Ambassadors from God

However decided might be the evidence, that an individual was a child of God, and had a gift, another element is ever kept in view as an attestation that he is truly commissioned from the Father—the power and anointing of the

Holy One transfused throughout his preaching, and giving it a moral effect which ordinary speech, however wise, would never carry. "Not in word only," however true and scriptural that word might be, "but in power, and in the Holy Ghost, and in much assurance." "The kingdom of God is not in word, but in power." "The preaching of the cross is to them that perish foolishness, but unto us who are saved it is the power of God." "My speech and my preaching were not with enticing words of man's wisdom, but with demonstration of the Spirit and of power, that your faith should not stand in the wisdom of men, but in the power of God."

Here we see the most highly gifted of the apostles clearly recognizing the fact that his success as an ambassador to sinful men lay not in the perfectness of his intellectual perceptions, nor in the mode in which he presented the truth to the intellectual view of those whom he addressed, but in a spiritual element of his preaching, as distinct from its intellectual characteristics as they were from its physical elocution, and as necessary, in addition to the intellectual presentation of truth, as was the latter in addition to a rush of words.

Without clear intellectual presentation of truth, any flow of words would fail to convince or to enlighten. Without the spiritual power, any exposition or argument would fail to awaken or regenerate. The work of Paul was nothing short of a commission to "turn them from darkness to light, and from the power of Satan unto God, that they may receive forgiveness of sins, and an inheritance among them that are sanctified"; and this he knew would never be effected except by "power and by the Holy Ghost," working in and through whatever truth he might utter as the bearer of God's great message.

Without this call from God, this gift from God, and this power from God, no one can be recognized as, in the scriptural sense, an ambassador from God. To dispense with any one of these essentials in the qualification of a minister, is to introduce a radical change into the institution of the ministry itself, and to set it up on a basis for which there is no scriptural precedent. These essentials being secured, the training is varied according to circumstances. In the case of the apostles and the Seventy, after our Lord had called them under the promise that He would make them fishers of men, He retained them near His own person, continually instructing them in the oracles of God, giving them the highest example of teaching and of a holy life; and this training He continued for three years.

After the call of St. Paul, we find that three years elapsed before he came up to Jerusalem, which time he had spent in Arabia and Damascus, in what manner we are not informed, but probably in study of the Holy Scriptures, tending to give him a fuller acquaintance with the revelation of God in Christ. It is certain, however, that he was also exercising his gifts; for even in Damascus, immediately after his conversion, he began to preach. The training of Apollos lay first in such light as he received as a disciple of John's baptism, next in the exercise of his gifts, and then in the further instruction of Aquila and Priscilla.

The training of Timothy lay in the early teaching of a holy mother and grandmother, the ordinary means of grace, study of the word of God, and then personal fellowship with the apostle Paul and his fellow-laborers on their journeys and in their toils. Whatever special training individuals may have been favored with, that which was essential in the training was common to all, namely, instruction in the Holy Scriptures, the exercise of their gifts in religious assemblies either of the church or of the synagogue, and the gradual development of those gifts, until fitness for the ministry was clearly proved.

Whatever value general education may have held in the eyes of our blessed Lord, or of the anointing Spirit, it is plain that even the apostles, in the height and glory of their Pentecostal preaching, were not gifted with any power which would cover the provincial peculiarities of their speech, or enable them to conciliate the refined by graceful enunciation. The educated ears of the scribes of Jerusalem at once recognized, in the workers of miracles and the teachers of an increasing church, "unlearned and ignorant men." But, as we noticed before, their want of learning related only to matters of polite education, not to the deep things of the word of God, the doctrines, facts, and promises of which they were commissioned to expound to the world. The general education of Luke and Paul was gained with a view to general purposes, and turned to the service of the church by the grace which converted them.

Both Gifts and Grace

We now come to the simple question, Are the call, the gift, the power, and the training of the Christian minister to continue to the end of time, as to essentials, the same as in the apostolic age? Are we to expect identity, in these particulars, between the ministry of our day, and that of the first century; or, dispensing with this, are we to be contented simply with a lineal connection?

To put out of sight the scriptural precedents and essentials of ministerial qualification, to give up the spiritual identity of the ministry, and be satisfied with a lineal connection, is a lamentable abandonment of the church's hope. If she does not obtain for the sacred office a succession of men able to teach, and endued with the Holy Ghost, she cannot preserve to herself, or transmit to future ages, the primitive and apostolic ministry. Though all the appendages of the office be preserved, if the spiritual essentials of the minister be lost, the pith and sap of the ancient tree are gone, though the bark and foliage may survive. It is for the church to see that unequivocal signs of grace, and gifts, and fruitfulness, mark out every candidate for the sacred office as one chosen of the Lord; and not to accept instead of these any substitute whatever, whether it be his own profession, or some qualifications supposed to replace the primitive ones.

Though no one formally professes that the Christian ministry has become a totally different institution from that which Christ founded—different in the qualification it requires, in the mode of induction, and in the source and fruit of its efficacy—yet all this is assumed in the current writings and thoughts of many, and the assumption is wrought into the framework and usages of different churches. For a call of God, delivered by the voice of the Holy Ghost, in the silence of a believing heart, and manifested by earnest efforts to save souls and to promote holy works, a formal commission from ecclesiastical authorities is relied upon. Instead of a gift from God—a gift of sacred and impressive speech, a "tongue of fire"—we have substituted a ritual; instead of a scriptural training, a high education; and instead of a power from God, some substitute intellectualism, and others propriety.

We are very far from decrying these things in their right place. The commission is good and needful as the church's seal and recognition of the Lord's call, but ridiculous and self-contradictory as a substitute for it. Learning is invaluable when associated with and adorning gifts from God, but lower than pitiable when offered as a substitute for the power of opening and enforcing the divine oracles. Propriety, intellectualism, and ritual have their honorable place; but when, instead of the power which penetrates the soul, we have only ceremony which fascinates the taste, or talent which regales the intellect, then are we fallen from the region of divine to that of human things, brought down from "the power of God" to "the wisdom of man."

For this substitution different classes are to be blamed; church authorities, chiefly for coveting the want of a call and a gift from God by a commission from man; and the multitude of professed Christians, chiefly for coveting not so much spiritual power, as propriety or intellectualism. Did the former adhere to the primitive idea of the ministry, they would no more commission, as a minister of God, a man who had not given proof, first of sincere godliness, and then of ministerial gifts, than would any naval board accredit a man as a pilot who had studied navigation and charts, but had never sailed the particular channel on which he was to be intrusted with valuable lives; or than would any medical board give a surgeon's diploma to a man who had read and heard lectures, but had never been in a hospital, or dealt with an actual patient.

To substitute education for the ministerial gift (even when grace is possessed) is, in fact, to set aside the question, Is this man called of God? And to substitute it for evidences of grace (even when gifts are possessed) is equally to set that question aside. True, it may be still retained in words; but if that is done, and yet, without proof of both gifts and grace, a man be inducted into the ministry upon the simple evidence of education, the question is deliberately evaded, and the sin of falsifying Christ's own institution is not miti-gated by the plea of forgetfulness, much less of ignorance; but, with both knowledge and memory of what it originally was, another thing, differing from it in the first and most

essential qualities, is hailed by its name, and invested with
its functions.

To constitute a Christian, three things are necessary—
faith, experience, and practice; to constitute a minister,
four—faith, experience, practice, and gifts. Without experience, knowledge or belief can no more qualify a man to teach
heart repentance, and heart faith, and heart holiness, than
book knowledge, whatever might be its amount, would qualify
a man to train soldiers, if he had never himself passed through
the process of military discipline. Without gifts, education and
experience would be together as insufficient a qualification as
if a soldier had ammunition and discipline, without weapons.

Remember the Ten Days

It is difficult to describe the evil done, when the church
overlays the essential qualification and training of the primitive ministry by exalting substitutes for the active power of
the Holy Spirit, and when she further sets before all men
a profession with high prizes, the door to which will infallibly be opened by a certain course of education, unless they
disgrace themselves, and thus allures them to make sacred
professions from secular motives.

On each individual who makes such professions without
due care, the guilt of voluntarily sinning must forever lie; but
how far has the church been his tempter, when she makes
overtures to him irrespective of qualifications which are
clearly laid down in the word of God, as those only which
attest the divine sanction and call?

It may be asked whether we are to expect that in all ages
a sufficient number of men will be raised up, bearing the
primitive marks of a call from God, and of gifts from God;
and our reply would be, simply, REMEMBER THE TEN DAYS.
There we see men whose commission had come from the

lips of the Lord Jesus, whose training had been under His own eye, who have forsaken houses, and lands, and all that could bind them to secular avocations, who are ready to set forth upon the work of calling and warning a world that is "lying in the wicked one"; and yet day after day the inhibition lies upon them, that they are to tarry until they are endued with power from on high.

As we look at that spectacle—sinners dying, time rolling on, the Master looking down from His newly ascended throne on the world which He has redeemed, seeing death bear away its thousands while His servants keep silence—there is in that silence a tone which booms through all the future, warning us that never, never, under the dispensation of the Spirit, are men to set out upon the embassy of Christ, *be their qualifications or credentials what they may*, until first the have been endued with power from on high, been baptized with tongues of fire.

Better let the church wait ever so long—better let the ordinances of God's house be without perfunctory actors, and all, feeling sore need, be forced to cry with special urgency for fresh outpourings and baptisms of the Holy Ghost, to raise up holy ministers, than that, by any manner of factitious supply, substitutes should be furnished—substitutes no more ministers of God, than coals arranged in a grate are a fire; or than a golden candlestick with a wax candle, which flame has never touched, is a light.

A Fruitful Church Is Her Own Nursery

It was the original design of the Lord to withdraw from the church the ministerial grace of the Spirit, and to leave her to the care of pastors, all whose qualifications were natural, or gained by natural acquisition, all whose authority was derived from human commission, without any "manifestation of the Spirit," either in gifts or moral power; it was clearly His purpose that His religion should essentially change its character, after its establishment in the world.

This change, also, would be not in the direction of improvement, but of degeneracy; not by progressive increase of communication with His redeemed flock, but by progressive increase of distance between it and Him; not by bringing earthly things nearer to heavenly, but by removing them further away. It would imply a design, on His part, to reduce the Christian dispensation lower, as to ministerial grace, than even the Jewish: for in it the prophetic spirit was constantly giving manifestation that there was *a God* in Israel; not merely that there was truth, order, priesthood, a church, but A GOD, a living Being, high, holy, and wise, who dwelt amid the people, and actively moved, through His servants, for the instruction, reproof, and holiness of all—"rising up early and sending" messenger after messenger. It would, in fact, imply, that while the dispensation of the gospel was the most favored as to truth, it would be the least favored as to tokens of actual intercourse between the Savior and His people: for even the days of the patriarchs were lighted with frequent manifestations of God. It is laid down as the principle of our dispensation, that the manifestations of God are to be by the operation and gifts of the Holy Spirit.

It is, therefore, consistent Christianity to expect no supernatural manifestations but of this kind. But is it consistent Christianity, or Christianity of any kind, not to expect these at all; not to count upon direct gifts from above, upon such wonderful working of the Spirit through the mind and tongue of messengers, as would compel all to feel that their endowments were not from nature only, but were indicative of divine power?

If it be not alleged that the Lord did indeed mean to withdraw ministerial grace, in every appreciable and practical form, on what other ground can the notion that the ministry is to be supplied by candidates, just as any other profession is supplied, be rested? And all that is necessary is, that fathers should decide that their sons are to be ministers, and not soldiers or lawyers; and should educate them; that then, after an examination in general knowledge and theology, the candidate shall be invested with an office which professes to be held by commission from God. On what other ground can one avoid the conclusion, that the first movement toward placing any one in the ministry, should result from proof given that the Holy Spirit had endued him with pastoral dispositions and pastoral gifts, and that every subsequent step in the same direction should be taken carefully, after confirmatory evidences of the same?

It is easy to say that we must not expect such clear cases to occur constantly; and must follow some definite mode of preparation. Yes, we must follow some definite mode; but defined on principles of faith, not of unbelief. "We must not expect a constant occurrence of clear cases!" On what principles must we not? On those of the New Testament, or of modern writers? On those of the church in the apostolic age, or of subsequent and degenerate ages? On those of Christ's uncorrupted Christianity, or those of fallen churches? On the principle of "I believe in the Holy Ghost," or on the principle of "I believe only in nature"?

The definite mode of perpetuating the supply of ministers should rest on the sole foundation of the Christian faith, rejecting every idea of distrust as resolutely as a chemist would reject every idea of inconstancy in the affinities of elements; rejecting every idea of substituting other action for that of the Holy Spirit as decisively as a gunner would reject the idea of aiding his explosion with mechanical force. If we have not the Spirit to raise up agents, we cannot preserve Christ's church alive; if we have Him, we may fully trust Him to do all that is not made to depend on our own fidelity. To doubt the supply of the summer heat, and to set ourselves to rear harvests in hotbeds, would not be doing more violence to the laws of the physical kingdom, than it is to the laws of the spiritual kingdom to doubt the supply of the Spirit whereby laborers fit for the field are raised up, and to set ourselves to furnish others.

Firm in faith, the church ought to set at the very entrance of the pathway toward the ministry, a gate which no family influence, no education, could open; which none could pass but they whom a number of serious and godly men—not ministers alone, but also laymen who had to hear, and feed, or starve, according to the quality of the ministrations—would deliberately conclude were worthy, at least, to be admitted to probation for the work of the ministry. Such a gate none could pass but one who was either in earnest, or a studious and practiced hypocrite.

Where the primitive training is maintained, all the members of the church exercise such gifts as the Spirit has distributed to them—prayer, and exhortation, and teaching, and mutual speaking one to another, and admonishing one another. Among the working believers of such a scriptural church, a suitable proportion will ever be raised up whose gifts will fit them to lead in all the offices. This is the real training school for Christian agents; a fruitful church is her own nursery. Meetings for fellowship of saints, for free-hearted prayer, for exhortation, are the legitimate means by which they whom the Lord is fitting for His high ministry shall be led to the development of their gifts.

This training must be held as indispensable, and of an essential importance with which no other training has any pretense to claim a comparison; and then general education must be held to have the same relation to the Christian ministry as a general education has to any other profession; and theological education the same as special education has to the other professions.

Classics and mathematics, history and logic, are of admirable use to a lawyer; but if, qualified by these, he is to attempt to conduct cases without having been specially trained in pleading, alas for his clients! They are of great use to a physician; but if, by their light, and without study of diseases and remedies, he undertake to heal, alas for the families which put precious life in his trust! To a minister their value is quite as great as to either of the others; but study of theology is as indispensable to him as study of law or medicine to them; and practical experience of that repentance, faith, and holiness which he is to enforce, is as necessary as practical treatment of disease in addition to study; or as practical acquaintance with a ship at sea is needful for a mariner, in addition to the science of navigation.

Were we forced to choose between two men, one of whom is an accomplished scholar without practical godliness, the other a holy and gifted man without refined scholarship; to ask us the question, which we should prefer for our minister, is about as respectful to our faith as Christians, as it would be respectful to the common sense of a shipowner, soberly to ask whether he preferred, as a pilot for his ships, a scholar from a nautical academy who had never walked a deck, or a rough sailor who had often sailed the very waters over which the precious freight must be conveyed.

Alas for those whose souls are watched over by unconverted scholars! And even if converted and gifted, the minister of Christ should not come to his office without having been practiced in prayer, in exhortation, in preaching, in all the art of healing souls, and that not in books only, not in schools only, but also in the lively meetings and labors of the church.

We not only acknowledge, but gratefully believe and record, that many of those who had been invested with the ministry without sufficient test of their fitness have, in the event, become burning and shining lights. But if this, on the one hand, deserves to be continually remembered as a proof of God's tender mercy to His church, it is, on the other hand, not less to be noted, that He has ordinarily allowed such unauthorized appointments to be followed by their natural consequences, until whole nations have come under the curse of a ministry who either taught another gospel than that of the apostles, or who, perfunctorily exhibiting the shell of the truth, set the example of denying its power; and that even where the church had been reformed, although primitive Christianity had not been generally revived.

What England was a century ago—what many Protestant churches on the continent are at this moment—sufficiently shows that if guards are not placed at the entrance to the ministry, such as will hinder the admission of any but spiritually minded men, the course of Providence is to allow the sin to work out its own punishment.

Power Belongeth Unto God

While ecclesiastical authorities may be justly blamed for too readily substituting a church commission for the genuine call and gift of God, the multitude of professed Christians are no less ready to accept, instead of the genuine moral power which is the true preeminence of the Christian minister, a substitute in either propriety or intellectualism.

A people whose idea of the ministry was formed by inspirations from the New Testament, would look and crave, with feelings amounting to hunger and thirst, for men "endued with power"—the true power of the Holy Ghost, awakening, converting, edifying power; power under which hearts would melt, lives would change, old men would put off the evil ways of a lifetime, and youth put on the wisdom of gray hairs, thoughtless revelry would give place to benevolent associations, and the whole neighborhood begin to breathe a purer and a nobler spirit. Nothing could to them compensate for the absence of this. Though all proprieties gratified the taste, though the intellect were charmed, yet would they pine and long for that power which lies beyond the ken of the eye, the taste, or the intellect; but which the moral nature at once feels and responds to, either by a stern moral resistance, felt to be a resistance to the voice of the Spirit, or by contrite acquiescence, felt to be the surrender of the heart to the constraining love of the Redeemer.

"Ye shall be endued," said our Lord, "with power from on high"—robed with power. This is the true robing and vestment of the minister of God—an invisible garment of power, which sits not upon his shoulders, but upon his spirit, shading him over with a moral dignity, as if he held office from the King of Kings, and conveying to every conscience before him the instinctive perception that he comes commissioned to deal with *it* on the things that affect its purity, and its relations with Him who planted it in man.

All power is indescribable, but at the same time appreciable. What it is, where it is, how it came, where it goes, its measure, movement, nature, form, or essence, no human skill can discover. We may ask the sunbeam, which has such power to fly and to illuminate; the lightning, which has such power to scathe; the dewdrop, that has power to refresh; the magnet, the fire, the steam, the eye that can see, the ear that can hear, the nerve that can convey the messages of will—we may ask all the agents we see exerting power to render us an account each of its own power, and all will be dumb. Not the cannonball on its flight, or the lion in his triumph, not the tempest or the sea, not even pestilence itself, can tell us what is power. If we ask death who has put all things under his feet, even he has no reply; and after we have passed the question, "What is power?" round a mute universe, we must say, "God has spoken once, yea, twice have I heard this, that POWER BELONGETH UNTO GOD."

Yet power, in itself so hidden and indescribable, is ever manifest by its effects. An effect demonstrates the presence of a power. Where gunpowder explodes, there must have been fire; where water shoots up through the atmosphere in steam, there must have been heat; where iron moves without mechanical force, a magnet must be; and the absence of the effect is conclusive evidence of the absence of the power from which the effect would have followed. The intellect at once recognizes the presence of intellectual power. The emotions, also, faithfully tell whenever an emotional power is brought to bear upon them; and no less surely does the conscience of a man feel when a moral power comes acting upon it.

Improper Propriety

In unconverted men a singular conflict goes on: they share the admiration which every man feels for moral power—an admiration which none can help feeling, even though he be so wedded to his sins that he is lashed into enmity when the action of such a power makes him fear that, after all, he will be converted into a saint; yet this feeling is combated by the natural aversion which men have for everything that crosses their earthly inclinations, and tends to lead their affections to holy things.

On the one hand, they feel that the man who preaches to them ought to be able to disturb them in their evil ways, as by a voice and a call from their Maker; and they are drawn toward him who has this character. On the other hand, they desire to continue longer in worldly ways; and it is comfortable to them, and welcome, when, instead of a trumpet peal which would break their slumbers, they hear a pleasant song that will help them to sleep on. With the great majority these latter feelings prevail, and, according as their own inclinations and training lead, they seek in the public ordinances of God's house either what they call an intellectual treat, or what they consider a well-performed and creditable solemnity.

With one class, the highest ideal of a Christian service seems to be, that nothing should pass that could, by any possibility, offend the taste of any human being who might look upon the whole scene as an assembly for some dignified purpose. As to the pulpit, their great desire is that the pulpit should "behave itself"; and in this country of ours many a service may be found which is

Faultily faultless, icily regular, splendidly null.

That is, "faultless" in such eyes—"faultless," if the idea of a Christian service be not a scene of penitence, fervent prayer, bursting adoration; a triumph of spiritual power; an assembly the atmosphere of which breathes of living souls and the present Spirit of God, of transgressors awakening, and penitents finding mercy, and saints standing truly nigh to the countenance of their Father; but, instead of all this, a number of well-dressed people decorously meeting, and celebrating something that affects no one, and coolly listening to something not formed to affect anyone, and, above all, not formed to offend any man, except him who wants to feel his own soul, and see the souls of his neighbors, moved to their depths as by a call from above.

The sanctuary of God ought, undoubtedly, to be the highest scene and model of propriety; the pulpit to be its foremost and most shining example. He who, under any pretext, introduces trifling, oddity, or coarseness there, strikes fearfully at a main support of power—true reverence. However offensive want of propriety may be elsewhere, it is doubly so in the house of God.

But the united praying of Christians, the delivering of a message from above, and the mingling of thankful voices in praise to the Most High, like all other peculiar actions, have a propriety of their own; and of all improprieties, none is more thoroughly alien to them than that, be it what it may—whether stiff form or elaborate literature—which gives to the place a savor rather of the wisdom of man than of the power of God.

At a marriage-feast the solemnity proper to a funeral would be an impropriety. In a company of friends the precision of military movement would be improper. The noise of instruments is propriety in a concert, the sound of grinding in a mill, the clatter of shuttles in a factory, the ring of hammers in a forge, the laughter of children in a nursery.

And so the house of God has its own atmosphere. Whatever would extinguish the reverent utterance of penitent or grateful emotion on the part of the simple and the poor, of the newly awakened or newly forgiven—whatever would train all Christian feelings to move there, in God's own house and in the assembly of His people, as if under the cold eye of a heathen world, is a more crying impropriety than those departures from *taste* which not only might flow, but must flow, from the utterance of feelings, where any multitude, composed of all classes, is deeply affected.

When the noble idea of Christian propriety gives place to the paltry idea of properness—when intense reverence and love and joy, meeting and stirring the breasts of a multitude, are distasted, and men are set on having everything square, well cut, and arranged beforehand, then we have little right to expect the highest of all proprieties—the breaking of sinful hearts as if in pieces under the hammer of God's word, and the cry of awakened sinners, "What must we do to be saved?"

In fact, many who call themselves Christians, and whose claim we readily allow, would regard the utterance of such a cry in the house of God as not less improper than if raised in a theater. The people may say, "Amen," if it be just by rule; may murmur a response, if just where good men, long since dead, marked, "Respond here"; but anything like the pentecostal scene—any general outburst of penitent emotion—would be intolerable; and even to see a solitary man, "unlearned and unbelieving," feeling himself judged and condemned, and "falling down upon his face and worshiping God," would be a disturbance of propriety, because it would make a fracture in that icy properness wherein a long continuance of cold has encased many a branch of Christ's church. Yet this scene is just as proper to the house of God as the crash of a falling tree is to the forest where the woodman is clearing.

The Mysterious Seal of Commission

A class very different from those who worship properness, set up intellectualism as the substitute for power. We are far from wishing, in any way, to undervalue that great gift of God, mental power. Some measure of this is always implied in the commission to preach the gospel; and the more of sense, pathos, imagination, of any real talent, that a minister may possess, the more is he fitted to give his office effect. The talk in which some good people indulge as to the great benefit of having weak instruments in the ministry, is without a tittle of scriptural foundation, the Scriptures being fairly applied to the case.

It is true that, to the wise of this world, the cross in itself is "foolishness"; but Christ never sent fools to be its heralds. The institution of preaching, as the means for regenerating mankind, is in itself "foolishness"; but none of the preachers sent of God were simpletons. Though they were despised by the great, and were of no account with the learned, every one of them was mighty through God to strike home to the consciences of sinners, and to confound gainsayers; the evidence of divine power working with them being all the more conspicuous by reason of their natural or educational defects.

Men who have no gift to teach, warn, or exhort, ought to betake themselves to whatever honest calling their Maker has fitted them to fulfill, and not whine about the Lord delighting to use foolish instruments, while every day proves that He is in no way using *them*, unless it be as an example to all not to assume an office without having proved their fitness. The men whom God sends may be without the accomplishments of scholars, but never without sense and utterance. They may be destitute of the talent which would enable them to treat secular subjects with oratorical or literary success—to allure the fancy, or exhilarate the emotions, to satisfy by logic, or illuminate by exposition, but never, never without power to act upon the conscience; and this, in the absence of other endowments, is often at once the scepter of a preacher's command and the mysterious seal of his commission.

He who speaks to us in the name of our God may bring statement as lucid and nervous as that of Moses or Matthew, wisdom as racy as that of Solomon, pathos as overwhelming as that of Jeremiah or John, argument as cogent as that of Paul, or imagination as gorgeous as that of David or Isaiah; any powers, however lofty, may he bring—any eloquence, however poetic, refined, or bold; only let him make us feel, as we always do under the hand of the prophets and the apostles, that all his powers are put in operation but to bring us nearer to our Redeemer.

Where the notion that the talent employed in Christian preaching ought to lie within a limited and humble range, without any high flights, any deep soundings, any glowing language, any metaphorical illustrations, or any masculine argument, can have originated, one would be at a loss to learn, were the Bible alone—Old Testament and New—the source of our information. There we see the power of the Holy Spirit, not allying itself with one order of mind, or with one stamp of composition, tamed down to a standard of properness, consecrated by the aesthetics of some small and proper men, but using every faculty that God ever gave to the human soul—every faculty of thought, illustration, and speech—hallowing by its fire all genius, all life, and all nature, touching everything and illuminating everything; so that there is not one scene of domestic life, and not one object of God's outer world, to which the tongue of psalmist or prophet, or the Great Teacher Himself, has not given a voice and made it speak to us in sacred poetry. From the grass beneath the mower's scythe, or the lily that a child has plucked; from the bridegroom's beaming face, or nursing mother's bosom, up to the lightning, the sun, and the stars, everything is hallowed by a ray from the Bible, and is hung round by its sacred associations.

We cannot but believe that this is the intentional model,
and that men of all orders, with talent of every possible shade,
are meant to be employed in God's holy ministry; and that,
therefore, any narrower view, founded either upon the ideal
of some prominent example in one class of preaching, on the
taste of a given age, or on any notion whatever of classic style
and propriety, is but an invention to cramp and trammel that
which must everlastingly be free—the utterance of men who
come to speak to us of all things infinite.

Intellectualism and Power

On the other hand, that which nowadays is called intellectualism does not appear so much to lie in the possession
and exercise of superior powers, as in the art of casting
common things in elaborate molds, and robing every familiar
truth, which, in a plain garb, all would recognize as an old
friend, in such array that those who do not look closely may
take it for a distinguished stranger.

It is true that thoughts which outgrow the ordinary
stature will naturally drape themselves nobly; but all haze,
or extravagance, in the style of wise men, will be in spite
of themselves. They will ever use their best endeavors, first
to clear their ideas in their own minds, and then to render
them clear to others. Often they will expend much labor in
reducing what gushed from their pregnant thoughts, from
its original splendor to something more simple and perspic-
uous, something perhaps less calculated to dazzle, but more
calculated to enlighten.

Some intellects are, among ordinary ones, what a
hothouse is in a garden—a special shrine which receives the
beams of heaven, through a medium of crystal, into an atmosphere of high temperature, within which bloom fruits and
flowers that would not grow in the ordinary ground; fruits

and flowers from brighter lands, and wondrous in our eyes; which, however, though at first nursed there, may, in time, be naturalized, and become familiar beauties in the homesteads of thousands.

It is manifestly the will of Providence to create such intellects; and even had we not the Bible to throw light on His design, it would certainly seem violently improbable that He should create them only to fringe with flowers the world's broad and downward way. Some men always treat richness of style as if it were the result of effort; just as if a plank, which always owes its color to nature, were to say to mahogany, or maple, or rosewood, "What labor it must have been to produce all the shadings!" No labor whatever; it is all in the grain.

At the same time, the intellectualism of our day is something so entirely apart from the exercise of power of mind, that it seems to us more like an attempt to invent great intellects, than like an honest endeavor to put out to the best account such intellect as God has given. The use of factitious power is to make common things loom up in misty grandeur, and the use of real power is to make strong, new, rare, or vast conceptions clear to the ordinary eye, or to bring what appeared cold intellectual abstractions home to the common heart.

If viewed only as a specimen of natural power, how wonderful the effect of that one stroke by which the simplest man in Christendom, from the time of our Lord down to this day, has been enabled to see in the fair drapery of a lily a pledge of providential care for his clothing, and to hear, in the glee-chirp of a sparrow, a pledge of the same care in feeding him and his children! Whatever is used with a view to clear divine truth to men's conceptions, to enforce divine law on the conscience, or to commend divine love to their hearts, that will the Spirit work with and quicken; but whatever is used merely to excite surprise or admiration at the powers of the speaker, must be forsaken by that sacred Power which moves, never to glorify one man in the eye of another, but to reveal the things of God to His wandering creatures.

It is very probable that not a few deceive themselves by Burke's idea of sublimity, to the effect that a clear idea is but another name for a little idea; a notion which he supports by quoting the vision of Eliphaz, and ascribing the sense of the sublime which that description at once conveys, to the haze and mystery wherewith the subject is invested. But he loses sight of the cardinal fact that the mystery lies not in the medium, but in the object. In language clear as the light of heaven, that object is presented to the mind; and, gazing through that pure and illuminated medium, we see what can be seen of the object.

That is only enough to tell us that it is no ordinary thing, but some mysterious being, an index of a whole world of invisible spirits: and this it is which carries with it the idea of the awful and infinite, and, therefore, of the sublime. Had he said that complete comprehension in our mind argued a finite object, he would undoubtedly have been correct; but, in order that our impression of the infinity of an object may be deep, some token of infinity must be clear.

Let those, then, who would wield a power over us present to our minds objects so great, if they will, that we can only catch a glimpse of some lower or hinder part, but let that glimpse be such as to convey to us an intimation of the whole as clearly as any stray flash of morning light carries with it the whole idea of sun and sky. Let their great thoughts be robed in any language, however simple, or however gorgeous, provided only that it be clear, that the medium obscure not our view of the object to be seen, and so confuse our sense either of its nature or dimensions;

and provided also it be plain, that their ruling idea is not a literary but a religious one, not to "acquit themselves well," and please their audience, but to produce instant and lasting religious impressions.

Let them bring before our souls the heights, the depths, the lengths, the breadths of God's revealed glories; and, whether they be plain in style as the homeliest peasant who passes our door, without one poetic idea in his mind, or one poetic phrase in his vocabulary, except those that his Bible has given to him—and many such plain men will ever be employed in the most eminent and glorious works of God— or whether all their expressions have the glow of superhuman fervor, or the luster of superhuman imagination, rivaling, in its wealth of imagery, in its purple, its scarlet, its gold, its precious stones, its frankincense, and its myrrh, the prophets of old, they will produce upon us healthy effects, will feed our spirits with angels' food, or enamor our contemplations with God's providence, His work of grace, or His eternal mansions provided for those who love Him.

Talent without Power

We repeat it, that it is not from any peculiar style, whether it be extreme plainness, or high elaboration, or what else, that we expect the ministry to acquire a world-renewing power. Let the style be ruled by every man's natural endowments; but, whatever these be, let them all be employed in the one direction of carrying out an embassy from God to the souls of sinful men. The greater the variety of talent and of style, the more will the pulpit be like the Bible—the more effectually will its work be done; but let no form of talent be ever accepted instead of power. For we must have power— power which the godly will welcome as meet to minister grace to the hearers—power which the ungodly will fear as certain to make them uncomfortable in their sins, or else force them to harden their hearts, as if they were refusing the voice of God.

Take away from the minister spiritual power, and, though you give us the fairest deportment, the richest eloquence, the most subtle and fascinating speculation, you leave us without any sense that we are hearkening to a man of God. Did the multitudes of the Christian church only set a due estimate upon this, and rank propriety and intellectualism in their proper place, the idea that a man could pass creditably as a minister merely by carefully performing a ceremony, or by weaving webs of curious and cunning language, would be as far from men's minds as is now the idea that one can obtain credit as a soldier without courage, as a painter without skill of hand, or as a musician without an instinct of tune.

The lowest effect (for less is no effect at all, or a negative one) which a Christian minister can produce, is merely to please his audience; next to that ranks astonishing them. Both of these effects terminate in himself. When a certain amount of admiration has been expended upon him, the whole harvest of his labor is reaped—a poor and scanty harvest, sufficing only to pass over the present hour, but yielding no seed for future sowing, no store for time to come. The creature who covets and earns the reward of being counted "an acceptable preacher"—a miserable praise, fit only for an impotent and soulless discourser—but shakes no sinner's heart, brings back to no father's arms a prodigal son, cheers no mother's soul by the conversion of her children, nor ever makes a believer feel that his preaching has formed a new and happy era in his spiritual life, may spin fine paragraphs for the winding-sheet of souls that are dying under his hands; may perform over dead souls the solemnities of

"Christian burial"; but when the body dies too, and then when the trumpet sounds, and the graves are opened, what reward will crown his resurrection?

As no variety of talent is effectual for the ends of the ministry without spiritual power, so, when accompanied by that power, every form of talent is. The refined are ready to demand a certain chastened style, in which there shall be no extravagance either in composition or in delivery. On the other hand, the poor are slow to recognize power unless it be accompanied by strength of voice and physical vehemence. Some will admit of little value in what is only exhortational or declamatory; others, again, cannot imagine that close argument, though it may enlighten, shall ever awaken or convert. Thus, most persons are in danger of forming a narrow ideal circle, within which they would have the Spirit to cooperate with the agency of man.

Each Is Best in Its Place

We are often told with great earnestness what is the best style for preaching, but the fact is, that what would be the very best style for one man, would perhaps be the worst possible for another. In the most fervid declamation, the deepest principles may be stated and pressed home; in the calmest and most logical reasoning, powerful motives may be forced close upon the feelings; in discussing some general principle, precious portions of the text of Scripture may be elucidated; and in simple exposition, general principles may be effectively set forth. Let but the powers given to any man play with their full force, aided by all the stores of divine knowledge which continuous acquisitions from its fountain and its purest channels can obtain for him; the fire being present—the fire of the Spirit's power and influence—spiritual effects will result.

The discussion about style amounts very much to a discussion whether the rifle, the carbine, the pistol, or the cannon is the best weapon. Each is best in its place. The point is, that everyone will use the weapon best suited to him, that he charge it well, and see that it is in a condition to strike fire. The criticisms which we often hear amount to this: we admit that such-a-one is a good exhortational preacher, or a good doctrinal preacher, or a good practical preacher, or a good expository preacher; but because he has not the qualities of another—qualities, perhaps, the very opposite of his own—we think lightly of him. That is, we admit that the carbine is a good carbine; but because it is not a rifle, we condemn it; and because the rifle is not a cannon, we condemn it.

Nothing can more directly tend to waste of power, than the attempt to divert the mind from its natural course of action into one for which it is unfitted. Instead of resorting to this with the idea of forming all after some preconceived model, it would be better to teach all to recognize in the variety of individual character another proof of the manifold wisdom of God.

Sometimes it is remarkable how small an amount of intellectual or literary power is combined with considerable, or even commanding, spiritual power. A man who by natural talent would impress an audience less than most men, yet by the superior unction of the Spirit may produce religious impressions, and raise up religious fruit, such as wiser and greater men might envy. Possessing this, his other defects are of comparatively little importance.

A general may have many defects in his character, temper, and habits, without losing command over his men: but if his defects be unsoldierly—if, above all, he lacks courage—then inevitably does his control over them decline. So a statesman may have a thousand defects not directly affecting statesmanship, and yet retain his ascendency over the mind of the nation; but let him show a lack of political sagacity, and at once his ascendency is gone.

So, if a minister of the gospel is justly described as "dry"; that is, if he gives godly and candid hearers the impression that he habitually delivers divine truths without any unction which either moves his own soul, or those of others, the fault is fatal. It is what cowardice is in a soldier, folly in a statesman, or lameness in a runner. The hold of such a one upon the conscience must hopelessly pass away. Rather let us have the man of humblest talent, or of plainest education, who can speak to us a word at which the soul within us thrills, than one who possesses no such power, though he can wrestle with every prejudice, or excite and fascinate every faculty.

The power of which we speak is the cooperation of the Holy Spirit with the preacher, that which is essential to its presence must lie, first, in the state of the preacher's heart; secondly, in the staple of his discourse. There must be a soul itself in communion with the Holy One, and there must be rays of truth—God's own truth—radiated from that soul to others, along which the Spirit's secret influence may be communicated from heart to heart. The preacher must first imbibe the divine fire, and then hold it in his heart, as a Leyden jar will hold the invisible electricity; and, this done, he must have a conductor to communicate it to those who are before him. Unless the truth of God be uttered and aimed in the right direction—aimed at the auditory, at their conscience, whether through the avenue of the imagination, the understanding, or the emotions—even had he himself the power of the Spirit, he could not convey it to others. There is but one conductor, and that is the Word of Life.

Suppose that a person, wishing to send a message from London to Edinburgh by lightning, knows how to construct an electric battery. When he comes to consider how he will transmit the impulse through hundreds of miles, he looks at an iron wire, and says, "This is dull, senseless, cold, has no sympathy with light. It is unnatural—in fact, irrational—to imagine that this dark thing can convey a lightning message in a moment." From this he turns and looks at a prism. It glows with the many-colored sunbeam. He might say, "This is sympathetic with light," and in its flashing imagine that he saw proof that his message would speed through it. However, when he puts it to the experiment, it proves that the shining prism will convey no touch of his silent fire, but that the dull iron will transmit it to the farthest end of the land. And so with God's holy truth. It alone is adapted to carry into the soul of man the secret fire which writes before the inner eye of the soul a message from the unseen One in the skies. Other proposed conductors may flash more in the showy light, but they will not convey the invisible fire.

Come with What Voice Thou Wilt Come

Again we repeat, that this fire may be combined with any form of talent, and with any style of composition. Who has not seen a tranquil man, whose tones seldom rose to passion, and never went beyond the severest taste; whose thought, demeanor, phrases, all breathed a gentle and quiet spirit; and yet, with the placid flow of instruction or exposition, a heavenly influence silently stole along, stole into the veins of the heart, diffusing a sacred glow, a desire to be holier, a sense of nearness to God, a refreshing of all the good principles within you, a check and a restraint on all the evil?

Again, you have seen a man who begins by some calm argument, passes to another point, closely reasoned, which again leads him to another well-pointed stroke at some error or prejudice; no by-play of imagination, no home-thrust to your heart, but one steady grapple with your intellect—a discourse which would be pronounced "dry," were it not for a mysterious power which accompanies it, not in the sentences, not in the syllogisms, not in the action, not in the tones, but a spirit infused through it all, that makes reasoning turn into a spiritual power, and seems to put God's law into your mind, and, at the same time, to write it upon your heart.

Again, you see a man who at once begins with pictures, and from history, from nature, from the Bible, from science, he strikes up before you a succession of bewitching or affecting scenes, playing with your fancy all the while as a poet might play with it. Yet every picture carries some sacred impulse to your soul, and leaves a moral lesson and moral strength behind. Another man moves simply on in a straightforward statement of some great doctrine, opening out its various branches, defining, setting guards upon his definition, shading from possible misconception, setting up fine distinctions, and seeming occupied principally with putting a truth into a compact and portable shape in your mind. Somehow this one truth, which he thus explains and defines, rouses within your breast the voices of all other truths, and evokes an appeal from every sacred thing you ever knew in favor of holy living.

Another assumes that you know all that need be known. Seizing upon the truths that are within you, upon your conscience with its light, upon your fear, or hope, or love, on your instinct of self-preservation, or on some other of the deathless principles of your nature, he pours upon you a succession of fervid declamation, exhorting you to that which is right; giving nothing to enlarge your knowledge, nothing to feed or even to exercise your reasoning powers, nothing to enrich the stores of your fancy, or to perfect your conceptions of truth. Yet his declamation brings a holy power which commands you more than the might of strong-minded men; and good resolutions and hopes that have often been vanquished in days gone by, rise up again at the voice of this simple man, and you follow him to the feet of the Savior.

Come, then, with what voice you will come, you power-clad messenger of my Redeemer! Come with thunder on thy tongue, or with a sweet "harp of ten strings"; come to us simple as a little child, or wise as a scribe instructed of God; but, O! let us only feel that fire in thy message which lies not in sentences, nor in tones, but in a heart itself inflamed from above, and pouring fire into our hearts!

Destitute of Divine Power

Just as we find all these types of men imbued with divine power, so do we find every one of them destitute of it. You have the gentle man, far away from anything extravagant, never bringing upon himself one word of blame, or giving to his auditory one feeling of trouble; but, O! how drearily years and years pass over him!—precious years, yet no souls are converted, no flocks grow larger; the field where he labors is never white unto the harvest, and it is always sowing time with him! Very probably he is content with this, and will tell you that in his sphere, though there is nothing extraordinary going forward, things are encouraging. Placidly does he pass on, although he knows well, and all who mark his course know well, that for long, long years it would be hard to say what spiritual life has flourished under his hand.

So, again, you may find the reasoner—clear, cogent, and forcible—enlisting you on his side, perhaps exciting you against everything which opposes his system; but no sinners are turned into saints by his reasoning; yet he reposes well pleased upon the miserable result of having argued his point ably—an advocate who has shown the jury that he is a master of law, but has lost his client's life.

And you may find the expositor, who will open up paragraph after paragraph with rare subtlety of analysis, while his auditory learn something of the Word of God, and so far become more prepared to be good Christians, if once converted. But with his exposition no converting power ever comes. Perhaps he does not think that it is his calling to convert sinners. You may also find the man of imagination, who plays brilliantly upon the various instruments of nature and science. His auditory are dazzled, perhaps enraptured; but who among them goes home to his closet to seek his Savior, or rises up in after life to bless the preacher? He was sent to fight, but he played off fireworks before the enemy, and, instead of flying or falling, they only said, "How grand!"

The declaimer you may hear, too, whose exhortations run apparently to the one point of producing a practical result; you have vociferation, and the swell and throe of great vehemence; but it is like the hollow report of a cannon without shot.

This absence of power is sometimes so clear that the soul that has come to the house of God seeking bread painfully feels that it is getting but a stone. Never is that feeling so painful as when all that ought to attend upon spiritual power is there—the truth, well understood and well stated—all the contours and outward form that would lead us to expect life; but, when we draw near, there is no breath in it. Sometimes one may see that this soulless thing is not a wax figure which never breathed, but a corpse from which the life has gone.

The truths, now uttered with such impotence, once thrilled through men as they fell from those lips; the appeals which now grate, like a chime of cracked bells, once carried multitudes before them. In days gone by many rose up to bless this man as a messenger of God. Today his words are as a tale twice told. Perhaps, conscious of the loss of the real power, he endeavors to compensate for it by a greater force of physical oratory, spurring himself to impetuosity, or swelling to lofty and solemn impressiveness; but it is only as when a ship in a calm makes her sails bulge by rolling. They flap and rustle, but there is no strength in them, as when filled by the silent wind they bore the vessel onward.

Every one of the effects flowing from the operation of spiritual power in the ministry is indescribably precious; and it must be grievous to God, as it is manifestly injurious to man, to underrate any kind of fruit. One professes to be so bent on attaining progress in the spiritual life, that preaching, which is effectual only to the conversion of sinners, is to him elementary and poor. Another is so exclusively occupied with the dark condition of the unsaved, that preaching which tends only to ripen the holiness of those already converted, is to him beside the mark. One specially looks for preaching which will tell upon the young, and another for what will content men of years and experience. But every one ought to learn that each variety of usefulness is far too estimable to be lightly dealt with. He who is in any way used as an instrument to benefit the souls of any of my fellow-pilgrims here, ought to be cherished by my heart as a precious friend of my own.

Where real spiritual power exists, it will not be wholly confined to one class of effects. He who leads on believers to brighter holiness will surely lead sinners to see somewhat of the sinfulness of their sins. And he who is the means of turning a sinner from the error of his ways, is the means, in that very act, of aiding the progress of all those around him.

Each one detached from the world and ranked on the side of godliness becomes a help to the general cause of Christianity in the land.

The Fields Need But a Reaper

In our own age and nation, we feel no hesitation in saying that the particular form of spiritual power for which we have most crying need is that whereby men who know the truth are brought to the point of deciding for God, and setting out in earnest on the way to heaven. We are in danger of laboring as if the ground still needed to be sown, while the fields are white unto the harvest, and need but a reaper.

We are in danger of preaching as if the people were either all serving God, or were all so far away from the possibility of being converted soon, that they must be approached as from a distance, and principles laid down and left to work which may bring forth fruit after some long time. Whereas the fact is, that everywhere the ground is sown.

We meet with comparatively few men in whose minds there is not enough of truth to awaken their conscience and point them toward the cross, were that truth only brought home to their hearts with power. Men fitted as instruments to use what the people believe and know, in order to bring them to a decision for God, are those whom the interests of our generation most loudly call for. Taught by Christianity, but led captive by sin, men are going downward by thousands and tens of thousands—at once in the light and in the dark, knowing their Master's will, but doing it not—downward to the punishment of many stripes. He, then, who can bring those multitudes to stop and think, to feel what they believe, to act on what they feel, to cry, "Lord, save me, I perish," he is most distinguished and most blessed of all the servants whom the Master honors.

To heal the leper, to open the eyes of the blind, to make the lame walk, and the paralytic strong, were great and blessed works. All these sufferers were living men, and great as was the work of healing them, to raise the dead was greater far. Blessed are ye among men, whom our Lord and Master honors to help or heal, or restore any of those souls which are living, but not in perfect soundness; but trebly blessed art thou, my brother, whose joyful lot it is to stretch thy soul over a soul that is dead, as Elisha stretched himself over the dead son of the Shunamite, and to raise it up breathing and calling upon God! O for a thousand men imbued with converting power! Better they than ten thousand times the number, however gifted, however learned, however pleasing, who are destitute of that crowning grace of the messenger of God!

Our Lord said, "He that believeth on Me, the works that I do shall he do also; yea, and greater works than these shall he do, because I go to My Father." By "greater works" He could not mean more wonderful miracles; for the wonders wrought by His own hands had reached the limits of possibility. Greater miracles than raising the dead and making the winds and the seas obey Him, were not to be performed. Besides, the "greater works" to be done are shown to have some special character from this, that they are to exist in connection with a new order of things, "Because I go to My Father."

We are at no loss as to that which was specially dependent on His ascension. It was the baptism of the Holy Spirit. We may therefore reasonably conclude that the "greater work" than all the other works which could be done was that work which He Himself from heaven announced to His servant Paul, as the purpose of his mission, "To open their eyes, and to turn them from darkness to light, and from the power of Satan unto God, that they may receive forgiveness of sins, and inheritance among them which are sanctified by faith that is in Me." This was the end of His own life and death, this was the crown of His own glory: "Thou shalt call His name Jesus; *for He shall save His people from their sins.*"

Only in men actually saved from their sins did His soul, afflicted and smitten, foresee the fruit of its travail, wherewith it should be satisfied. Only in men actually saved from their sins while in the flesh, while surrounded by temptation, could He foresee the possibility of glorifying His Father upon earth, by His own branches bearing much fruit, by His own life, "the life of Christ, being manifest in mortal bodies." Only by this could He see that which He so dearly purchased, a holy church formed out of Adam's fallen sons. Only by this could His own special joy, the joy set before Him, the joy of "bringing many sons to glory," ever be secured. To this one result His whole work pointed; upon this all the interests of His kingdom turned.

No glory of the Eternal One is higher than this, "MIGHTY TO SAVE"; no name of Godhead more adorable than that of "SAVIOR"; no place among the servants of God can be so glorious as that of an instrument of salvation. "He that winneth souls is wise." "They that turn many to righteousness shall shine as the stars forever and ever." Under the new dispensation, the Lord's messengers, abundantly replenished with the Spirit, having the cross for their theme and the baptism of fire for their impulse, were to go forth as men with whom God would work, and would accompany His word with signs following it.

It was great to cast out devils from the body; it is greater to cast them out of souls and out of society. It was great to heal the sick or to feed the poor; it is greater to heal the sources of disease and want, by turning sinful hearts to purity. He around whom are continually springing up new converts from sin to holiness—he, the sound of whose voice many bless as having been to them the trump of God, who at the great day, will have for his crown of rejoicing tens, or hundreds, or thousands, to whom many others were "teachers," but only he a "father"—he rises to such joy and dignity that he may look back upon the best and most honored of God's ancient servants, and feel that, in comparison with them, he has only to be thankful for his own more blessed lot. He need not envy Moses his rod, or David his harp, or Elijah his mantle, or Solomon his wisdom; for his own crown and his own prize are the highest to which man may aspire. How close the servant is brought to the Master! The Master is Savior, the servant the instrument of saving!

Judged by the Fruit of His Labor

When we speak of ministerial power, we are not implying that any amount of power in the minister will *necessarily* subdue his hearers. What may be fully relied upon as the result of power dwelling in the minister is that he will make every hearer feel that a spiritual power is grappling with him, and bringing him either to yield to the voice that warns him, or to set up a conscious resistance. "Almost thou persuadest me," is the language of one who can scarcely prevent himself from yielding to the force that is impelling him toward Christ. Felix trembled, and said, "Go thy way for this time; when I have a convenient season, I will call for thee." Here is a man consciously under the impulse of a power which is urging him to a result that he dreads. To escape its influence, he adopts the ordinary plan of "putting off for a while." But the very awakening of this conscious resistance, the setting up of this struggle in the breasts of men, is in itself a proof of power. He who can do this, although he will have his Agrippas and his Felixes over whom to mourn, will undoubtedly have numbers of others over whom to rejoice.

A farmer who all his lifetime has been sowing, but never brought one shock of corn safe home; a gardener who has ever been pruning and training, but never brought one basket of fruit away; a merchant who has been trading all his life, but never concluded one year with clear profit; a lawyer who has had intrusted to him, for years and years, the most important causes, and has never carried one; the doctor who has been consulted by thousands in disease, and has never brought one patient back to health; the philosopher who has been propounding principles all his life, and attempting experiments every day, but has never once succeeded in a demonstration—all these would be abashed and humiliated men. They would walk through the world with their heads low, they would acknowledge themselves to be abortions, they would not dare to look up among those of their own professions; and as for others regarding them with respect, pity would be all they could give.

Alas! are there not cases to be found wherein men whose calling it is to heal souls, pass years and years, and seldom, if ever, can any fruit of their labors be seen? Yet they hold up their heads and have good reasons to give why they are not useful. Those reasons generally lie, not in themselves, but somewhere else—in the age, the neighborhood, the agitation or the apathy, the ignorance or the over-education, the want of gospel light or the commonness of gospel light, or some other reason why the majority of those who hear them continue unconverted, and why they should look on in repose, without smiting upon their breasts, and crying day and night to God to breathe a power upon them whereby they might awaken those that sleep. Probably they have wise things to say about the undesirableness of being too anxious about fruit, and about the advantage of the work going on steadily and slowly, rather than seeking for an excitement, and a rush of converts. But while they are thus dozing, sinners are going to hell.

It is pitiable to see a minister who has all his life, when judged by the fruit of his labor, been destitute of the power of the Spirit; but there is something even more touching to see, as, alas!—sometimes we *do* see—one who in his early days had truly a gift of God in him, becoming weak, like other men, without unction, and without fruit. The gift, not stirred up, has passed away; the power, not renewed and renewed again by fresh supplies, has forsaken him. Perhaps, desirous of more efficiency, he has heaped up knowledge—not too much knowledge, for none can have too much; but he has not maintained a due proportion between his acquisitions of knowledge and his acquisition of spiritual power. He is like one who would pour coals upon a feeble fire with the idea of making a great one, until the few live coals were smothered under a black mass.

Perhaps another has gone just to the opposite extreme; and, fearing to damp his lively fire, has allowed it to flame on, without constantly feeding it with truth, and knowledge, and experience, and thought; and his fire has burned out. Perhaps another, beginning to distrust his simple weapon, which had no adornments, and could only strike right home, has got for himself a jeweled sword with a golden blade, but finds that the edge is turned by the least resistance. Perhaps another, who used to thunder as a second Baptist, and make the truths of the eternal law, of the resurrection, of judgment, and of the world to come, ring in the ears of slumbering souls with a supernatural and awakening power, begins to desire something more alluring, less distressing to the sensitive, more acceptable to the sedate, more "attractive," as the phrase is. Now you may find him an absurd combination of strength and feebleness—a gunner working heavy guns, but with silver barrels, and scented powder, and balls of frozen honey.

In the progress of a man's life it will often happen that great variations appear in his usefulness. If he walk with God, maintain his integrity, and make steady progress in knowledge and in faith, although the form of his usefulness may change, it will never change into uselessness. When the flush and glow of youthful ardor disappear, they will be replaced, not by vapidness or tameness, but by more of the unction that elevates and hallows.

There is a law of mechanics, the moral counterpart of which we see in such men, that what is lost in velocity is gained in power. And yet such men, though they may be blessed with great usefulness, if they see not conversions such as rejoiced their earlier days, will ever look back with yearning and humiliation. Never will they fail to honor, above all their brethren, those whom God honors by making them the instruments of many conversions, or to covet, with a coveting more eager than they could feel for any other distinction, or joy, or gift, the restoration to them of the power to persuade sinners to be reconciled to God.

A more pitiable thing cannot be than to see a man who, himself destitute of ministerial power, not only is unconscious how miserable a creature he is, but is even ready to make light of the usefulness of others; and, in his ordinary conversation, to set down those whom the Lord honors as the instruments of converting sinners, below what he calls "intellectual" men, fine soliloquizers, or curious speculators, who deal out dainties from the pulpit, but do no work that will live when they are dead.

This style of depreciating the useful and the earnest, painful in anyone, becomes appalling when it falls from the lips of a man who at one stage of his own life was remarkably useful, but who has lost his fire. One who, instead of mourning, and seeking to recover it, can even make light of those who have retained theirs. "It is not hard to convert servant-maids," and such depreciating expressions, may lightly drop from an unthinking lip, but they will affect hearers, and will be remembered in the great day. How differently will the two men appear—the one whose humble labor has been the means of converting servant-maids, and the one whose envy and whose wit were vented in making light of the work!

O, let those of us whose history too plainly tells that no extraordinary power of God has rested upon us; who can look back to years of labor which, if not absolutely barren, yet, in comparison with what others have reaped, must be called years of barrenness—let us not fail to bless and to honor, in our own hearts, those who have been, in the meantime, doing us good by the news that has reached us, every now and then, of the fruit of their labor. Above all, let us look back on our years of barrenness with most tender and contrite humiliation, crying earnestly to God to take away our reproach from among men, and to give us many, many children!

A minister can never be responsible for success, but he is responsible for power. He is responsible not only for presenting the truth to the people—in which many seem to think that their responsibility terminates—but responsible also that the truth he presents be not dry, but accompanied with some energy of the Spirit. If the Spirit be in the man, shining upon his soul with the light of God, more or less of holy fire will go with the word.

A frame having muscular strength, without nervous energy—a countenance with linear grace, without expression —a needle for the compass, without magnetism, are not more defective than is the statement of religious truth without the accompanying power of the Holy Spirit. This power was presupposed in the man's first entrance on the ministry. He stands there by virtue of his solemn declaration before God and men that he felt it in his heart; and he is bound to stir up the gift of God within him, to keep his lamp trimmed, and his light burning, and evermore to be replenishing with holy oil.

This power has but one source—the Spirit of God in the soul of man. It is the one thing that cannot be feigned. A hypocrite may possess the truth, and clearly explain, and powerfully urge, and passionately apply it. He may feign tenderness, feign ardor, feign all the passions, but he cannot feign the power that searches the conscience, that makes men feel, "God is in you of a truth," that leads them in the silence of their own closets to wet their couch with their tears, and spend long nights in repenting before God. You may as well attempt to feign life in a dead eye, or music in a cracked voice, as to feign the power of the Holy Spirit in a soul that does not habitually wait at the throne of grace, until endued with power from on high.

Giants Refreshed with New Wine

Those of us who are manifestly not endued with great power, who cannot flatter ourselves that anyone looks upon us as blessed messengers of God, or in any light higher than that of well-meaning and useful men, by whose ministry, perhaps, now and then, at rare intervals, such a thing may be heard of as a sinner being converted, and who yet feel disinclined to take any blame to our own heart on account of our barrenness, can best judge how much time has been spent in our closets, in deploring the state of the souls that are perishing under our sight, in strong crying and tears to God for their deliverance, in importuning and imploring that we might be robed with power, and made mighty to blow an awakening blast, and rescue multitudes from the grasp of the devil.

We can, each for himself, best tell whether or not the results of our labors do very fairly correspond with the depth, intensity, and continuity of our secret search after the coworking fire of the Spirit. If on a review it should appear clear to us that far, far more might have been done in our private walk with God toward having our own souls imbued with the Spirit of Christ and of Christ's apostles, then let each of us conclude for himself, whether much more might or might not have been done to "save those that hear him."

And should the conclusion on our mind be clear that more might have been done, much more—that it ought to have been done—that we are very guilty by reason of supineness, of unbelief, of feeble and ineffectual prayer, of duplicity in our aim, or of any other defect in the keeping our own souls as God's ambassadors, let our penitence be deep, our cry for forgiveness pressing and earnest; but not for one moment let it take that form which strangely unnerves and debilitates a man, namely, the state of mind in which one takes pleasure in talking of his own feebleness and unworthiness, or, at least, finds sufficient relief in talking of it. Rather let us feel sure that the God of grace and mercy will hearken to our voice, will answer our prayer, will forgive our past unfaithfulness, will draw near to us with new and gracious power, will enable us to go forth as giants refreshed with new wine, to bear away from the arms of the adversary, in triumph and with shouting, many a lamb that is ready to be torn to pieces.

We cannot be content to look upon the minister of this actual hour as anything less, in the intention of our God and Savior, than an instrument "of the mighty power of God"— the power which is unto salvation. We do not expect the gift of tongues or of miracles, because these were not essential to the work of the ministry; but the active cooperation, the abiding unction of the Holy Spirit is.

If we were forced to believe either that all the primitive manifestations of the Spirit were now attainable, or that all had now passed away, we could a thousand times rather look for the tongues and the miracles, with the gift of prophesying, than dismiss the hope of this last with that of the other gifts. Better the excess of faith, a thousand times better and more rational, than unbelief in any promise that stands clearly for all generations. Better to suppose that the Lord designed every sign and token of His presence to continue with His church to the last; than suppose that they were all to be called back, and that the Christians of the latter day were to suffer a total privation of the Holy Spirit's ministerial gifts.

We will covet, earnestly covet, the Lord's good gift of prophesying; and we will covet, also, the "manifestation of the Spirit to profit withal," not only in the pastors of the church, but in the members; giving to one the word of wisdom, to another the word of knowledge, to another the spirit of grace and of supplications, that men with fire in their hearts may go everywhere, and publicly or privately preach the word, the Lord working with them, and confirming the word by signs following.

Let us look up and hope to see, not one, or two, or three, not merely an occasional and extraordinary man, shining in the churches as with a light from on high; but let us soberly, and steadily, and in prayer, expect companies of preachers, each differing from his brethren, yet all of them manifesting in some form or another that an anointing from the Holy One abides upon them, teaches them in all things, and enables them to appear before men, not only saying in words, but by their commending fruits saying to the conscience, "Now, then, we are ambassadors for Christ, as though God did beseech you by us: we pray you, in Christ's stead, be ye reconciled to God." One such man is better than a thousand, and two of them will put ten thousand to flight.

We Are Promised the Same Mighty Power

Intimately connected with the question of ministerial power is another vital question—whether or not the church is to retain the converting influence of the Holy Spirit on anything like the original scale. Here, again, we do not confine ourselves to combating formally stated opinions, but deal with vague, undefined, unexpressed, or but half-expressed sentiments, not embodied in the creed of any church, but perceptible in the ordinary tone equally of religious conversation, literature, and preaching. Is it not a prevalent state of feeling, that to look for a very large number of conversions at once is extravagant; that for any minister to expect a great many to be converted while he is delivering the sermon then in hand, argues a mind scarcely balanced; that sudden conversions have much to be said against them; that we ought to be content if the work of God proceed slowly, and to be elated if the good men of any community bear some respectable proportion to the numbers who forget God?

It is manifest that the conversions effected by the primitive church were very numerous, compared with her agencies and facilities; varying greatly in different times and places, but, in the main, going onward with accumulative power.

The difference between the conversion of a Jew to the faith and holiness of the gospel, and the conversion of a nominal Christian to the same faith and holiness, is a difference, not of kind, but of degree; and the degree is not so great as might at first be supposed. The Jew believed the oracles of God, and the truths therein contained, as far as he knew them. So does the nominal Christian. Both hold the truth in unrighteousness—the unrighteousness of frank rebellion, or of Pharisaical self-righteousness. Both are brought to learn God's love in redeeming man, to repent, to believe on the crucified Messiah as their Savior, and to walk in fellowship with the Father and the Son.

The conversion of a heathen involved much more of intellectual enlightenment, and, on the whole, presented a greater difficulty, and a greater change; but we do not find that the apostles ever point out any difference in the operation of the Spirit in the conversion of a Jewish scribe, and of a heathen necromancer, of a Roman centurion, and of a widow in Jerusalem. The same mighty power convinced them all of sin, of righteousness, and of judgment, and brought them to a level by the wounds of a smitten spirit. Then like those with various maladies, who came to Christ, and were all healed—came barbarian and Scythian, bond and free, Jew and Greek, learned and unlearned.

If we take the hundred and twenty disciples of whom the church consisted on the day of Pentecost, and then take the number of Christians before the first century was ended, we see how "mightily grew the word of God, and prevailed." Then suppose, for one moment, the possibility that, by the same spiritual power, the church had multiplied her converts in equal ratio. Few ages would have elapsed before the whole earth would have been renewed in righteousness. But the saint-making power abated, and crowds of Christians became little better, though still better, than crowds of heathen. Was this loss of efficiency owing to the unfaithfulness of men, and, therefore, capable of being recovered by a return to the original means of importunate prayer and strong faith? or was it owing to a design of the Head of the church, and therefore irrecoverable?

On a question so vital to the interests of mankind, no mind ought to float on the prevailing current without adopting a deliberate conviction. Was the conversion of thousands in Jerusalem, of crowds in Ephesus, in Samaria, Antioch, Corinth, Rome, and elsewhere, a proof, once for all, of what God could do toward the saving of this lost world, which He designed never to repeat, and which His children would be presumptuous in expecting to see again?

Were those multitudes, so speedily gathered out of the world, to represent, in future ages, only small companies of true believers, to whom accessions were to be very gradual, and who were never to gain the overwhelming majority? If so, then the Christian dispensation was deliberately planned above to begin in sunrise, but, instead of shining more and more to the perfect day, speedily to pale into twilight; and then darken to a long, long night, in which stars would thinly spangle a wide space of gloom.

Would not many who recoil from this conclusion stare at a man having a congregation of a thousand people before him, any one of whom would feel perplexed if you asked him, "Could you confidently lay your hand on fifty persons in this congregation who are living like heirs of heaven?"—if he, simply telling them their state, would go on to say that they might all that very morning become children of God, and live for "the rest of their time" a new and blessed life?

Were it done with the official formality which at once indicated that it was just a thing proper to be believed, and even to be said now and then, very probably it would excite no remark; but if it were done with the downright air of a man who thoroughly meant what he said, and was then and there looking for corresponding results, would not many be startled? But why? If it be not true that God has withdrawn from Christianity the converting power of the Holy Ghost, why? Either affirm your principle, or abandon the habit of thought which you have formed on the assumption of that principle. If you see that there is death to the church, or death to souls, in the principle, why not see that there is death, too, in assuming it and acting upon it as clearly announced, without affirming it?

Some who would be gratified to see an expectation of one conversion, or of a few, would nevertheless be disturbed by the manifest expectation of a great number. Why should this be? If the minister of the gospel is not now to go before a multitude with a frank and earnest assurance that every one of them who will only repent and believe may "receive the gift of the Holy Ghost," it must be because our dispensation has been fearfully changed since its opening.

The first multitude who stood before a preacher of Christianity can never be regarded as representing itself alone. When the cry arose from it, "What must we do?" it was not the men then present only who inquired. It was you, and I, and every man who ever comes to a preacher of the gospel to hear what he has to say on the great subject of our salvation. The answer which Peter rendered to that multitude was not to them alone, but to us and our children, to all of every age and every nation who put the question which they put. That answer was, "Repent, and be baptized, every one of you in the name of Jesus Christ for the remission of sins, *and ye shall receive the gift of the Holy Ghost.*" He does not promise them that they should be admitted as members of the church merely, accounted Christians merely, or that after death they shall inherit eternal happiness; but, in plain, strong words, he tells them that they shall receive that blessing which constitutes the substance of the gospel: "Ye shall receive the gift of the Holy Ghost"; and this, not "*some* of you," but "*every one* of you," with no condition whatever but that they "repent, and be baptized."

Is it to be supposed that Peter would have altered this reply, had you, and I, and our children been there? or that, had the image of future generations risen to his eye as standing behind those he addressed and represented by them, he would have qualified his grand promise, and taken care to falter something guarded, instead of plainly saying, "Ye shall receive the gift of the Holy Ghost"? Let those who fear to regard this promise as equally applicable to us as to them, only read the words with which he follows it up: "For the promise is unto you, and to your children, and to all that are afar off, even as many as the Lord our God shall call." On the next occasion when he addresses a multitude, he holds this language: "Unto you first God, having raised up His Son Jesus, sent Him to bless you, *in turning away every one of you from his iniquities.*" Here the converting grace of Christ is without hesitation proclaimed to all who stand before him.

It is to be remarked that what he states here to be Christ's mode of blessing men lies in conversion itself, in the "turning away" of a man "from his iniquities." Whatever the gospel may do indirectly for the enlightenment and elevation of a man, so long as he continues the servant of sin, it has conferred upon him no eternal advantage. "His servants ye are to whom ye obey," is a word that must stand forever. He that is still doing the work of Satan is his servant and with him must take his reward. It is also notable that he speaks of Jesus having been sent to bless them after He had been raised, thus announcing a mission of Christ subsequent to His resurrection, yet having already taken place in those days. This must be that presence of Christ which He promised them when He was about to depart from them, saying, in the very act of leaving them, "I am with you always, even unto the end of the world."

"With them," no longer in that body which confined Him to the very spot in which the Twelve were, but "with them" by the power of His Spirit, which is represented in the Apocalypse as the "eyes of the Lamb." "And I beheld, and lo, in the midst of the throne and of the four beasts, and in the midst of the elders, stood a Lamb as it had been slain, having seven horns and seven eyes, which are the seven Spirits of God sent forth into all the earth" (Rev. 5:6). Here we have the Lamb enthroned, yet, "as slain," with the tokens of death and atonement upon Him; yet, again, "having seven horns," the signs of universal kingship, "and seven eyes, which are the seven Spirits of God sent forth into all the earth."

Majesty, mediation, and spiritual presence "throughout all the earth" are here gloriously set before us. The Lamb, though no longer bodily present with one group of disciples, is present with all, by His Spirit, which is moving in the hearts of those who serve Him, as if it were the glance of the Lord. He ascended that He might be with us all and with us always, just as a Prince, on the eve of the battle, would retire from any one division of his army, and go above them, that he might be present with all. He would be present with every battalion that he had under his sight. And as that Prince would dart his own spirit by his eye into the breast of every follower, so does our King dart His into the breast of all who wait before His throne.

The one blessing, then, which the exalted Mediator has to confer on this world is, in "turning men from their iniquities," in converting sinners from the error of their ways, in bringing those who are far from God close to Him, and making those who are now living in sin to be "heirs of God, and joint-heirs with Christ"; restoring, in fact, the image of God upon earth, manifesting the divine ideal of humanity in our "mortal bodies," rearing up communities who shall be properly called "the children of our Father who is in heaven"—communities, whose ruling nature shall not be that of fallen Adam, but who shall have that mind in them which was also in Christ, being made partakers of the divine nature, and, in proof thereof, loving those that hate them, blessing those that curse them, praying for those that despitefully use them and persecute them; and thus, by returning good feelings for bad feelings, good words for bad words, good deeds for bad deeds, showing themselves the children of their Father in heaven. The triumph and glory of Christ lies in so renewing the face of the earth, that this image of God shall be the prevalent characteristic of humanity, that peace and goodwill shall take hold of nations, righteousness and truth flourish in the homes of all.

The accomplishment, to a considerable extent, of this great purpose formed the singular glory of the early church. To a community in the city of Rome it could be said, "Ye were the servants of sin. . . . But now, being made free from sin, and become servants to God, ye have your fruit unto holiness, and the end everlasting life." To another company in the city of Corinth it could be said, after describing the various classes of sinners who could not see the kingdom of God, "Such were some of you; but ye are washed, but ye are sanctified, but ye are justified in the name of the Lord Jesus, and by the Spirit of our God."

To some in the city of Ephesus it could be said, "And you hath He quickened who were dead in trespasses and sins; wherein in times past ye walked according to the course of this world, according to the prince of the power of the air, the spirit that now worketh in the children of disobedience: among whom also we all had our conversation in times past in the lusts of our flesh, fulfilling the desires of the flesh and of the mind; and were by nature the children of wrath, even as others. But God, who is rich in mercy, for His great love wherewith He loved us, even when we were dead in sins, hath quickened us together with Christ (by grace are ye saved); and hath raised us up together, and made us sit together in heavenly places in Christ Jesus: that in the ages to come He might show the exceeding riches of His grace in His kindness toward us through Christ Jesus" (Eph. 2:1–7).

To some in the city of Colosse it could be said, "Giving thanks unto the Father, which hath made us meet to be partakers of the inheritance of the saints in light: who hath delivered us from the power of darkness, and hath translated us into the kingdom of His dear Son" (Col. 1:12–13).

To some in Thessalonica it could be said, "And ye became followers of us, and of the Lord, having received the word in much affliction, with joy of the Holy Ghost: so that ye were ensamples to all that believe in Macedonia and Achaia" (1 Thess. 1:6–7). And when our Lord looked down from Heaven upon the Seven Churches of Asia, even His eyes of flame, looking upon the Church of Sardis itself, saw there were "some names in Sardis which had not defiled their garments."

To suppose that this power to regenerate man, and thereby to ameliorate human society, has been withdrawn from the church by the will and appointment of her adorable Head, is to suppose, in fact, that *the one practical end of Christianity has been voluntarily abandoned*—that end which lies in glorifying God upon the earth, and in saving the souls

of men. If Christianity cannot renew men in the image of
God, she ceases to have any special distinction above other
religions, except the one of more wisdom and more virtue.
Her mission here was to overcome Satan in the realm in
which he had hitherto triumphed, to reestablish the empire
of God over the hearts and lives of a race that had wandered
from Him, and to prepare out of the children of that race
heirs fit for a pure and an immortal kingdom.

Servants of God

Not only would this practical end be abandoned, *but the
standing evidence to Christianity would be discontinued.* The
miracles and prophecies of the past time are an evidence to
Christianity as a system of truth; but if she be only a system
of truth, and not also a power unto salvation, she but adds to
the guilt of men here by increasing their light, and to their
misery hereafter by increasing their stripes.

No miracles, no prophecies, no accumulation of arguments under heaven can demonstrate to our neighbors at
this moment that Christianity is a power which can actually
make men superior to their own circumstances and their own
sins; which can take men of this nineteenth century, men
with sin in their blood, sin in their bones, sin in their habits,
sin in their down-sitting and their uprising, sin against God,
sin against their neighbor, sin against themselves, sins of
self-interest and sins against self-interest, sins for happiness,
and sins that wreck happiness—and out of these men, still
living in the very circumstances wherein their past time has
been spent, make "servants of God, free from sin, having
their fruit unto holiness, and the end everlasting life."

The evidence of this, the only real and effective evidence,
is living men who have been regenerated, and whose good
works plainly declare them to be of our Father who is in

heaven. We, too, can say that "God has sent His Son Jesus to bless" our neighbors, "in turning away every one of them from his iniquities." How unimpressive would be our saying it, were there none to whom we could point them, and add, "There are our epistles, known and read of all men!"

Peter, recurring again to the kingly state of the Savior, said, "Him hath God exalted with His right hand to be a Prince and a Savior, for to give repentance to Israel, and forgiveness of sins. And we are His witnesses of these things; and so is also the Holy Ghost, whom God hath given to them that obey Him" (Acts 5:31–32). Here is the double evidence, that of apostles and that of the Spirit in living converts. We of this day are also Christ's witnesses that He is "exalted a Prince and a Savior, to give repentance and forgiveness of sins"; but our witness must be corroborated by those who, having received the Holy Ghost, live in the Spirit and walk in the Spirit.

Peter, in speaking of the witness which the prophets bore to Christ, sums it up thus: "To Him give all the prophets witness, that through His name whosoever believeth in Him *shall receive remission of sins.*" When we bear this witness, we ought to expect the same attestation of it which Peter saw in his Gentile audience, and which he afterward used to prove that they also had received salvation as well as the Jews; namely, God "put no difference between us" (the first Jewish converts) "and them, purifying their hearts by faith." Wherever men can be pointed to, whose hearts have been purified by faith, whose lives are a manifest example of salvation from sin, there is the standing evidence that Christianity is "the power of God unto salvation"; and no other description of evidence, as we before said, can prove this. Is it supposable that Christ has withdrawn from His church or diminished that power which would show continually that He "saves His people from their sins"?

Converting Power: the Church's Great Attraction

The converting power is also the *church's great attraction*. It is true that some would attract men by ceremonies, or talent, or the charms of architecture or music—attract them that they may convert them; whereas the true order is: convert, that you may attract. The one is the order of the charlatan, who trusts to factitious allurements for attracting the public in the hope that he may cure some; the other, the order of the true physician, who trusts to the fact of his curing some as the means of attracting others.

Whenever the church sends into a family one new convert glowing with love and joy, she kindles a light which will, in all probability, give light to all that are in the house. Whenever she is the means of making one shopman turn from his sins, and exhibit to his comrades a picture of holy living, in all probability she will soon have others from that shop at her altars. Whenever she brings one factory-girl to sit, like Mary, at the feet of Jesus, very probably in a little while other Marys will be with her.

In every situation, new converts are the most powerful attraction that ever acts on those who are still in the world. There seems a peculiar spiritual power connected with the first love, and an impressiveness in the words of new converts, enforced by the manifest change in them, which nothing else can exert. That house of God which becomes noted in a neighborhood as a place in which many sinners have been "transformed by the renewing of their minds," will, by a certain instinct of our redeemed humanity, soon become a center of attraction, not only to those who, with scarcely any light, are groping after the truth, but even to men who are still hardily going on in sin. The greatest fame of Christianity is the fame of the cures she works, her greatest glory the glory of the saints she trains, her own unshared renown, the renown of sinners renewed in the image of God. Wherever works of this kind are noised abroad in any community, there the preacher will not be in want for hearers, there the sower will not be without a field.

Converting Power: Raising the Standard of Morals

The converting power is also *the principal lever which Christianity can use for raising the standard of morals in nations*. Instruction is the basis of all moral operation; but instruction in morals, like instruction in science, is of little force unless backed by experiment. Say all you can to men about the duty of returning good for evil, they will scarcely have a clear conception of it, until they see some man deliberately benefiting one from whom he has received deliberate injury.

One tradesman converted, and manfully taking ground among his companions against trade tricks once used by himself, casts greater shame upon their dishonesty than all the instructions they ever heard from pulpits; or, rather, gives an edge, a power, and an embodiment to them all. One youth whom religion strengthens to walk purely among dissipated companions sends lights and stings into their consciences which mere instruction could not give, because it shows them that purity is not, as temptation says, unattainable. And so with all the virtues: it is but by embodying them in the persons of men that they become thoroughly understood in the public mind.

It is but too well known that there are nations of the highest civilization, in which all that need be said about truthfulness has been said for ages, till the word "truth" is on the lips of every one; yet it is next to impossible to find one being who has anything like a just conception of what manly, consistent, continual truth-telling is.

Just in proportion as the number of converted men is great or small, will be the amount of conscience in the community generally. Viewed in this light, each conversion facilitates future conversions. Each new convert adds somewhat to the moral influence existing among men, and each additional thousand greatly improves the public conscience and weakens the ties which bind men to sin. Where no one is godly, moderately correct persons are almost ashamed of their lack of badness. Where a tenth of the adults are godly, even ordinary sinners are ashamed of their lack of goodness. Where a fifth, or a third of the adults are godly, the hindrances to the conversion of the rest are as nothing, compared with those that exist where the great masses are still living in their sins.

Converting Power: Raising Up Agents

The converting power is also *the only means whereby Christianity raises up agents for her own propagation.* That which is wanted in an agent, above all, is zeal—zeal for God, burning desire to save sinners. This zeal is never a matter of mere conviction, but always a matter of nature. It is "Christ in you." It is "the love of Christ constraining you." It is the divine nature, which delights to communicate, to bestow, to purify, to save, breathed into the soul of man, and impelling it in the same course wherein Christ Himself moved. Agents with this nature we can have only by successive outpourings of the Spirit of God, by constant accession of new converts.

When great sinners are themselves converted to God, having been forgiven much, they love much, and frequently become mighty instruments of winning others to Christ. For the high work of the ministry, either we must content ourselves to make ministers by factitious process, or we must look to see them springing up from amid multitudes of new converts, who in youth turn to the Lord and devote themselves to do His will.

When conversions are not few, but many—when "numbers turn to the Lord"—when the inhabitants of one town say to those of another, "Come, let us go speedily to seek the Lord, and to pray before the Lord of hosts"—when there are many repenting, and many rejoicing, saying, "We have redemption in His blood, even the forgiveness of sins"—then will assuredly appear some with plain marks that the spirit of the prophets is in them, and that they are called to spread, far and wide, the glorious salvation of which they themselves partake.

Nothing so reanimates the zeal of old Christians as witnessing the joy and simplicity, the gratitude and fervor, of those who have been lately born of God. While the old disciple is to the young one an example of moderation and strength, the young is to the old an example of fervor; the one shedding upon the other a steadying influence, while he receives in return a cheering and an impelling one.

It is also wonderful how much the occurrence of conversions heightens the efficiency of men already employed in the ministry, or in other departments of the work of God. The preacher preaches with new heart, the exhorter exhorts with revived feeling, he that prays has double faith and fervor; and the joy of conquest breathes new vigor into all the Lord's host.

While the importance, and in fact the necessity, of the converting power of the Spirit may be admitted in the abstract, all its practical value may be set aside by cherishing dislike to the idea of sudden conversions, or numerous conversions. It is deemed sober to expect conversions some time, but not so to expect them now. As the "now" perpetuates itself on, and on, and on through the lifetime of a generation, the time to look for their conversion never comes, and the next generation succeeds to the same chill law of unbelief; each one living in the doomed "now" when the converting power is not to be looked for without fanaticism.

The preference so carefully and even ostentatiously displayed by many good men for what are called gradual conversions over sudden ones, may have some foundation— but not in Scripture. All the conversions we find mentioned in the New Testament are sudden. That of Lydia is the only one that is ever cited as being gradual, and yet it took place under one sermon. The expression, "The Lord opened her heart," cannot imply, at the very most, more than that the action upon her heart was a gentle one. The door was opened, not burst in; but it did not take three months to open it—it was done in a day.

The sudden conversion is an operation manifestly divine. It brings with it a token of something supernatural; and when the afterlife attests its genuineness, there is in the very fact of its suddenness a perpetual memento of "the mighty power of God." The natural aversion of the heart to everything which forces upon it the consciousness of a spiritual and supernatural power moving in this present life, sufficiently accounts for the tendency we all feel to prefer some mode of operation which would appear less supernatural than the sudden, not to say miraculous, transformations from sin to godliness, which form the commonplace chronicles of the early church.

As to the question whether those who are suddenly converted are or are not as stable as those upon whom the work is more gradual, few are in a good position to judge. Every one who is suddenly converted is sure to have many eyes upon him, and if he draw back, the notice of all these is excited; whereas many who gradually take up a religious profession gradually drop it again, and scarcely any notice is taken.

But, be the question of stability settled as it may, it is certain that the scriptural examples of conversion are sudden, and equally certain that, if we are to look only for gradual conversions, we must deliberately make up our minds to see millions upon millions of our countrymen die impenitent, who, if sudden conversions are multiplied, may yet be brought to God before they end their days. The jailor was found at the extremity of sinfulness, just in the act of suicide; yet that very night salvation was preached to him, embraced by him, and filled his heart with holy joy.

Gaining by Degrees

Some would not so much object to sudden conversions, if many of them did not take place at a time. But there is something unaccountable in the feeling with which even godly men look upon any movement in which it would seem that a large number of sinners have been simultaneously turned to God. First, they can hardly believe that the work is real. They begin to prophesy that it will not be lasting. Then, if they find that it has lasted, they still incline to think that they had better not look for anything so extraordinary among their own neighbors, but go on steadily, as they say, gaining by degrees.

One simple objection to this theory of "going on steadily" (that is, slowly) is that it coolly consigns whole generations to hell, and leaves us with the dreadful feeling that the best progress of the work of God is a progress which leaves the great majority of those now alive hopelessly in their sins.

Another objection to this "going on steadily" is that it is not Pentecostal; it is not primitive; it is not after the example of "the mighty power of God." In the early church, conversions were by the hundred and the thousand. The word spread, not with the moderation dear to small and proper men, who are always afraid of being charged with extravagance, but with the sweep and power of a divine movement, the agents in which were borne onward as on the wings of the wind, willing to be a laughing-stock to men, willing to hear an outcry from the world which they were turning upside down.

When conversions are very numerous, in proportion to the human instruments, the agency of God is much more strikingly manifested than when they are few. Although the man who, by his own experience, knows what it is to pass from darkness to light, will see an evidence of the power of the Holy Ghost in any and every true conversion. Those who have no such experience, easily avoid concluding that a supernatural power is in action so long as they can trace an imagined proportion between the agency and the results.

If a few people are turned from their sins by many preachers, it seems no more than natural. If a few holy men are found in a multitude, it is only another proof, they think, of the fact that there will always be a certain number of good people among the wicked. But if a large number of thoughtless youths, or confirmed sinners, become devoted to God through the instrumentality of some one preacher, and if this extend to neighborhood after neighborhood, a feeling falls upon spectators that it is not to be accounted for by reasoning about proportion, but by the operation of a superior power.

Let but the results of preaching as to the number and suddenness of the conversions pass a certain point—let the number be thousands, and the time one day—and the idea of attributing this to the power of some men would not enter the mind. Who ever thought, on reading that three thousand Jews were converted on the day of Pentecost, and lived holy lives afterward, of exclaiming, "What a preacher Peter was!" The magnitude of the effect at once suggests a superhuman cause.

Had the result been small, the man would have been glorified; but when it took such proportions, he was thrown into the shade, and "the mighty power of God" alone occupies the mind. When a flash of light falls on our path in the street in the evening, we should at once think of a lamp, because the surface illuminated in itself indicates some such origin. But if we see a light fall upon a hill, and sweep over successive hills, until a whole countryside is brightened, we think of the sun.

Too many conversions now take place, too many really converted men are to be found, to permit anyone to believe that the converting power of the Spirit has been wholly withdrawn from the church. His presence in the midst of us is attested by many witnesses, but the practical question for us is: Is it contrary to the design of God that true believers now should multiply themselves as rapidly, in proportion, as they did after the day of Pentecost? If it be, then, no matter what means may be used, that result cannot be obtained; but, if it be *not*, then we are bound to hope that, the same means being used—the same prayer, faith, and zeal being put forth on the part of the church—the same blessing of the Holy Spirit will be vouchsafed.

On the whole question as to what permanent benefits remain to the church from the dispensation of the Spirit, we contend that everything substantial implied in the gift of the Holy Ghost remains unimpaired. Whatever is necessary to the holiness of the individual, to the spiritual life and ministering gifts of the church, or to the conversion of the world, is as much the heritage of the people of God in the latest days as in the first.

We do not see that the miraculous effects which followed the Pentecost are promised to all ages and all people, and therefore we do not look for them to reappear. But we feel satisfied that he who does expect the gift of healing, and the gift of tongues, or any other miraculous manifestation of the Holy Spirit (in addition to those substantial blessings of which these were the ushers and the heralds), has ten times more scriptural ground on which to base his expectation, than have they for their unbelief who do not expect supernatural sanctifying strength for the believer, supernatural aid in preaching, exhortation, and prayer, for pastors and gifted members, and supernatural converting power upon the minds of those who are yet of the world.

CHAPTER 6

Practical Lessons

At one time we meant to dwell at considerable length upon practical lessons connected with our subject; but this book is already larger than we wished it to be, and we will therefore touch only three topics. We may learn a lesson on THE SOURCE OF POWER; one on THE WAY TO OBTAIN POWER; and one on THE SCALE ON WHICH OUR EXPECTATIONS OF SUCCESS SHOULD BE FRAMED.

The Source of Power

In the application of any instrument, no error can be more fatal than one that affects the source of power. To recur to an illustration before used, any reasoning upon explosive weapons which assumed elasticity to be the source of power must lead completely astray. If this is to be noted in all things, it is especially to be noted in what affects the regeneration of the world. In merely natural processes, persons proposing to affect the sentiments of mankind must depend largely on their influence, their wealth, and their facilities. Christians frequently permit themselves to fall into a state of mind in which the want of all or any of these is taken to be fatal to their prospects of success, and the acquisition of them to be the first step toward making any impression. But wealth, influence, and facilities, however great, never yet secured results in the spiritual conversion of men while the most notable triumphs of Christianity have often been gained in the total absence of them all.

Others, or the same men at different times, would rather allow their hopes to rest on order, talent, or truth. But neither are these the source of power. Order is as necessary in Christianity as are bones, ligaments, and skin in a man; talent is as necessary as brain, and truth as blood. But you may have all these, and have a paralytic; ay, have them all, and have but a corpse. You must have both the breathing spirit and that indescribable something we call "power."

The order of the Christian church ought to be such, her outward framework so constructed, that she shall not be as a building, which, though it looks more cheerful when there is life within, yet will stand when there is none; but rather as a body, which falls the moment the spirit forsakes it, and tends to decomposition. No church ought to be otherwise constructed, than in entire dependence on the presence of the living Spirit in all her ministerial arrangements. Her frame ought to answer to no definition that would suit an inorganic body; but to answer exactly to the celebrated definition of an organic one, namely, "that wherein every part is mutually means and end." The pervading presence of the Spirit should be assumed, so that, if it be absent, the pains of death shall instantly take hold upon her, and the cry be extorted, "Lord, save, or I perish!"

We must again recall to mind that most wonderful silence of ten days—that long, long pause of the commissioned church in sight of the perishing world. Never should the solemnity of that silence pass from the thoughts of any of God's people. It stands in the very forefront of our history—the Lord's most memorable and affecting protest beforehand—that no authority under heaven, that no training, that no ordination could qualify men to propagate the gospel, without the baptism of the Holy Ghost.

Each successive day of those solemn and silent ten, the perishing world might have knocked at the door of the church, and asked, "What waitest thou for, O bride of the ascended Bridegroom? Why dost thou not say, 'Come'? Why leavest thou us to slumber on uncalled, unwarned, unblessed, whilst thou, with thy good tidings, art tarrying inactive there? What waitest thou for?" And every moment the answer would have been, "We are waiting to be 'endued with power from on high'; we are waiting to be 'baptized with the Holy Ghost and with fire.'"

This is the one and the only source of our power. Without this, our wealth, influence, facilities, are ships of war and ammunition without guns or men. Our order, talent, truth, are men and guns without fire. We want in this age, above all wants, fire, God's holy fire, burning in the hearts of men, stirring their brains, impelling their emotions, thrilling in their tongues, glowing in their countenances, vibrating in their actions, expanding their intellectual powers more than can ever be done by the heats of genius, of argument, or of party; and fusing all their knowledge, logic, and rhetoric into a burning stream. Every accessory, every instrument of usefulness, the church has now in such a degree and of such excellence as was never known in any other age; and we want but a supreme and glorious baptism of fire to exhibit to the

world such a spectacle as would raise ten thousand hallelu-
jahs to the glory of our King.

Let but this baptism descend, and thousands of us who,
up to this day, have been but commonplace or weak ministers, such as might easily pass from the memory of mankind,
would then become mighty. Men would wonder at us, as if we
had been made anew; and we should wonder, not at ourselves,
but at the grace of God which could thus transform us.

Suppose we saw an army sitting down before a granite
fort, and they told us that they intended to batter it down.
We might ask them, "How?" They point to a cannonball.
Well, but there is no power in that; it is heavy, but not more
than half a hundred, or perhaps a hundred, weight. If all the
men in the army hurled it against the fort, they would make
no impression. They say, "No; but look at the cannon." Well,
there is no power in that. A child may ride upon it, a bird
may perch in its mouth; it is a machine, and nothing more.
"But look at the powder." Well, there is no power in that.
A child may spill it, a sparrow may peck it. Yet this powerless powder, and powerless ball, are put into the powerless
cannon. One spark of fire enters it, and then, in the twin-
kling of an eye, that powder is a flash of lightning, and that
ball a thunderbolt, which smites as if it had been sent from
heaven. So is it with our church machinery at this day: we
have all the instruments necessary for pulling down strong-
holds, and O for the baptism of fire!

The Means of Power

As to the way in which this power may be
obtained, here we have only to recall the lesson of the
Ten Days—"They continued with one accord in prayer
and supplication." Prayer earnest, prayer united, and prayer

persevering—these are the conditions; and, these being fulfilled, we shall assuredly be "endued with power from on high." We should never expect that the power will fall upon us just because we happen once to awake and ask for it. Nor have any community of Christians a right to look for a great manifestation of the Spirit, if they are not all ready to join in supplication, and, "with one accord," to wait and pray as if it were the concern of each one. The murmurer, who always accounts for barrenness in the church by the faults of others, may be assured that his readiest way to spiritual power, if that be his real object, lies in uniting all, as one heart, to pray without ceasing.

Above all, we are not to expect it without persevering prayer. Prayer which takes the fact that past prayers have not yet been answered, as a reason for languor, has already ceased to be the prayer of faith. To the latter, the fact that prayers remain unanswered is only evidence that the moment of the answer is so much nearer. From first to last, the lessons and example of our Lord all tell us that prayer which cannot persevere, and urge its plea importunately, and renew, and renew itself again, and gather strength from every past petition, is not the prayer that will prevail.

When John in the Apocalypse saw the Lamb on the throne, *before that throne* were the seven lamps of fire burning, "which are the seven Spirits of God sent forth into all the earth." It is only by waiting before that throne of grace that we become imbued with the holy fire; but he who waits there long and believingly will imbibe that fire, and come forth from his communion with God, bearing tokens of where he has been.

For the individual believer, and, above all, for every laborer in the Lord's vineyard, the only way to gain spiritual power is by secret waiting at the throne of God for the baptism of the Holy Spirit. Every moment spent in real prayer is a moment spent in refreshing the fire of God within the soul. This fire cannot be simulated; nothing else will produce its effects. No more can the means of obtaining it be feigned. Nothing but the Lord's own appointed means, nothing but "waiting at the throne," nothing but keeping the heart under "the eyes of the Lamb," to be again, and again, and again penetrated by His Spirit, can put the soul into that condition in which it is a fit instrument to impart the light and power of God to other men.

When a lecturer on electricity wants to show an example of a human body surcharged with his fire, he places a person on a stool with glass legs. The glass serves to isolate him from the earth, because it will not conduct the fire—the electric fluid. Were it not for this, however much might be poured into his frame, it would be carried away by the earth; but, when thus isolated from it, he retains all that enters him. You see no fire, you hear no fire; but you are told that it is pouring into him.

Presently you are challenged to the proof—asked to come near, and hold your hand close to his person. When you do so, a spark of fire shoots out toward you. If thou, then, wouldst have thy soul surcharged with the fire of God, so that those who come nigh to thee shall feel some mysterious influence proceeding out from thee, thou must draw nigh to the source of that fire, to the throne of God and of the Lamb, and shut thyself out from the world—that cold world, which so swiftly steals our fire away. Enter into thy closet, and shut to thy door, and there, isolated, "before the throne," await the baptism. Then the fire shall fill thee, and when thou comest forth, holy power will attend thee, and thou shalt labor, not in thine own strength, but "with demonstration of the Spirit, and with power."

As this is the only way for an individual to obtain spiritual power, so is it the only way for churches. Prayer, prayer, all prayer—mighty, importunate, repeated, united prayer. The rich and the poor, the learned and the unlearned, the fathers and the children, the pastors and the people, the gifted and the simple, all uniting to cry to God above, that He would come and affect them as in the days of the right hand of the Most High, and imbue them with the Spirit of Christ, and warm them, and kindle them, and make them as a flame of fire, and lay His right hand mightily on the sinners that surround them, and turn them in truth to Him. Such united and repeated supplications will assuredly accomplish their end, and "the power of God" descending will make every such company as a band of giants refreshed with new wine.

The Scale of Success

If the source of our power, and the way to obtain it, be so plain, how can it be that the "tongue of fire" is so rare? *What are the hindrances?* Is it because, as many would seem to think, nothing is so difficult to obtain as the grace of the Holy Spirit? We often hear it said, all effort must be unsuccessful without the blessing of God, without the accompanying power of the Spirit. The tone used indicates that it is therefore proper not to look for any great results, as if the accompanying power of the Spirit was the only thing not to be counted upon. The recognition of our impotency without the Spirit, and of the absolute necessity of His presence and His power, is as needful as the recognition of the fact that, without sunshine and rain, all labor and all skill would fail to preserve the human race for one season. But the sunshine and the rain are precisely the things which cost nothing, and on which we may constantly depend.

So it is with the baptism and the power of the Holy Spirit. Freer than the air we breathe, freer than the rich sunbeams, freer than any of God's other gifts, because it is the one which has cost Him most, and which blesses His children most, that gift is ever at hand. When we have done what the Lord lays upon us to do, it is dishonoring to Him to cherish a secret feeling as if He, being good, not evil, was backward to pour out His Spirit, and to do good to His children.

This feeling of unbelief, wherever cherished, must, on the principles of the gospel, be fatal to all power. He alone who magnifies the freeness, the fullness, and the present efficacy of the Lord's grace, can by the Holy Ghost accomplish wonders. Trust, firm trust, straightforward, childlike trust, is the everlasting condition of all cooperation with God. He will not use, He will not bless, He will not inhabit the heart that, at the moment when it offers Him a request, says, "I doubt Thee."

In this age of faith in the natural, and disinclination to the supernatural, we want especially to meet the whole world with this *credo*, "I believe in the Holy Ghost." I expect to see saints as lovely as any that are written of in the Scriptures—because I believe in the Holy Ghost. I expect to see preachers as powerful to set forth Christ evidently crucified before the eyes of men, as powerful to pierce the conscience, to persuade, to convince, to convert, as any that ever shook the multitudes of Jerusalem, or Corinth, or Rome—because I believe in the Holy Ghost.

I expect to see churches, the members of which shall be severally endued with spiritual gifts, and every one moving in spiritual activity, animating and edifying one another, commending themselves to the conscience of the world by their good works, commending their Savior to it by a heart-engaging testimony—because I believe all in the Holy Ghost.

I expect to see villages where the respectable people are now opposed to religion, the proprietor ungodly, the nominal pastor worldly, all that take a lead set against living Christianity—to see such villages summoned, disturbed, divided, and then reunited, by the subduing of the whole population to Christ—because I believe in the Holy Ghost.

I expect to see cities swept from end to end, their manners elevated, their commerce purified, their politics Christianized, their criminal population reformed, their poor made to feel that they dwell among brethren—righteousness in the streets, peace in the homes, an altar at every fireside—because I believe in the Holy Ghost.

I expect the world to be overflowed with the knowledge of God; the day to come when no man shall need to say to his neighbor, "Know thou the Lord"; but when all shall know Him, "from the least unto the greatest"; east and west, north and south, uniting to praise the name of the one God, and the one Mediator—because I believe in the Holy Ghost.

Unbelief and neglect of prayer generally go together as preventatives of spiritual power. Let all of us who are painfully conscious that the results just indicated, will never be attained by the instrumentality of men, in the condition in which we are, simply ask ourselves: How long, how often, how importunately have we waited at the throne of the Savior for the outpouring of the Spirit? Let our closets answer. "The eyes of the Lamb," that are looking through us now, have noted. O! is it any wonder that ofttimes we have been powerless, and ofttimes have had but "a little strength"?

Want of true faith and neglect of prayer are sure to make place for faith in the instrument, instead of in the power. When we are not living near the throne, our minds become occupied with questions of order, of talent, or of truth; or, if we sink into yet a lower state, with questions of facility, or influence, or wealth. This church reform will be followed by great good; the clear development of such or such a doctrine would bring us revival; more luster or strength of talent in the ministry would ensure progress. We only wait the removal of such and such hindrances to open this door; for the supply of pecuniary means, and we shall see good done there; or for the accession to the church of some person of influence, and God's work will prosper yonder. Faith is sadly wasted when bestowed on such things. Give them their right value—never underrate them—place them where God has placed them; but the fact that you trust in them shows that your heart is wrong. Wait not for these—for the power is not in them—but for the baptism of fire.

Hindrances to the Tongue of Fire

The Tongue Itself. Among the hindrances which will prevent any one from having the "tongue of fire," none acts more directly than any misuse of the "tongue" itself. If the door of the lips be not guarded, if uncharitable or idle speech be indulged, if political or party discussion be permitted to excite heats, if foolish "talking or jesting" be a chosen method of display, it is not to be supposed that the same tongue will be the medium wherein the sacred fire of the Spirit will delight to dwell. Who has ever worn at the same time the reputation of a trifler and of a man powerful to search consciences?

Sensual Indulgence. Another fatal hindrance is any kind of sensual indulgence. Whatever gives the least ascendency to the body over the spirit must gradually subdue, and ultimately extinguish the fire in the heart. This applies to all sloth, to every luxurious habit, every artificial appetite, and all the pleasures of the table. It is not a little remarkable that while, at the day of Pentecost, the people, on seeing the excitement and animation of the Christians, said, "They are filled with new wine." Paul himself says to us, "Be not drunk with wine, wherein is excess; but be filled with the Spirit." In both these cases there is a suggestion, however indirect, yet unquestionably a suggestion of some analogy between the condition of being "drunk with wine" and that of being "filled with the Spirit."

Nor do we need to seek far for the grounds of that analogy. To men of the world wine is a resort when they want something above their natural strength of mind or body, and in it they seek three things—strength, cheering, and mental elevation. Under its influence they will do more work than they could otherwise. They will cast off their cares, and their mental powers will reach a state which they themselves call "inspiration." That worldly orators, even of the highest reputation, often seek in wine such animation of their powers as is necessary to great success, is only too well known. The physical tendency to seek elevation in such a source cannot be even slightly yielded to, without fatally affecting the "tongue of fire."

Every Christian who wishes to retain the life of God in his soul must hold all the enjoyments of the table under a strict law of regard to health and to temperance. For strength, for cheering, and for mental elevation, such as an extraordinary affliction or public effort may demand, he must look alone to power from on high—to the strength, and comfort, and inspiration of the Holy Ghost. The bare idea of seeking any of these in wine implies a heart already far fallen into the bondage of the flesh.

Even without going so far, one may easily pass the bounds of moderation, and drink, not for health, but for pleasure. If the man who drinks to intoxication is miserable and pitiable, he who has learned the bad secret of "how far he can go," and who even acts upon it, although he may never be drunk, is daily intemperate. In one aspect, his social influence is the most dangerous of all; for, while one who totally abstains, and one who drinks under a rigid rule of regard for health and moderation, may each contend that they are setting the wisest example that can be set, and while the drunkard may truly say that his very excess is a warning to all about him, he who habitually shows that he drinks as much as is safe, is a lure and an enticement to push indulgence as far as it can be done without wreck of character.

Aiming at Literary Effect. Another fatal hindrance is what may be called "aiming at literary effect." When preaching, praying, or any other religious exercise of the tongue is ruled by the idea of composition, it loses the character of a divine gift. Under that idea, utterance especially is by the aid of the Holy Spirit. With those who look at Christian preaching as an exercise of natural talent, we enter into no discussion. We speak only to those who are seeking the "tongue of fire," who believe that real Christian preaching is effected only by the help of God. To them, and to ourselves, we say, that nothing will more surely steal away the fire from our sentences than anxiety to deliver them just as they were precomposed, or to precompose them with studious regard to literary grace.

Study of style, of words, of the force, forms, and laws of language, we of course recommend. Efforts on the part of every one to gain the best style of which his nature admits—the tersest, strongest, clearest, briefest—we equally recommend. Seeking, like Bunyan, for "picked and packed words," is the instinct of a teacher. Even the study of the art of speaking, against which the vulgar prejudice is so strong, we would, with Wesley and Whitfield, encourage. Mouthing elocutionists may have brought it into disrepute, but that is no reason why hundreds of us should be maimed in health before mid-life by public speaking, when we might have done as much work, and done it better, without the least injury, had we availed ourselves of the science of those who have philosophically studied and taught upon the voice.[1]

Intellectual Pleasure and Care of Words. While, however, we contend that it is the duty of all who take any part in teaching, to labor to the uttermost for every qualification helpful to their work, two things are to be forever and guardedly shut out. The one is aiming at giving intellectual pleasure, instead of producing religious impression; the other, being careful about words in the pulpit, so as to interfere with dependence upon God for utterance.

In the study, attention to style ought to be with a view, not to beauty, but to power. In the pulpit, all thought of style is thought wasted, and even worse. The gift of prophesying in its very ideal excludes relying for utterance upon a manuscript or upon memory. It is the delivery of truth by the help of God. The feeling of every man standing up in the Lord's name ought to be, "I am not here to acquit myself well, nor to deliver a good discourse; but after having made my best efforts to study and digest the truth, I am here to say just what God may enable me to say, to be enlarged or to be straitened, according as He may be pleased to give me utterance or not."

With this feeling of the preacher all appearances ought to correspond. It ought to be manifest that, while he has done what in him lies to be thoroughly furnished, he is *trusting* for utterance to help from above, and not *ensuring* it by natural means—either a manuscript or memory. We put these two together, because we do not see that any distinction really exists between them. The plea that the manuscript is more honest than *memoriter* preaching, has some force, but certainly not much; for he that reads from his memory is, to the feeling and instinct of his hearers, as much reading as he who reads from his manuscript.

In neither case are the thoughts and feelings gushing straight from the mind, and clothing themselves as they come. The mind is taking up words from paper or from memory, and doing its best to animate them with feeling. Even intellectually, the operation is essentially different from speaking, and the difference is felt by all. For literary purposes, for intellectual gratification, both have a decided advantage over speaking; but for the purposes of pleading, entreating, winning, and creating a sense of fellowship, for impelling and arousing, for doing good—speaking is the natural, this is the Creator's, instrument.

We never say, nor think of saying, that God will not bless sermons read, either from the manuscript or from the memory; for we are sure that both these modes are resorted to by holy and earnest servants of His, who seek His blessing, and obtain it to the saving of many souls. All we say of reading, either from the manuscript or the memory, is, that it is not scriptural preaching. It is not ministering after the mode of Pentecostal Christianity; it is a departure from scriptural precedent, an adoption of a lower order of public ministration, and a solemn declaration that security of utterance gained by natural supports, is preferred over a liability to be humiliated by trusting to the help of the Lord. It has its clear advantages, and its clear losses. It secures a gain of elegance, at the cost of ease—of finish, at the cost of freedom—of precision, at that of power—and of literary pleasure, at that of religious impressiveness.

A literary ideal of preaching is vicious. Half-educated people pride themselves on admiring what they consider intellectual, or "splendid." To men of real mind, and real education, aiming at literary effect is as distasteful, on the one hand, as are traces of carelessness, looseness, or vulgarity, on the other. Men of great talent or refinement, when speaking great truths, under holy inspiration, must be eloquent, or pleasing.

Eloquence Comes from the Spirit of God

But an "intellectual treat" is far from being the ideal of preaching. We have heard efforts of this kind greatly praised, even by aged and venerable ministers, which, when we look back upon them, after years have elapsed, we feel ought not to have been called sermons at all. They were discourses which showed how a certain subject could be treated, but which were never meant to do any work. An acute and profound philosopher, looking upon the pulpit from the chair of the historical professor, treats this point in the following remarkable words:

> Compare, I pray you, gentlemen, the sacred eloquence of the sixth century with modern pulpit eloquence, even in its most palmy days in the seventeenth century. I said just now, that in the seventh and eighth centuries the character of literature had been that it ceased

to be a literature—that it had become in fact a power, that in writing and speaking men concerned themselves only with positive and immediate results, that they sought neither science nor intellectual pleasure, and that on this account the age had produced nothing but sermons or similar works. This fact, which shows itself in literature in general, is imprinted upon the sermons themselves. Those of modern times have a character evidently more literary than practical. The orator aspires much more after beauty of language, after the intellectual satisfaction of his auditory than to act upon the deeps of their souls, to produce real effects, notable reforms, efficacious conversions. Nothing of this sort—nothing of the literary character in the sermons of which I have just been speaking to you; not one thought of expressing themselves nicely, of combining images and ideas with art. The orator goes to the point; he wants to do a work; he turns, and turns again in the same circle; he has no fear of repetition, of familiarity, not even of vulgarity. He speaks briefly, but recommences every morning. THIS IS NOT SACRED ELOQUENCE; IT IS RELIGIOUS POWER."[2]

Whenever we are tempted to think that fruitfulness is only to be looked for in connection with superior attainments, the image of Peter preaching in Jerusalem, and of that vast multitude in tears before him, should rise into our view. With what reverence, not unmixed with sorrow, do we often look back on preachers of days now gone, perhaps on some whom our own ears have blessed when we heard them; but more on those of whose mighty voices we have caught faint echoes, sounding in the bosoms of hoary men who heard them in their youth, and have never ceased to hear them, though their tongues have long been silent!

When noting our own poor efforts; when seeing how tamely the precepts of Sinai or the songs of Bethlehem have fallen upon men from our lips; seeing that, after our closest thinking, we have seemed as those who beat the air; that, after seeking converts, we have only gained credit; that, when looking for multitudes to be seized with the thought, "What must I do to be saved?" we have only sent them away to discuss our faults or our merits, with perchance here and there a heart touched and contrite;—when years have thus passed away, and no stronghold of sin brought down, no province completely conquered from the Prince of Darkness, no great awakening to show that there was a power and a God in the midst of the church;—when we have seen all this, and much more alike thereto, has not our disposition often been to open a calculation as to our own abilities and the difficulties before us, concluding, on the whole, that such as we need not expect to do things which only the mighty could do?

How could lips like ours move mankind? True, apostles and prophets moved them. True, Whitfield and Wesley, and hundreds of their coadjutors, near to our days, and in our own country, moved them. But then they were the wonders of their age, the seraphim of earth. But what made them seraphim? They were once no mightier than others as to converting souls. Unbaptized with fire or but slightly touched, their tongues might have charmed, fascinated, set the world discussing their gifts and extolling their abilities; but they would never have shot fires into the souls of men, burned by which the stolid would roar, and the stoical melt, the sedate smite upon his breast, and the corrupt cleanse himself "from all filthiness of the flesh and of the spirit."

Perhaps without the baptism of fire they would never have gained even the airy fame of orators. Their very eloquence may have come chiefly from the Spirit of God. At all events, it was that fire which raised the orator into the apostle, and made their words sound as if Christ's first messengers were risen from the dead.

The spectacle of Peter preaching at Jerusalem answers ten thousand arguments of unbelief. Who is that Galilean peasant, and who are that group beside him? They are men of like passions with ourselves. In nature, in gifts, in early opportunities, they cannot be ranked above the average of mankind. Even though they have been favored with the personal teaching and society of Christ for three whole years, they had not, up to this period, shown any extraordinary superiority of character. They have not been even without faults; they have had their disputes among themselves, their unbelief, their faint-heartedness, their strifes about the things of the world, their "false brethren"; yet are they endued with a power of speech which passes all previously conceived reach of eloquence.

Is it rational, when looking up to the Spirit which wrought this in them, to doubt whether or not it is within His power to baptize His servants now living with such a baptism as would change the ordinary into the extraordinary, the feeble into the mighty? Whether is it easier for Him to say, "Speak with many tongues," or to say, "I will give thee a mouth and wisdom which all thine adversaries shall not be able to gainsay or to resist"? The former He has said, and common men at once received the power; the latter He has said, and the same common men received the power. The former power we do not seek; but all of us who have any heart for our Master's service, any real intention to bear a part in the battle for the rescue of mankind, do desire in our very hearts—yea, long with mournful longing for a tongue of fire—to tell of the love of the Savior, and of the woe of sin, in such tones that the dead ear shall tingle.

Is He not able to give the gift now as He gave it then? Is the distrust of His power in this respect, which we find so common; this counting on our own impotence as a life-long companion; this speaking of what we ought to expect, as if our power must halt where our natural abilities halt; this thinking it really humble to expect little or no fruit; this thinking it meek to be happy without fruit—is all this a fit answer to the baptism and a fit memorial of the tongues of fire? Do we not there see the Spirit answering forever all doubts as to what ordinary men can be made, and proclaiming to all who would bear a message from God, that if they will only wait until they are "endued with power from on high," the effect which of all others will show the working of that power within them will be this— that they shall be raised above themselves, and made to speak with a mouth and wisdom which, all who know them will know, were not within their natural endowments or attainments?

The Scale to Which Our Expectations Should Be Framed

There Is *a Supernatural*

AS TO THE SCALE ON WHICH OUR EXPECTATIONS SHOULD BE FRAMED. In our age, invention by aid of natural science often seems to leap almost within the bounds of the supernatural. The impossibilities of our fathers are disappearing, one becoming a traffic and another a pastime. This has produced a state of mind in which nothing seems impossible to natural science. Concurrently with this has arisen a tendency to bring spiritual progress and action within natural bounds.

We are proud of our knowledge of the laws of the natural kingdom, and impatient of any phenomena which cannot be judged by them. Yet we do not object to judging the vegetable kingdom by laws totally different from those which we apply to the mineral, and the animal by laws totally different from what we apply to the vegetable, and the pervasive fluids[3] by laws different from those we apply to any of those three kingdoms. To shrink from the marvels of vegetable life because they are unaccountable on chemical principles, or from those of instinct because they are unfathomable mysteries on botanical principles, or from those of intellect because they are inexplicable by the laws of natural history, or from the mysteries of light because they cannot be metaphysically analyzed and conditioned, would not be more unreasonable than to shrink from marvels in the spiritual kingdom, because they cannot be judged by the laws of the natural. The supernatural has its own laws, and there *is* a supernatural.

Instead of seeking to keep down spiritual movements to the level of natural explanation, in an age when natural marvels reach almost to miracles, we ought rather to be impelled to pray that they may put on a more striking character of supernatural manifestation. Today more by far is necessary to carry into the mind of the multitude a clear conviction, "It is the hand of God," than was necessary in other ages. When men saw few wonders from natural science, they readily ascribed each wonder to divine agency; but now that they are accustomed to see them daily, moral wonders must swell beyond all pretext of natural explanation, before they are felt to be from God.

Is our footing firm? Do we stand, or do we tremble? Is Christianity to seat herself in the circle of natural agency, or to arise from the dust, and prove that there is a God in Israel? Are we to shrink from things extraordinary? Are we to be afraid of anything that would make skeptical or prayerless men mock? Are we to desire that the Spirit shall use and work in us just to such a degree as will never bring a sneer upon us—to pray, as a continental writer represents some as *meaning*, "Give us of the Holy Spirit; but not too much; lest the people should say that we are full of new wine"?[4]

Age of Opportunity

To Christianity, this is preeminently the age of opportunity. Never before did the world offer to her anything like the same open field as at this moment. Even a single century from the present time, how much more limited was her access to the minds of men! Within our own favored country a zealous preacher would then have been driven away from many a sphere, where now he would be hailed. On the continent of Europe, the whole of France has been opened to the preaching of the word, though under some restraints. In Belgium, Sardinia, and other fields, it may now be said that the word of God is not bound.

A century ago, the Chinese empire, the Mohammedan world, and Africa, containing between them such a preponderating majority of the human race, were all closed against the gospel of Christ. China is open at several points. The whole empire of the Mogul is one field where opportunity and protection invite the evangelist. Turkey itself has been added to the spheres wherein he may labor. Around the wild shores of Africa, and far into her western, eastern, and southern interior, outposts of Christianity have been established. Wide realms beyond invite her onward.

In the South Seas, several regions which a hundred years ago had not been made known by the voyages of Cook are now regularly occupied. Could the churches of England and America send forth tomorrow a hundred thousand preachers of the gospel, each one of them might find a sphere, already opened by the strong hand of Providence, where a century ago none of them could have come without danger.

The age, if not so remarkable for agency as for opportunity, is yet very remarkable in this respect, when compared with any that has preceded it. While, on the one hand, we may well humble ourselves that, after so long a lapse of time, Christian men are so few, and Christian operations so feeble, yet, measuring our own day with that of the generation that went before us, we may devoutly magnify our God. Any one of the three great divisions of Christians in England—the Established Church, the Methodists, or the Dissenters—can this day furnish a number of faithful ministers teaching the truth in the fear of God, and wishful to be the instruments in saving souls, supported by a number of spiritually minded laymen ready for every good work, such that, could they have been presented to John Wesley as the entire force of godly men in the country, would have made him feel as if the army for the whole world's conquest was already raised.

Scotland alone could now produce a host of loyal soldiers ready and able to wage the Redeemer's war, such as in his day would have appeared to him almost sufficient to conclude the conquest. Ireland, too, would offer in this respect an amazing advance. In France, where, at the conclusion of the great Peace, scarcely any earnest preachers could be found, they may now be counted by hundreds; and in Germany, notwithstanding all its mists and its blights, not a few are growing up in vigor.

Whether for the direct labors of the pulpit, for united movements of enlightenment, or the ministering of gentle relief to the wants of human society, never, never did the sun shine upon so much agency, so much organization, so much liberty, so much earnest effort. Could we indulge ourselves by forming our own world, and only think of all the good men, good societies, and good works, on which the eye may rest, we might rejoice with unbroken joy, proclaim the full advent of the kingdom of God, and feel ourselves launched on a benign and brotherly age.

But alas! alas! the vast world rolls on, a turbid and a freezing stream. When we look first at our own little land, then at the broad earth, we find, for one who fears God and works righteousness, there are thousands who forget God and work wickedness. Christian agency is not, therefore, as some amiable theorists would seem to think, chiefly for training those who are born Christians, or made Christians in baptism, and who need nothing more than church ordinances, and an open heaven when they die. It is an agency raised up to carry out the great work of conversion which the Lord has begun within the lands of Christendom, and then bear onward the banner until every nation under heaven bows under it.

Age of Progress

It is also an age of progress, as much as of opportunity or of agency. What an advance has Christianity made, as to impress upon our national manners, within the last century! On our highest classes and on our lowest, on those who love God and those who love Him not, she has imposed many restraints.

The vices which remain are every day made more hideous to the public eye. How different the amount of piety in officers and men developed by the horrors of the late war, from what was ever known in an English army before! How different the spiritual condition of many of our rural and manufacturing districts from what they were a century ago! What a change in the morals of the court, in the temperance of private entertainments! How much more promising the aspect of Ireland! How much more animated the religion of Scotland! What an incalculable advance in America! And within that time the West Indies, Australia, New Zealand, the Society Islands, the Sandwich Islands, the Friendly Islands, the Navigator's Islands, a considerable part of Fiji, and tracts of Southern and Western Africa, may be written down as provinces added to Christendom. Though in some of these place much ungodliness remains, yet in most of them a far more promising state of things exists than was known in any country between the first days of Christianity, and the last century.

In other countries, beginnings have been made and firstfruits gathered; as, for instance, in India, China, and Northern Africa. At the same time, every system of religion not calling itself Christian has decayed. Mohammedanism, Brahmanism, Buddhism, and Paganism have lost territory, adherents, and power. Altogether it may be questioned, whether even the progress of the first century has not been equaled, as to positive amount, by that of the last. But, when we look at the agents, means, and facilities enjoyed during the last century compared with the first, and at the rapidity with which believers have multiplied themselves in both periods, we at once feel that, as to propagating power, in the face of adverse circumstances and small resources, there is no comparison between them.

What Remains to Be Done

It is, on the one hand, as wrong and as dangerous to overlook the success which God has given to His word in the last age, or the unparalleled openings which promise to the church future conquest, as it is, on the other, to repose on our present possessions, as if the conquest was achieved. What has been done is enough to excite our liveliest gratitude; but if we dwell on it alone, we become enervated and careless. What remains to be done is enough to excite our deepest solicitude; but if we look at it alone, we become dispirited and powerless. Even in England everything is stained; our commerce corrupt; our politics earthy; our social manners chiefly formed after the will of "the god of this world"; our streets crying shame upon us; our hamlets, many of them, dark, ignorant, and immoral; our towns debauched and drunken.

Amid this, much good exists, in which we do rejoice, yea, and will rejoice; but O! the evil, the evil is, day by day, breaking thousands of hearts, ruining thousands of characters, and destroying thousands of souls! Looking abroad beyond the one little sphere of Britain and America, which we proud boasters of the two nations are prone to look upon as being nearly the whole world—though we are not one-twentieth of the human race—how dreary and how lonely does the soul of the Christian feel, as it floats, in imagination, over the rest of the earth! That Europe, so learned, so splendid, so brave—what misery is by its fireside! what stains upon its conscience! what superstition, stoicism, or despair around its deathbeds!

And yonder bright old Asia, where the "tongue of fire" first spoke—how rare and how few are the scenes of moral beauty which there meet the eye! Instead of the family, the harem; instead of religion, superstition; instead of peace, oppression; instead of enterprise, war; instead of morals, ceremonies; instead of a God, idols; instead of refinement and growth, corruption and collapse; here, there, thinly sown and scarcely within sight one of the other, a school, a book, a man of God—one star in a sky of darkness.

And poor Africa! What is to become of the present generation of her sons? Thinly around her coasts are beginnings of good things; but O! the blood and darkness, and woe, the base superstition, and the miserable cruelties, under which the majority of her youth are now trained, amid which her old men are going down to the grave!

All this existed a century ago, but was not then known as we know it now. The world is not yet explored by the church, much less occupied; but the exploration at least is carried so far, that we know its plagues as our fathers knew them not; and if our hearts were rightly affected, we should weep over them as they never wept; for, although the spread of Christianity has greatly multiplied the number of Christians, the increase of population has been such, that more men are sinning and suffering now, than were a hundred years ago.

Taking the forces of the church, comparing them with the length and breadth of the world, and then asking, "Are these ever to be the means of converting all?" we feel that only the promise of God could inspire such a hope. But that promise is so confirmed, illustrated, and exalted by the success of the past century, that when we look back to the few faithful men in this country and in America, men in different circumstances and of different views, who then began in earnest to call the churches to their work, and see how far their labors and those of their spiritual sons have advanced the kingdom of Christ beyond where it stood then, we are led to say, "Suppose that all the good men, now loving God and desiring His glory, were but to be multiplied in equal ratio during the next century, as those few have been during the last century; what an amazing stride would be made toward the conversion of the whole world!"

Is this too much to expect? Are we to conclude that the force of the animating Spirit is spent, and that an age of feebleness must succeed to one of power? To do so is fearfully to disbelieve at once the goodness and the faithfulness of our God.

Some say that, because populations have become familiarized with the truths of the gospel, we are not to expect the same converting effects as when those truths were new. If this be so, we had better make way for a generation of rationalists and formalists, to prepare the ground again for spiritual cultivation! Some say that, because the age is so educated, intellectual, scientific, and inquisitive, men are not so susceptible of the influence of Christianity. Then shall we wait for an age less enlightened and less educated? Some say that the age is so unduly active, forcing enterprise and commerce to the point of absorbing every man, till religion is pushed aside.

Must we then wait for a duller and more lethargic time? Some say that the Lord does not give us great success lest we should be uplifted. Is it His way to promote humility by giving small results to great agencies, or by giving great results to small ones? And would not results after the Pentecostal scale make any of our agencies seem small? These are miserable withes wherewith to bind the giant church of God.

Away with them every one! After going round all the reasons which one hears ordinarily assigned for the greater direct success of preachers in the last century than now, our mind finds rest only in that one reason, which carries a world of rebuke and of humiliation to ourselves. They produced greater effects, simply because of the greater power of God within them.

When the Fruit of Their Sowing Comes to Be Reaped

Every ray of gospel truth that exists in any man is on our side. All intelligence, all intellectual activity, all vigor of character, are more for us than their opposites would be. In fact, they are very much the fruit, the indirect and secondary fruit, of the past triumph of religion. It is impossible that true godliness shall spread among any people, without stimulating their intellectual and social energies.

It is hard to imagine a satire on the gospel more bitter than that it should be powerful when new to men, and impotent when familiar; that it should be good for the half barbarous, but not for those whom itself had refined; capable of captivating the inert, but incapable of commanding the masculine and the energetic. We expect age not less instructed in Christian doctrine, but far more instructed; not intellectually duller, but more active; not darker as to science and literature, but inconceivably brighter; not slower as to invention, enterprise, and progress, but more vigorous by far.

And am I to return to "the glorious Gospel of the blessed God," whereto I feel that I and mine, my kindred, my country, the race from which I have sprung, the lands in which I have traveled, are all indebted for their purest and brightest things—and say to it, "When these bright ages come, thou shalt lag behind, perhaps recollected as one of the infantine instructors of the world, but distanced by the progress of man"? Let those who assign reasons for our want of fruitfulness which fairly sow the seeds of rationalism prepare to render an account when the fruit of their sowing comes to be reaped.

There is a natural tendency in any movement to lose intensity as it gains surface. When godliness becomes the habit of large numbers, it is not according to the laws of human nature that it should retain, in every individual, all the fervor which it must maintain, in order to exist at all, when it is the peculiarity of an extremely few. But if this fact is to be recognized, it must be remembered that the disadvantage which it presents is easily overcome by the power of grace. Indeed, a natural counterpoise to this subduing tendency, in practical religion, is offered in an equally natural accumulative tendency.

That decrease of distinction between the church and the world which is so often noticed, does not wholly arise from the church becoming less Christian, but partly from the world becoming less wicked. The testimony of a large number of decided men gradually and silently imposes on the world a respect for Christian principles, till the world tacitly accepts many of its moral laws and social standards at the hands of the church. Every concession of this kind is an advantage to those Christians who mean to conquer all, while it is a seduction to those who repose in the idea of converting a small section of the people, leaving the rest to live in sin.

Put the ungodly in a minority, then vice becomes a social as well as a spiritual blemish, and religion an outward as well as an inward comfort. As the multitude of Christians goes on increasing, there is accumulative power of example, accumulative power of teaching, accumulative power of prayers, accumulative power of Christian training in families, accumulative power of purity in habits, all tending in the one direction—to bring the public sentiment under the dominion of Christ.

Towns and villages exist in this country where, within the memory of living men, very few godly persons were to be found; but now one-tenth, one-seventh, and even one-fifth in some cases, of their adult population are professing to follow Christ and living more or less worthily of that profession. Can any man help feeling that the unconverted people in such a town are much more likely to be converted than those living where the proportion of the godly is not more than one in a hundred, or one in a thousand?

Who could not feel—who would not practically acknowledge the feeling—of the accumulative power of Christian progress, if he had to decide in which of two towns his unconverted son should settle for life—one with a believer to every thousand of the population, or one with a believer to every ten? He would instantly say, "In the latter place the prospects of my son's conversion are vastly greater than in the other."

What we should feel in an individual case, we ought to feel on the great scale—to gather strength and hope, not feebleness, from past successes, and to become especially impatient of the continuance of sinners in those fields where notable triumphs of grace have already been achieved. What the Canaanites were to the Israelites of old, the unconverted dwelling in our towns and villages are to us at this day. They confuse and weaken us, they allure, they ensnare us, they lead our children astray, they rob us of the fruit of our schools, they dampen the zeal of our young converts, they entice families into worldly practices, they tempt our tradesmen, they infect our churches; and never, until they are totally uprooted, can peace and righteousness flourish in our coasts.

Impatient of their obstinacy everywhere, we ought to be especially so where victories, won by those who have preceded us, leave us comparatively little to do. The uphill fight has been fought, the vantage ground gained, and now for the power to complete the triumph! The entire conversion of England and America, within the next fifty years, would not be so great a work for the Christians now existing, as the progress made within the last hundred years has been for the Christians then existing. Is it rational to believe that God will less bless His servants in this nineteenth century than in the one that is gone, if they be equally faithful? Or that He will shower on this generation of ours less-marked benedictions than He did on the one to whom we are indebted for so much?

Good News for Every Creature

The single consideration of past progress suffices to prove that, on the ground of experience, we are not warranted to conclude that the conversion of the whole world is impossible. Much as may be argued from the slowness of the past progress of Christianity, the last century has so changed the aspect of affairs as now to cast the weight of the argument from experience decisively into the scale of hope.

Many, however, will continue to look upon any consistent expectation of the general conversion of men as illusory; the objections of some resting on their views of the constancy of human nature, certain, they think, hereafter as heretofore, to present great numbers of unconquerable opponents to holiness; while others take higher ground and believe that the general conversion of our race is contrary to the purpose of God.

When the question, "Is the conversion of the whole world possible?" is fairly put, the plain answer to it is obviously this: "It is possible, unless it be contrary to the will of God." If He has ordained that it is not to be, an infinite obstacle opposes it; if He has not so ordained, the obstacles which oppose it are finite, and therefore conquerable. Christians can overcome all things but a decree of God.

Has He, then, given us any declaration that He does not intend to renew the earth, as a whole, in righteousness? We do not mean to hold any controversy with those who have deliberately adopted the view that the Christian dispensation is a kind of interlude between the Lord's lifetime upon earth and a future earthly reign, meanwhile, bearing witness in His name—a witness, for the conversion of a few, and the condemnation of the many. We leave them with the praise of being perfectly consistent, in expecting small results from the preaching of the gospel, and with the responsibility of looking on that gospel in a light which warrants little faith.

We deal with those who regard the gospel as *bona fide* "good news" for every creature; "good news" which those who heard it before me were bound to tell to me; "good news" which I am bound to tell to every creature living, according to the extent of my opportunities; "good news" to the effect that "the grace of God, which bringeth salvation to all men, hath appeared"; news which could not be told to me as good, if it left any doubt whether it was or was not for me; "good news" to every creature, "a Gospel for thee."

We take the first two announcements by a preacher under the Christian dispensation, to audiences of sinners, as intended for our instruction and imitation: "Repent, and be baptized, EVERY ONE OF YOU, in the name of Jesus Christ, for the remission of sins"; "God, having raised up His Son Jesus, sent Him to bless you, in turning away EVERY ONE OF YOU from his iniquities." Declarations less direct, personal, or comprehensive than these, we have no manner of authority to deliver. We are to "command all men everywhere to repent," to call upon every one of them to believe, to assure every one of them that Christ is "sent to bless him in turning him away from his iniquities."

Nor are we to make such proclamations under the feeling that, although it is our duty to do it, there is no intention on the part of God to second our testimony and give it effect. Hope in the result sustained the apostle in his work, according to his own avowal. He says, "Therefore we both labor and suffer reproach, because we trust in the living God, who is the Savior of all men, specially of those that believe." This trust in the God and Savior of all was enough to animate any man in labor and under reproach, and such a trust we should never cast away.

The question, whether or not the conversions of the first ages ought to be looked back to by us, as a standard at which to aim, is settled by one of the passages already quoted. After joyfully describing the conversion of the church in Ephesus, where "the word of the Lord" so "mightily grew and prevailed," St. Paul says, that God has done this, "THAT IN THE AGES TO COME HE MIGHT SHOW THE EXCEEDING RICHES OF HIS GRACE, in His kindness toward us through Christ Jesus." We are living in what were, then, "the ages to come." On us the light of those "exceeding riches of grace" is shining—shining for our encouragement—shining that we may believe that in heathen cities, where great Dianas are adored, we also shall see "the word of God mightily grow and prevail," heathen rites abandoned, bad books consumed, and the craft of idol-makers destroyed.

While this collective number of conversions is given to us as an encouragement, the most remarkable of all individual conversions is placed before us in the same light. "Howbeit," says St. Paul, "for this cause I obtained mercy, that in me first Jesus Christ might show forth all long-suffering, *for a pattern to them which should hereafter believe on Him to life everlasting.*" Thus we are deliberately forewarned to take the most singular conversion that ever occurred in the early church, not as a discouragement because of its specialty, but as an intentional manifestation of the wonderful grace of the Redeemer, by which every sinner in all ages, who would fain "find mercy," may encourage himself.

The persecutor Paul, converted and forgiven, is for a pattern to individual believers in "the ages to come." The great multitude of "children of wrath" in Ephesus who were made to "sit in heavenly places in Christ Jesus," are also to us, of "the ages to come," a pattern of the "exceeding riches of grace." Whether our faith be tried in respect to the possibility of the conversion of an individual as unlikely as Saul, or of a number as great as the Church of Ephesus, in either case we should believe that the ancient grace is free and mighty this day. Thus trusting in "God, who is the Savior of all men," we shall both cheerfully "labor and suffer reproach."

The same relation which we have shown to exist between hope and labor, is also pointed out to us, as existing between hope and prayer. "I exhort, therefore, that, first of all, supplications, prayers, intercessions, and giving of thanks, be made for all men." Here no one doubts that we are literally commanded to pray for every human being; but if we did not carefully attend to the context, we might run away with a vague idea that we were only to pray as an expression of goodwill, and that for temporal and national blessings, especially as allusion is made to "kings, and all that are in authority"—that, in fact, the "prayers, and supplications, and intercessions, and giving of thanks, for all men," do not mean that we are to pray, supplicate, and intercede, that all men may be saved and come to the knowledge of the truth; for that would only be asking what God wills should never be, and therefore what could not be acceptable to Him.

But, as if expressly to anticipate this unbelief, the apostle adds, "For this is good and acceptable in the sight of God our Savior; who will have all men to be saved, and to come unto the knowledge of the truth. For there is one God, and one Mediator between God and men, the Man Christ Jesus; who gave Himself a ransom for all, a testimony in due time."[5]

Here our encouragement in prayer, supplication, and intercession for all men is grounded first on the clear declaration that such prayer is "good and acceptable in the sight of God our Savior"; "our Savior" giving intensity to the expression, as if reminding us that He who has saved us, must be one to whom it is good and acceptable, that we should seek the salvation of all.

It is further grounded on the express declaration of His will regarding others, that He "will have them to be saved, and to come unto the knowledge of the truth." Here is not only the assurance that we are right in praying that they may be saved, but right in praying that the truth may be brought to all, and that they may be saved through its instrumentality; praying, in fact, for the universal diffusion of Christ's gospel, and the universal salvation of men in consequence. It is further supported on the ground of the unity of God, the unity of the Mediator between God and men, and the unity of man as regarded by His mediating atonement: "One God, and one Mediator between God and men, the Man Christ Jesus, who gave Himself a ransom for all, a testimony in due time."

We have, then, the clear example of the first preachers, the express declaration that the early conversions were as a pattern for the ages to come, the statement that trust in God as the Savior of all men was the animating strength under apostolic toil and shame, the command to pray for all, and the most formally stated warrant for such prayers boldly to lay hold upon the promises of God.

The Free Agency of Man

Many who will admit that the scriptural argument points in this direction, yet, looking at human nature, the present condition of mankind, the proportion of Christian agency to population, and the past career of man, will, on the whole, conclude that the conversion of the world is not to be expected. They will also ask us how we can reconcile such an expectation with the free agency of man. We will no further answer them than by recalling the fact, that every additional conversion to some extent, however slight, changes the condition of society, and, in so doing, affects the motives which act upon the unconverted, throwing a greater weight upon the side of goodness. A few more decided advances on the part of the church, in some countries of Christendom, would cast a preponderating weight of social motives on the side of godliness, leaving little to be contended against but the natural depravity of man's heart, which, even in the purest condition of society, would be enough to demand the most zealous care for the conversion of each human being.

This bears first on the general question of natural motives, next on the particular one as to reconciling faith, for the general regeneration of men, with their free agency. We readily admit that, logically, we cannot reconcile them, and certainly we are not anxious to attempt it. All the difficulties which meet us in soberly expecting the conversion of the entire world, equally meet us in soberly expecting the conversion of an entire family.

Every question of free agency, motives, human nature, past experience, which enters into the one, enters into the other, though on a smaller scale. But it is only the scale that differs; the elements are the same. Yet who that has felt the faith and love of Christ within him, and has kindred dear to his own heart, has not again and again pleaded that they might all appear, "no wanderer lost, a family in heaven"? Who does not feel that to exercise faith that such a prayer shall be answered, is good and wise, and acceptable to God? In fact, all the difficulty exists as to faith for the conversion of any one individual.

The difference between preaching the gospel with a full expectation of doing no more than saving small companies of saints from amid multitudes of sinners, on whose shipwreck no influence is to be exercised beyond holding them a light to sink by, and of looking upon every converted man as one rescued from a common danger, who is immediately to join in rescuing the rest—is such, that in the one case, when a little is accomplished, it is looked upon as what the gospel was sent to do; while, in the other case, every little is taken as but an earnest of the great, and the great as an earnest of the universal. While we aim at few, we shall win but few; for, that our successes shall take their proportions from our faith, is the universal law of the service of Christ.

Work, Work, Work

Should we be wrong in our views; should it be contrary to the design of our Lord to convert all our race by the preaching of His word, and the outpouring of His Spirit; should it be His purpose to leave the earth much as it is until He concludes its mournful story in thunderclaps of judgment; should that consummation be nigh, and the last trumpet be already beginning to fill with the breath of the archangel, yet surely, if we, under the illusion of our belief, are found panting, praying, laboring, if by any means we might save some, that blast might cause us a pang for the multitudes whom it found unwarned; but no pang because we had been busy in warning, exhorting, entreating; no pang because we had done so in faith, that our Lord willed all men to come to the knowledge of the truth.

Suppose, on the other hand, that there is even a possibility of our being right; that the grace of God which has appeared to us really is "good tidings" for every creature; that the truth so precious to our nation and to our own souls is not decreed away from any part of the human family by the great Savior above us; that He does mean that literally every creature should hear it from the lips of His servants, that literally the whole earth should be filled with the knowledge of the Lord, that literally "the ages to come" should take the early conversions as the type of their expectations, and should embrace all men in their supplications and their labors.

Should all this be true, and we spend our strength in observing the clouds, and the judgments, and the trumpets, telling those who are calling the nations that they may call, but they will accomplish little thereby—as far as in us lies stealing the nerve from their arm and the fire from their voice; should we in the midst of this die, and find "ages to come" yet advancing, then, perhaps, we might feel as if the Scripture had been neglected by us, which says, "He that observeth the wind shall not sow, and he that regardeth the clouds shall not reap." Futurity, judgments, and providential design, lie within the unshared province of God. None need make it his chief concern to settle or to ascertain them. A world of sinning and suffering men, each one of them my own brother, calls on me for work, work, work. I may trust the future, and the time of restoring Israel, to better hands than mine.

In hope, or without hope, let us be up and doing. Encouragements are on every hand, and so are menaces. The enlightened, the true, the zealous, are many. The wicked and the slothful are fearfully more. The number of the former has been growing by conversions, the number of the latter growing faster by the natural increase of population. The appliances for Christian propagation are vast; the faith of many in their efficacy feeble. The doctrines of Christianity are known and prized by multitudes who never knew them before. On the other hand, there are few of the churches, in the very heart of which those doctrines are not betrayed.

One would rob us of the incarnation of God, another of the Spirit of God, another of an atonement, another of providence, another of prayer; some of regenerating grace, some of ministerial unction, some of primitive fervor, some of a Lord's Day; some would launch us on a sea of thought without an inspired guide; others on a moral universe without punishment for wrong; thus nearly every truth that distinguishes the system of Christianity from earthly inventions is attacked by mining or by battery. We are not sure but truth is sometimes spoken when little good ensues; we are sure that error is never issued into the world without doing harm; and there are strong men now doing work over which, unless others, made stronger by the might of God, undo it, generations to come will have reason to weep.

For all who cannot bear to see the cross betrayed, the Holy Ghost grieved, the oracles of God degraded, the work of the Spirit in the human soul reduced to a process of motives and emotions, and every divine tie that connects us, as a redeemed race, with a redeeming Father, skillfully cut asunder. For those who are not prepared to see the churches of England and America pass through blights such as have befallen the churches of Switzerland, Germany, and other Protestant regions of the continent, this is a moment when the air seems full of trumpet notes, when every step taken on doctrinal ground raises the echo of warning. Alas, many who dogmatically repel error evaporate in intellectualism; others decay, under a silvered mildew of respectability; and others, professing to seek the old Christianity, content themselves with garnishing the sepulcher in which the Middle Ages buried her, instead of seeking that her first preachers, in the persons of other men, but in the "spirit and power" of Peters and Pauls, should be raised up once more!

We will bless every laborer for any service done toward the maintenance and advance of the truth, for every good word spoken, every sound argument uttered from the pulpit, every page of evangelical truth written, and every rebuke administered in any way to those who would falsify our faith. Let them be assured that more than all other services, turning many away from iniquity will counterwork and confound attempts to reduce Christianity from a divine to a human system. This is the practical answer to difficulties and objections. Let us only have multitudes of newborn Christians, fervent in faith and hope, full of love and of good works, and rationalists may account for the phenomenon as they will; but the common conscience of mankind will feel that God is in it. "Beholding the man which was healed standing with them, they could say nothing against it."

The one reason for being zealous for Christian doctrine which so far surpasses all others that beside it they become as nothing, is that given by St. Paul to Timothy: "Take heed unto thyself, and unto the doctrine; continue in them: for in doing this thou shalt both save thyself, and them that hear thee." What a motive! Saving, first, ourselves—then, those that hear us. The sublime can go no farther!

Here we have set before our hearts, soliciting us onward, motives which we acknowledge have already moved the very heart of the Godhead. To save! as an instrument, it is true; but O, how infinitely glorious, even as an instrument, to save! and that, not only ourselves, but others! While, on the one hand, guarding "the doctrine" is the only means of retaining saving power in the church; on the other, no guard upon the doctrine will ever be effectual unless we can raise up a succession of saved men.

Creeds, catechisms, confessions, are not to be treated as is now the fashion in many quarters to treat them. When kept in their proper place, as human and fallible, and strong only when they accord with God's holy oracles, they have a high utility. The idea of relying upon these for conserving the truth in any church, is as well-founded as would be the idea of relying on a good military code for defending a nation. An army of cowards would interpret any code down to their own level, and churches and unconverted men will equally lower any confession of faith.

For rescuing souls, for rebuking blasphemy, for building up God's holy church, for glorifying the Savior's name on earth, for our own joy and crown of rejoicing, for the bliss of covering a multitude of sins, for the eternal delight of having saved a soul from death, let us aim at one work—bringing sinners from darkness to light. Of all the records of praise which our merciful Lord will give His servants, who would not most covet that his record should be?—"The law of truth was in his mouth, and iniquity was not found in his lips. He walked with Me in peace and equity, AND DID TURN MANY AWAY FROM INIQUITY!"

You that are lights and fathers in the ministry, whose very name is a power, whose tone decides that of many young evangelists, whose standard of faith and success regulates the practical expectations of many humble Christians—O show us the way to victory, lead us to downright conquests over this cold and sinful world! What if, ere you go hence, you should leave to your successors a glorious tradition of multitudes broken under the power of the word, of notorious sinners suddenly transformed into bright examples of grace, of throngs of inquirers asking the way to heaven with tears, of churches once dying easily, roused, through your instrumentality, to apostolic zeal? If you but leave behind you such traditions to be told, and told again, to children, and to children's children, your "tongue of fire" will be multiplying itself in the homesteads of your people, when your voice has long been silent; and the fruit of your labor will go on propagating itself, until the trump of the archangel sounds.

Those who are entering into the work of the ministry, or are as yet young in its ranks, choose, among all those who have gone before you, whose fame you would prefer. Take the host of those who have trifled with the cross, with inspiration, with the fall and the redemption of man, with the work of the Spirit, or any of the other vital doctrines of our religion. If you find among them one man whose name, after ages, is dear to a nation, sacred in the homesteads of thousands to whose ancestors he was a blessing—then follow him. If you find among those who gave themselves to intellectual pleasures, and were above the plain, rough work of revivals and awakenings, one who has left a memory which is to this day blessed, raising up even now spiritual children to perpetuate his fruit to other generations—you may follow him.

But surely you would never think of following in the track of those whose labors have been succeeded by a blight, or whose names, if remembered at all, are remembered, not as a blessing to the world, but simply as an example of talent! Surely you would wish rather to be one of those whom grandsires shall speak of to their grandchildren, as having been the means of saving such a man, of kindling such a revival, of introducing a new religious era into the history of such a village, or of first carrying the gospel to some people to whom Christ was a stranger. You will find that all those upon whose memories the blessings of living men rest, were those who most gave themselves to accomplish the salvation of sinners, who gloried in the cross, who trusted in the Holy Ghost, and who, whether their tongue was that of a Boanerges, or that of a Barnabas, ever took care, by solitary waiting before the Redeemer's throne, to have it so imbued with the Holy Ghost, that it was, at least, a "tongue of fire."

We do not feel that we have said what we had to say. In looking over this little book, we can hardly believe that it is all that the feelings and thoughts with which we began it have produced. But, such as it is, let it go out to the world, to be rebuked where it errs, to be unheeded where it is feeble, to be blessed where it is true and strong.

And now, adorable Spirit, proceeding from the Father and the Son, descend upon all the churches, renew the Pentecost in this our age, and baptize Thy people generally—O baptize them yet again with tongues of fire! Crown this nineteenth century with a revival of "pure and undefiled religion" greater than that of the last century, greater than that of the first, greater than any "demonstration of the Spirit" ever yet vouchsafed to men!

Notes

1. It is often assumed, that speaking is a natural exercise, and therefore, needs no instruction. The word "speaking" covers a fallacy. Conversation in a moderate tone, and at short intervals, is a natural exercise of the voice; public speaking, in an elevated tone, and for an hour together, is an artificial one. Except in very rare cases of persons singularly favored by nature, this artificial exercise is never performed with the ease of the natural one; and how often it impairs, and even destroys health, is too notorious to need any mention. Such writers as Mr. Cull, and Dr. Rush, show that under

proper training public speaking may become as easy and as healthy for persons of sound organs as singing is; and to the neglect of this we owe the loss, in their prime, of many of the best and ablest preachers that ever lived.

2. Guizot's "*Histoire de la Civilisation*," Vol. II., p. 24. Sixth Paris edition.

3. Water, air, light, electricity, etc., which cannot be conveniently classed under any of the three divisions—vegetable, mineral, and animal—usually taken to comprise all natural objects.

4. Pasteur Augustin Bost.

5. We give the marginal reading, which is a literal translation; the other is, "to be testified in due time."